HOW TO HAVE A HEALTHIER DOG

HOW TO HAVE A HEALTHIER DOG

The Benefits of Vitamins and
Minerals for Your Dog's Life Cycles

Wendell O. Belfield, D.V.M.
and Martin Zucker

Doubleday & Company, Inc.
Garden City, New York
1981

Library of Congress Cataloging in Publication Data

Belfield, Wendell O
    How to have a healthier dog.

    Includes bibliographical references and index.
    1. Dogs—Food. 2. Dogs—Diseases. 3. Vitamins
in animal nutrition. 4. Minerals in animal nutrition.
5. Nutrition disorders. I. Zucker, Martin, joint author. II. Title.
SF427.4.B44   636.7'0852
ISBN: 0-385-15992-7
Library of Congress Catalog Card Number 80-1081
Copyright © 1981 by Wendell O. Belfield, D.V.M. and Martin Zucker

To all my clients over the years at the Bel-Mar Veterinary Hospital who trusted their pets to an animal doctor doing things a little differently.

Contents

Foreword

The value of vitamins to human beings and domesticated animals has been recognized for more than sixty years. It was just one hundred years ago, in 1881, that the Swiss biochemist Lunin found that mice died when they were fed a mixture of purified protein, carbohydrate, fat, and minerals, whereas mice fed the same diet with the addition of some milk survived. Lunin concluded that a natural food such as milk must contain, in addition to the known principal ingredients, small quantities of unknown substances essential to life. Other investigators reported similar results, and by 1940 most of the vitamins that are now known had been discovered.

The Food and Nutrition Board of the National Academy of Sciences–National Research Council makes recommendations about the recommended dietary allowance of vitamins and minerals for human beings, and similar recommendations are made also for domesticated animals. In making their recommendations, these groups of scientists and physicians have attempted to answer one question. This question is, what amount of each of these nutrients is needed in order to keep the person or the animal from dying of the corresponding deficiency disease? The disease arising from a deficiency of vitamin C is scurvy, that arising from a deficiency of vitamin B_1 is beriberi, and that arising from a deficiency of niacin is pellagra. The Food and Nutrition Board and the other agencies have given good recommendations about these amounts.

There is, however, another question that can be asked. This question is, what amount of each of these nutrient substances, especially of the vitamins, is needed in order to put the person or the cat or the dog in the best of health; what amount will decrease most effectively the incidence of disease; and what amount will be of the greatest benefit in the treatment of disease? The optimum intakes of these nutrients have been recognized only recently as being much greater than the intakes needed to prevent death from deficiency diseases.

In his book Dr. Belfield discusses the question of the amounts of vitamins and minerals given to dogs in order to put them and sustain them in the best of health, and also the way in which these substances can be used in the treatment of disease. Dr. Belfield himself deserves great credit for his discovery that massive doses of vitamin C, as great as a half gram of sodium ascorbate intravenously per pound of body weight twice a day, have great value in the treatment of viral diseases in dogs and cats.

Vitamin C is indeed an extraordinary substance, somewhat different from the other vitamins. A striking difference between vitamin C and the other vitamins is that animals of most species synthesize their own ascorbic acid (vitamin C) in the cells of either the liver or the kidney, with man and a few other animal species being exceptions. Accordingly most animals do not die of scurvy when they are completely deprived of vitamin C. On the other hand, the other substances that man requires for life—that is, the other vitamins—are also required for life by essentially all animal species.

An indication of the amount of vitamin C that is needed for good health is provided by determining the amount of this substance made by various animal species. It is found that the amount made is approximately proportional to the body weight. The average animal weighing 16 pounds makes between 200 and 2,000 milligrams of vitamin C per day, with animals of some species synthesizing the smaller amount and those of other species synthesizing the larger amount. Dogs and cats are in the first group, in that they synthesize only about 200 milligrams of vitamin C per day (for a 16-pound animal), only about ⅕ as much as animals of most other species synthesize. It is probably for this reason that a large amount of supplementary vitamin C is important for the preservation of the best of health in dogs.

This book by Dr. Belfield provides much information that should be of value to every owner of a household pet.

—**Linus Pauling**
Palo Alto, California

Part One

WHY YOUR DOG NEEDS EXTRA VITAMINS AND MINERALS

A New Therapy Is Born

Great oaks from little acorns grow, they say. So it is that a small and even routine event in one's life can change a way of thinking or a way of living.

In my case it was a small black and tan mongrel dog, a terrier and cocker cross. A Mexican farm worker brought him into my office one evening about fifteen years ago and the man, his wife, and the five children who trailed along were visibly worried.

I examined the dog and quickly saw the usual symptoms. Mucus and pus oozed from the nose and eyes. High temperature. A bad cough. Listlessness. Diarrhea.

In my poor Spanish I told the Mexican and his family there was nothing I could do for their dog, that he was very sick and going to die.

The dog had distemper, a common viral disease highly contagious and deadly to all breeds of dogs. Animals that have it are usually put to sleep. The veterinary textbook says there is no effective treatment.

Talking in broken English, the Mexican wanted to know why I couldn't help. I was the animal doctor and supposed to cure sickness and that was why he was in my office.

"You have to fix the dog because my children love him," he said.

I said there was nothing I could do but destroy the dog. My Spanish vocabulary contained nothing so sophisticated as expressions of regret and sympathy, so I used all the body and facial language I could manage.

The man turned to tell his family. The words were no sooner out of his mouth than the children began to cry.

In the very beginning of my veterinary practice, whenever I put an animal to sleep I keenly felt I was failing in my role as a healer. This sense of failure would always be aggravated by the genuine grief of a family or an individual who had lost something very precious. Even though I never became immune to the tears, with time and experience I acquired more confidence in my skill and knew that when I had to put an animal away, I had done all that was possible.

I had been practicing for some three years when the Mexican bracero and his mongrel dog came into my hospital. I was a very orthodox veterinarian, living by the textbook, doing what I had been trained to do at the Tuskegee Institute School of Veterinary Medicine. I had by this time put many dogs to sleep. And I had seen many tears.

I don't know what made this time different but I got that old feeling of failure again that I hadn't experienced since I was a rookie veterinarian. I have often reflected on that incident, looking for the factors that made it transcend routine, for it was routine and yet it changed my career. It led me onto a path, a way of thinking about medicine, that would put me at odds with my colleagues and brand me a maverick.

In looking back, I think it was the faces of the children of that poor migrant farm worker. The dog was more than a plaything to them. It was continuity, a steady source of love and warmth in a life of uprootedness and uncertainty. As they moved from place to place, farm to farm, they carried their little dog with them.

I felt I had let them down. I felt suddenly impotent over my inability to help and over the inability of my profession to help. I felt an urgent need to look elsewhere, beyond the textbooks, beyond my teaching, to find some enlightenment.

I began researching viral diseases. One day in some minor journal I came across an article about a North Carolina doctor who used large doses of vitamin C to cure people of polio, hepatitis, and other serious viral conditions. Dr. Fred Klenner was his name, and he had been achieving remarkable results back before the potent vaccines were developed.

To appreciate the significance of Klenner's work you have to understand that doctors are essentially taught to treat disease with commercial drugs, not vitamins. To treat viral conditions with vitamins, as Klenner began doing back in the forties and as Dr. Linus Pauling has championed in more recent times, is to welcome ridicule by the orthodox medical establishment. In cancer and mental illness and a host of other conditions, promising work with vitamin therapy is similarly opposed in this country.

Klenner was years ahead of the field in showing that vitamin C has great therapeutic antiviral powers when given in massive doses and has great preventive powers when taken in lesser, maintenance doses.

There were no medical textbooks to point the way for Klenner. He did it on his own.

Reading about Klenner's work, I immediately wondered if this approach might work with distemper, also a viral disease. There was nothing in the veterinary books about using vitamin C. And for good reason, it seemed. Most animals, including dogs, produce their own supply of vitamin C through a biochemical process in the liver. The exceptions, the nonproducers, are few: the guinea pig, a few species of birds, the apes and you and me. Humans.

Furthermore, I found out, when subjected to stress or when their bodies are invaded by some virus, most animals can produce many times more vitamin C than normal. Vitamin C is a key chemical in the body's defense system.

Even though the idea seemed unlikely, a real long shot in fact, I decided to give Klenner's concept a try on small animals. When I mentioned this to a colleague, he laughed at me.

"Forget about it," he said. "There is nothing to be done when the animal has distemper. There is no cure. And certainly vitamin C is no cure, even if one existed."

The man was probably right, I thought. The animals made their own vitamin C. Why would vitamin C from the outside be any good? Still, Klenner's work showed that massive doses of vitamin C had tremendous antiviral powers.

The test came when a very sick poodle was brought into the office with a bad case of distemper. Sidney Golinsky, a pharmacist friend, had found me an injectable vitamin C product and now I fingered it diffidently, feeling a little bit of the fool and at the same time a little bit of the adventurer. I really had no idea what the results would be. I did know, though, that I was not hurting the dog. This was no cruel animal experiment, for the dog had a disease that the entire profession regarded as hopeless. In effect, I was trying to save a dead dog.

To my utter delight and surprise, the poodle responded dramatically and in several days was well on the way to regaining its health. I tried the vitamin C on other distemper cases and the recovery rate was similarly impressive. By now I have seen scores of recoveries from this "fatal" disease for which the textbook still says there is no successful treatment.

My experience with vitamin C was so positive that I began to apply it to other conditions besides distemper. Then I began to work with other nutrients such as vitamins A and E, the B complex group, with zinc and other minerals.

I doubt if anybody ever told you to go out and buy vitamins and minerals for your pet to treat or prevent disease and common ailments. But that precisely is my message to you if you love your animal and want to see it active and happy and enjoying maximum health for as long as possible.

If somebody had told me years ago, before the office call of the Mexican farm worker, that dogs needed extra vitamin C or other supplementation, I would have been very skeptical. I might even have laughed in his face, just as the other veterinarian laughed at my apparent folly when I mentioned the vitamin C–distemper connection. I would have agreed that there were certain well-defined deficiency conditions that responded to certain vitamins. This we were all taught in veterinary school. But routine supplementation? Vitamin C? No way.

I have never received any research money to conduct the kind of expensive and elaborate studies that medical science likes to see when new findings are presented. But on my own, in my one-man practice and on the basis of hundreds of clinical cases with show dogs, hunting dogs, working dogs, and plain mutts, I have learned just how great a difference extra vitamins and minerals can make in improving the quality of a dog's life.

The continual good results quickly erased an initial sense of insecurity over doing something different from standard veterinary practice. I found real meaning in the words of Henry J.

Kaiser, the great industrialist, who once said, "When your work speaks for itself, don't interrupt."

If the idea of giving your dog vitamins and minerals sounds a little silly, consider the following examples:

— A little brewers' yeast, mixed in your dog's supper bowl, will keep the fleas off him. Brewers' yeast is a rich source of the B complex vitamins and produces a taste in the dog's skin that fleas don't like. There is nothing silly about a flea-free dog.

— A pregnant German shepherd bitch on supplements will deliver her pups in under ten hours. Normally the whelping can take up to twenty-four. That's not silly.

— Hip dysplasia is a dreaded crippler of large-breed dogs. It has long been thought to be a problem of genetics. Extra vitamin C, the same vitamin C that these animals are supposed to produce themselves in sufficient quantity, stops hip dysplasia. The veterinary community first thought it was nonsense when I published a paper on this connection in 1976. Now other practitioners as well as breeders all around the world are using it successfully.

— Have you seen a frisky dachshund felled suddenly by a ruptured disc? It's a fairly common occurrence with the breed. Vitamin C or vitamin E will prevent it.

— Does your dog scratch endlessly and you can't figure out why? Try putting the animal on a good regimen of vitamins and minerals. Both you and your dog will be grateful.

Consider, too, what vitamins and minerals can do for old and debilitated dogs.

Hoss was a ten-year-old Great Dane and in pretty bad shape when he was brought—literally carried—into my office. Like many large-breed dogs in their middle and later years, Hoss was suffering from spinal myelopathy, a degenerative disease of the spine.

The dog was barely mobile, a weak, sorry shell of a once magnificent animal. He could no longer manage steps or rear up on his hind legs. You would touch him on the hind quarters and he'd go down like a kayoed boxer. He urinated and defecated where he lay.

A dog like this is usually put to sleep.

I gave the animal injections of vitamin B complex and C. I instructed his owners to follow up with oral doses.

The improvement was noticeable almost at once. Hoss, the dying dog, gradually became more mobile and friskier than he had been in a long while. He lived on for another year but without the terrible previous agony. His owners were happy to have had that extra time with him.

Bea Barlow, a lady from Bowie, Maryland, called me about a similar case involving her ten-year-old Doberman, Kurt. She had taken the dog to a big university veterinary school and was told the animal would have to be euthanized. She had read about my work and asked me if vitamin C would help. I said it couldn't hurt, but without seeing the animal I couldn't say for sure if it would clear up the condition. She said she had nothing to lose and would try to find a veterinarian in her area who would inject the dog with vitamin C.

Some time later she telephoned to say she was having no luck finding such a veterinarian. They just didn't believe in vitamin C, she said. I told her to try vitamin C by mouth, using powder or tablets. This approach would take longer to yield results than an injection but it might work. She said she would try anything.

Several weeks later, after starting the dog on oral vitamin C and other vitamins and minerals according to my instructions, she called back. She said Kurt was turning over by himself. Previously she used to have some kids come in and turn the dog over because he couldn't do it himself and the animal was too heavy for her to move.

After two months, the dog was up and walking about. A happy and bubbling Bea Barlow telephoned to tell me the news. She said also that she had taken the animal back to the veterinary school. The doctors examined Kurt and passed judgment: "spontaneous recovery."

Three years later I received a letter from Maryland. Kurt had just died of a heart attack. He had been active until the last minute.

Nothing is more saddening and depressing than watching your once-active dog become a helpless cripple and then being told there is no medical hope for the animal. Bea Barlow loved Kurt too much. She refused to see him deteriorate in front of her eyes without trying all possible therapies, even one so "unorthodox" as vitamins. In recent years, I have not seen this rather common condition in any aging animal that is routinely on a vitamin and mineral program.

Rusty, a declining Irish setter of sixteen years, was brought in by his owner. This dog had a stiff gait, poor appetite, a scruffy hair coat, and growths around the rectum.

I put him on 100 International Units (IUs) of vitamin E for the first week and upped that to 200 for the second week. Within ten days he began to show new life. In two and one half weeks, owner Phillip Clark of San Jose reported that Rusty was back to eating twice a day, "as he used to do when younger." He was taking longer walks despite an arthritic sacroiliac and a lame left hip.

After six weeks, Mr. Clark wrote to say that the hair coat was better than it had ever been during the dog's entire life. Swelling and protruding growths outside the rectum were diminishing. Rusty had even resumed his old habit of lively barking around 5 P.M., which was the dog's customary way of saying, "I'm hungry, where's my tasty snack of meat?" The barking had stopped several months before.

"Actually," said Mr. Clark, "we figured he'd be quite dead by now the way he was going. What has happened is really quite remarkable."

Rusty lived on for another year. I felt we were able to stimulate him in those last days to the maximum for his age and condition with the simple introduction of vitamin E.

2

Preventive
Veterinary Medicine:
Getting at the Cause
of Problems

While you may be your dog's master, the purpose of this book is not to make you your dog's doctor as well. Neither you nor this book can replace a skilled veterinarian trained to deal with animal disease. However, I can show you how to enjoy your animal more and save veterinary bills that absolutely can be avoided.

I will give you the same simple directions I have given hundreds of dog owners. I will explain how to handle a number of common conditions with inexpensive vitamin and mineral products readily available in drug stores, health food stores, pet stores, supermarkets, and even in your veterinarian's office.

Even more important to me is to teach you how a simple daily supplementation program can prevent or minimize physical distress and disease. By simple I mean it can be done in a matter of seconds. By following my instructions, by taking the few seconds every day to supplement their animals' diets, many of my clients have been able to save themselves medical bills. And you can do the same thing.

In Part Three I lay out a general prevention plan and show you just how easy it is to follow. The plan is divided into cycle of life sections that will tell you what, why, and how much supplementation is needed at certain periods of your pet's life. You will also receive advice on how to choose and how to use the supplements. Then, in Part Four you will find descriptions of specific canine conditions and information on how vitamins and minerals can be utilized in dealing with them.

I believe that prevention is the name of the game. It is what medicine should really be about, whether humans or animals are involved. Doesn't it make more sense to prevent the disease from happening rather than waiting around to treat disease once it strikes and inflicts damage? It was H. E. Sigerist, the leading historian of the medical profession, who said, "The ideal of medicine is the prevention of disease, and the necessity for curative treatment is a tacit admission of its failure."

But medical schools—both the human and veterinary kind—are totally geared to disease. There are no courses in "wellness" to teach doctors how to make apparently healthy beings into optimally healthy beings.

Among the ancient Chinese, health was regarded as so important that the people paid their physicians to keep them healthy. And they paid only while well. There was no payment for treatment of illness.

Hippocrates, the father of medicine, told his medical students 2,500 years ago, "Let thy food be thy medicine and thy medicine be thy food."

In looking at the present state of the art, it doesn't seem like the Chinese or Hippocrates had much influence.

One leading medical school official told the Senate Select Committee on Nutrition and Human Needs that probably 90 percent of today's medical school graduates couldn't describe an adequate, nutritious diet that was appropriate for people at various stages of life. The graduates "know more about heart transplants than they do about basic nutrition," he said.[1] And yet, doctors will say you don't need extra vitamins because if you eat an adequate diet you get all the vitamins you need. They don't even know what an adequate diet is!

The situation in veterinary medicine is not much better.

Nutritional education in veterinary medicine is an "impoverished area," Dr. Robert Wilson of Washington State University's Department of Veterinary Medicine told the same senate committee. He attributed the situation to the emphasis on diagnosis and treatment.

"Something in our psychological makeup leads us to enjoy the role of the old family doctor who is always on hand to help out in an emergency," he said, "but we seem to find less satisfaction in preventing problems."[2]

Dr. Lyle Baker, a veterinarian for large animals in California's agricultural central valley, put it this way: "During my eight years of college, I was taught virtually nothing about nutrition and prevention of disease. As a matter of fact, the slightest mention of the possibility that something you ingested might exert some control over any disease was justification for branding one an oddball, out of step with the times."[3]

From my own veterinary school days, I remember only one course in livestock feeds. There was nothing on small animal nutrition. There was fleeting familiarization with the relationship of classic disease syndromes and specific nutrient deficiencies. We heard nothing about what types of food were better than others and certainly nothing on vitamin supplementation. How could we, coming out of this background, expect to advise clients about correct nutrition for their pets? How could we understand the impact of any particular food on any particular animal? How could we diagnose the low grade and subtle symptoms of nutritional deficiencies when all we were taught was to recognize the blatant terminal symptoms? The answers are all the same. We couldn't . . . and we still can't.

Today, twenty-five years later, it is still pretty much the same way. Young graduates emerge with little more knowledge of nutrition and prevention than when I received my degree in 1954.

Despite all the wonderful equipment and techniques and diagnostic precision we have, we also have—sad to say—a continual rise in the rate of deaths from chronic disorders. A lot of this disease is preventable. Certainly the millions of people who are out in the streets jogging every day think so. And the people who are sacrificing the joy of sweets and alcohol and the junk food they grew up unhealthy on also think so.

We humans have a free choice to do something about the quality of our lives. We can attempt to prevent disease. Our pets can't. They have to eat the man-made food we give them (and I will have plenty to say about that in the next chapter). They have to live in the environment we place them, which is often confined quarters without room to romp and exercise. They have to breathe the air we pollute. We have domesticated the dog and he is as dependent as a young child. The animal himself can't prevent disease. But you, his owner, can do something about it. And that is what this book is all about. It is my attempt to help you help your dependent animal.

At my San Jose animal hospital, I do all the things that other veterinarians do. I diagnose and treat disease. I perform spays and neuters and other surgery. I am proud of the fact that two surgical procedures I originated are today widely used in small animal veterinary practice. I give immunizations. I pull out the odd burr that dogs manage so skillfully to imbed in their ears. I set broken bones. I also administer drugs.

Drugs, of course, relieve symptoms and acute distress and are necessary to the medical practitioner—be he or she a doctor who handles humans or handles animals. But drugs don't cure. They don't eliminate the cause of the symptom.

Drugs also have side effects. They are, after all, powerful foreign substances put into the body. You may knock out the symptom—let's say it is chronic headaches—but often you have to give another drug to combat a second symptom caused by the first drug. Meanwhile, the cause of the original symptom is still at large and bound to raise hell elsewhere in the body if it is not corrected.

The situation is akin to having a hole in your roof and instead of looking for the hole and patching it, you put a bucket on the floor when it rains in order to catch the water. Effective, yes. You solve the immediate problem of water. But the cause is still there.

When people have headaches they take aspirin. That helps with the immediate problem, just like the bucket. But it doesn't get at the cause and the cause of the headache is surely not a lack of aspirin in the body, just as the cause of the leak is not a lack of buckets.

To get at the cause of the problem, I do something that most veterinarians don't do. I provide my animals with vitamins and minerals.

My idea of preventive veterinary medicine is a first cousin to a new branch of human medicine founded by Linus Pauling, the two-time Nobel Prize winner. It is called orthomolecular medicine.

The big word means "right molecules in the right amounts." The idea is to provide optimal amounts of substances that are normally present in the body to achieve optimal health conditions or to treat disease. Vitamins and minerals are such substances. Drugs, obviously, are not. They are not found in the body.

The vitamins and minerals combine, react, and transform with other internal ingredients in an endless number of known and unknown biochemical processes that fuel the machinery of body and brain. However, because of stress, poor diet, aging, and environmental and genetic factors, they often become depleted and thus are not available in sufficient quantity or quality. The result is less than optimal health . . . or varying degrees of disease.

Orthomolecular medicine provides these natural substances in the form of vitamin and mineral supplementation. The whole body is treated—and benefits—in this way. All systems are strengthened, revitalized. An optimal level of health is achieved. If disease is present, the whole body is bolstered and fortified to fight the disorder and get on with the process of healing.

This is as true for pets as it is for humans.

I cannot guarantee that a supplementation program will entirely eliminate all disease, but what it doesn't prevent it will minimize. Clients who follow my program tell me they have animals living longer and almost disease free. These dogs maintain their teeth and good vision longer. They are hardier, healthier, and do not come down with the problems that might otherwise be expected. When I see these animals for routine checkups, they seem to be saying, "Hey, Doc, look at me! I have no aches and pains. I am not worried about my hips or my spine. I feel great!"

If a bitch is on supplements she delivers in half the normal time. The puppies are going to be healthy. You won't see litter runts, bad hips, open craniums, or sudden death.

If the puppy gets his vitamins from the start he is benefiting from extra protection that he can really use. Puppyhood is trauma time. The stresses are endless and often exact a sad toll in the form of illness and debility from a tiny animal struggling to survive.

One breeder I deal with in Southern California raises golden retrievers. She decided to put her animals on the supplementation program in an attempt to stop the hip dysplasia that had been a chronic problem for her.

After several litters she told me that she had not only been able to eliminate the hip dysplasia problem but now she was getting pups far superior to anything she had been getting before.

One day, a woman who had bought one of these retriever pups brought the animal in for immunization. The dog was about twelve weeks old. By coincidence, another client with a golden retriever the same age was also in my office. The latter animal came from a pet shop and had not received any supplementation.

The difference between the two young dogs was striking. The supplemented pup was about a fourth larger than his counterpart, his hair coat was richer and shinier, and he appeared much more alert.

Anne Rogers Clark, of Cecilton, Maryland, has for years been one of the country's leading professional dog handlers and kennel operators. She informs me that for more than twenty-five years she has maintained her animals on a multivitamin and mineral supplement.

"I have found over generation and generation of animals that we get a better looking, more tightly constructed dog," she says. "Whenever a litter was produced during a period when for some reason or another we weren't supplying the supplement, it seemed that the young were not as tight and hard. The form and muscle were not quite as good."[4]

Irving Eldredge operates the Tirvelda Kennel in Middleburg, Virginia. In his forty-five years of breeding and handling Irish setters, his animals have won something like 125 championships. Two years ago he started his dogs on vitamin C.

"The dogs seem to be in terrific health and bloom," he says. "My wife, watching me take one of my dogs through its paces during a show, commented that the animal really seemed to be in so much better condition and looked so much more healthy compared to the other setters in there."[5]

I repeatedly hear these kinds of stories. They tell me that the supplements are bringing out the maximum that any particular breed has to offer.

A good prevention program of vitamins and minerals translates directly into economy: you save time and money. Short of routine vaccinations, spaying, checkups, and genuine emergencies, you shouldn't have to spend time and money visiting your vet. Too many people will run to the animal hospital at the drop of a sneeze. The vitamins should prevent the sneeze.

What is a genuine emergency? Obviously you should head straight for the vet if your dog has an accident, if it is bleeding profusely, if somebody squashes its tail under a rocking chair, if it has a convulsive seizure, has difficulty breathing, is unconscious, gets injured in a dogfight, snags a burr in the ear, or gets hit over the head with a baseball bat.

Besides the love and attachment between dog and owner, there is also a very real cost factor involved in obtaining and maintaining an animal. Ten years ago, you could buy a pedigreed German shepherd for $50 to $100. The same dog now will cost you $300 to $500. The average pedigreed dog bought from a pet shop costs $250 to $300. I know of a loan company here in the San Jose area that will even finance the purchase of your dog.

Once you have an animal you have to feed it. Each year in this country we spend more than four times as much money on pet food than we do on baby food. So you are paying for the pleasure of a pet even if you obtained the animal for free. And for your money, you want a healthy and happy pet.

On the other side of the coin, breeders and pet shop owners are concerned about the health of their animals. Their reputations and businesses are at stake. They have to replace an animal or return payment if the dog dies or is defective in any way.

One breeder of German shepherds told me that sometimes she had to replace three and even four animals from a single litter because of hip dysplasia. Like the golden retriever lady, she tried supplementation and has no more problems.

I know breeders who incorporate into their sales agreements a clause stating that the pups are guaranteed dysplasia-free as long as they are kept on a regimen of vitamin C.

Often a client will ask me, "Doctor, does my dog *really* need vitamins and minerals? Isn't he supposed to get all he needs in his food?"

"No," I answer, "your dog doesn't need vitamins and minerals supplementally to survive. It is only a matter of how you want the animal to survive. Do you want him without kennel cough when you go away and board him for two weeks? Do you want him without hip dysplasia? A dysplastic dog will survive, but in what shape? Do you want him scratching all the time? Full of fleas?

"Your dog is supposed to be getting all his basic nutrient requirements in the man-made food he receives. Yet what I have seen over the years is that supplementation is making the difference between a sickly or apparently healthy dog and an optimally healthy dog. Which kind of dog do you want?

"Remember too that we often live in very close contact with our animals. Our children play with them. Kiss them. Love them. Hug them. Some people even sleep with their pets. Bacterial and viral infections can be easily passed between man and dog at this kind of close range. A weak dog, a stressed dog, is going to be more prone to infection and disease. That means more risk to you, the owner. Therefore, I am talking about a program that will not only protect the dog but will also protect the dog's owner."

There are many gaps in the veterinarian's knowledge of canine nutrition. We are taught very little about it. This book contains lessons I have learned from my clinical experience and information I have learned from research. This book too may have its gaps. There is so much more to be known about this subject. But whatever its shortcomings, I hope this book will in some way stimulate the veterinary medical establishment to begin looking at nutrition in a new light—not from the traditional standpoint of vitamin and mineral deficiencies, but from the standpoint of creating optimal health.

3

What the TV Commercials Don't Tell You About Dog Food

There is mounting evidence that a lifetime of eating commercial pet foods can shorten your pet's life, make him fatter than he ought to be and contribute to the development of such increasingly common disorders as cystitis and stones (in cats), glaucoma and heart disease (in dogs), diabetes, lead poisoning, rickets and serious vitamin-mineral deficiencies (in both cats and dogs).

—From Consumers Digest,
November–December, 1979[1]

Unfortunately, the most prominent source of nutrition education for pet owners and veterinarians alike currently available is the Madison Avenue merchant acting on behalf of the pet food industry through mass media advertisements. When dawn comes up over Manhattan, these fecund salesmen begin to stir and scratch and dream up new ways of promoting a product that may bear little relation to pet nutrition. Much of the information . . . on how best to feed your pet . . . is misleading and primarily designed to sell a product . . . often with very little if any supporting evidence to back the claims made by the manufacturer. The pet owning public and in many cases the veterinary profession has thus been at the mercy of the mass media adver-

*tising, often to the detriment of the health of the animal and
increased cost to the client.*

*—Dr. Paul M. Newberne,
Department of Nutrition and Food Science,
Massachusetts Institute of Technology*[2]

Once upon a time there were no cheese-flavored burger dinners,
no tender chunk-sized puppy chow, and no canned chicken,
liver, and egg combinations on the face of this earth. This was an
age before any dog had set eyes on multicolored biscuit snacks
or eaten out of red and yellow plastic bowls or even appeared in
a TV commercial.

For the dog, was this unprocessed past a time of nutritional
deprivation or was he better off foraging and hunting and collecting scraps at his master's table?

Many, including myself, feel that man's best friend probably
did better on his own before the bags and cans of man-made
food came into his life.

In the past, dogs ran wild or lived predominantly out of doors.
While some still do today, many have been highly urbanized,
most have been highly domesticated, and practically all of them
made totally dependent on man for food.

Dogs used to roam and kill their own food. An animal in nature has instinctual intelligence for his nutritional needs. The
first course of food after the kill is the innards. The dog would
open up the abdomen of his prey and eat the liver, the spleen,
the kidneys, and the intestinal matter of undigested grain,
greens, and nuts. These visceral parts are rich in vitamins and
minerals. The liver, for example, is an extremely rich source of A,
C, and the B complex group.

The last thing the dog would do is eat the muscle tissue—what
we humans call steak—which contains considerably less in the
way of nutrients. An animal in the wild might return hours later
perhaps to munch on this lesser meat. It is unlikely he would
have anything to do with the gristle, hair, lungs, tails, and other
odd parts that are routinely incorporated in commercial food.

These predatory canines knew what they were doing. They
knew what their bodies needed. They foraged and rooted around
for vegetables and berries, good sources of vitamins and min-

erals. Wolves, coyotes, and dogs are not true carnivores like the cats. They prefer meat but will eat most anything. The dog that fended for himself would appear to have had more of a balanced diet because he sought what he needed.

Today, we confine these animals to a backyard or an apartment and buy them food that is cheap and convenient to store and administer. We are dictating the dog's diet, or, to be more precise, providing a diet that is dictated by the pet food manufacturing industry.

The industry says the food it makes covers an animal's nutrient requirements. Does it really?

I have seen no end of dogs in varying states of unwellness and discomfort and traced the problem directly to nutrition.

Does the commercial food harm a dog? Quite often, yes. I see diet involved often enough as the cause of a dog's diarrhea, scratching, skin problems, kidney ailments, and other disorders.

Does the commercial food make an optimally healthy dog? Absolutely not.

As far as I am concerned, most commercial products are suspect. I am convinced they do not give the dog everything he needs and I know they give him some things he definitely doesn't need.

Many breeders are wise to the shortcomings of commercial food and abundantly supplement their animals' diets with vitamins and minerals to bring them to maximum condition. Most pet owners, however, are ignorant of the problems of store-bought pet food. They see the commercials on television and that generally is their sole source of nutritional information.

I don't expect pet owners to enroll in classes on animal nutrition. I don't know where they could go even if they were so motivated. We are all convenience-minded and for this reason there is a practical dependence upon commercially available food. My message is *caveat emptor!* Let the buyer beware! All is not as rosy as TV advertising would have you believe.

My intention is not so much to jolt you, which I probably will, but to make you a little wiser and show you how to compensate for the flaws in commercial food. I want to share with you some of the conclusions I am drawing after a nearly twenty-year, six-day-a-week parade of dogs in my practice. The animal hospital, you see, is the front line of battle. This is where I—and other veterinarians—see and treat the casualties of commercial pet foods.

There have been tremendous differences of opinion about the nutritional components of dog food and particularly how much meat and protein a dog should have. The high protein argument has been raging for years among veterinary nutritionists and it is not my intention to get involved in this squabble. I will leave it for future human wisdom to divine a dog's precise protein needs.

One thing is certain: many dogs are actually allergic to beef. This could be the result of the protein-converting enzyme system breaking down because of an excess diet of meat. Another fact: many older dogs suffer from seriously impaired kidney function and a large part of the blame is the prolonged overload on the kidneys to handle the wastes of excess protein metabolism.

Until the time comes when the protein question and other issues concerning dog food are cleared up, I will continue to dispense the same kind of advice: no matter what your dog is eating, the addition of vitamins and minerals will prevent or minimize disease.

Six out of ten families in the United States maintain pets in their households. There are about 50 million dogs and nearly 40 million cats. That's a huge captive market that needs to be fed and the pet food industry spends a ton of money advertising packaging gimmicks and making vague nutritional claims that will appeal to animal owners. In 1978, the pet food industry spent upward of $150 million on TV advertising alone. If that seems an enormous figure, then stop and consider the sales. In 1979, according to industry statistics, pet owners paid over $3 billion to feed their animals, an amount accounting for 7 percent of all food sales. In comparative terms, that is nearly four times as much as was spent on baby food and more than double the amount spent on cereals, flour, and macaroni products for people. "Today," says *Consumers Digest* magazine, "pet foods have replaced coffee as the number one mover on supermarket shelves."[3] The British are said to spend more on pet foods than they do for their beloved tea.

The average consumer is interested in convenience and economy. For sure, unless you have an ultraexpensive dog, a show dog, or a working dog with unusual feeding needs, you will be feeding your animal primarily out of the convenient and economical sacks, packages, and cans you find on the market shelf.

Pet food is usually fortified with vitamins. This is because the natural ingredients do not come up to the nutrient requirements as defined by the Subcommittee on Dog Nutrition of the National Academy of Science's National Research Council (NRC). Moreover, the processing and storage of the finished products are known to result in substantial losses of vitamins. Vitamins are sensitive to heat, moisture, light, and oxidation. They lose potency under these conditions. Vitamin B_1, also known as thiamine, is well-known for losing strength during processing and storage.[4]

The degradation of vitamin content occurs both in the natural ingredients and even in the vitamins that are actually added during processing—the so-called fortifying vitamins. One of the major suppliers to the pet food industry has published data showing these losses to be substantial. In order to compensate for this loss, the producers are urged to fortify their products with amounts of vitamins above the NRC levels.[5]

But overage or not, a sack of dry food is going to be less fresh and less nutritious after being opened a dozen times than when you first brought it from the store. Every time you open the bag, there is air, there is heat, there is moisture, and there is going to be a little less potency and nutrition each time.

"Complete and Balanced"

You have no doubt seen some products that claim to be "complete and balanced." But what exactly does it mean? I put the question to one official at the U. S. Food and Drug Administration's Animal Feeds Division, which oversees the advertising claims of pet food manufacturers.

"If a product claims it is complete and balanced then that claim has to be substantiated," the official said. "The Association of American Feed Control Officials is composed mostly of state feed control officials, and they have set out a whole group of regulations. They specify a pet food cannot be called complete and balanced unless it complies with the nutrient requirements of the NRC or the product has undergone testing according to their protocols. The role of the FDA is to make sure that a label cannot have anything false or misleading. A product better be able to substantiate that it is complete and balanced."

I wanted to know if the products do indeed come up to these standards.

"Most of them do if they say complete and balanced," the official said.

I asked if they are checked for vitamin content.

"No, in general no," the official said. "But if there was any question about the vitamin content we would check."

"And how do you know then if they have in there what they are supposed to have?" I wanted to know. "Aren't you the judge of those standards?"

"The FDA isn't going to go out and check every food that is on the market," was the answer. "We only check things out if there is reason to."

"Then most of the products that claim to be complete and balanced are taken at face value?"

"That's right."

"There is no way of knowing then if they have indeed met the NRC standards?"

"No," said the official, "everything is going to be based on the word and the integrity of the pet food companies. For the most part, from what I have seen of big plant operations, they have been very good about controlling themselves. There have been some problems in the past but in general the pet food companies are very wary about the government getting involved in their business."

My impression from this conversation was that controls are pretty lax. The more I learned about pet food the stronger this impression became.

What exactly are the NRC standards that pet food manufacturers are supposed to meet in order to call their products complete and balanced? And just how lacking are the products that don't make this claim?

The Subcommittee on Dog Nutrition is composed of veterinary nutritionists. The group reviews and publishes every several years updated information relating to nutritional requirements. Other subcommittees do similar work with other species, including humans. The opinion of these groups are registered in the form of RDAs that you hear so much about. RDAs are the recommended daily allowances.

Writing in a veterinary publication, MIT's Paul M. Newberne commented that the NRC standards are minimum requirements that have proven to be adequate for canine maintenance. But, he points out, years of scientific investigation of these requirements has led to a situation where "we know more about the minimal requirements essential to the maintenance of the dog than we do about maximum or optimal requirements. . . . The minimum requirements are just that, and cannot be construed as optimum." Moreover, he adds, the requirements for special needs, such as those associated with pregnancy, growth, or illness, have not been precisely determined.[6]

In a 1973 publication entitled *Dishing Up the Dog Food,* the FDA points out that the "complete and balanced diet" claim on the label does not mean that the product can be used as the sole diet for every dog. What this means is that the product provides the minimum diet to assure that the animal will maintain its body weight and size, with a normal amount of exercise. This is called a "maintenance diet."

The publication suggests that a pet owner may want his dog to have more than a maintenance diet for a number of reasons. For instance, it says, more protein is required for puppy growth, pregnancy, lactation, and other situations of stress.[7]

Another admirable reason to supplement the animal's diet is to elevate the dog from a minimum and maintenance standard to one of optimal health. It is obvious to me that the commercial products are adequate for maintaining nothing more than a minimal state of health. By themselves these products seem to fall short in protecting an animal from the normal stresses encountered in life and the abnormal stresses of chemical toxins, drugs, parasites, trauma, and environmental pollution. The body requires more nutrition than usual in times of stress and if this is not provided, the stage is set for nutritional deficiencies and trouble.

How can a commercial diet that is geared to minimal requirements safeguard an animal through a lifetime of stress? The answer is clear. It can't. Whenever I supplement animals with a vitamin and mineral program they respond as if born again.

The 4-Ds

After graduation from veterinary school and before going into private practice, I spent seven years as a veterinary meat inspector for the Department of Agriculture and the U. S. Air Force. During this time, I was assigned to a number of major slaughterhouses, first on the East Coast and later in California.

The job of the veterinary meat inspector is to inspect the animals and carcasses that are intended for human consumption and to give them the "USDA Inspected" stamp if they pass scrutiny. By no means though does every animal pass inspection. An animal comes along with a head full of pus, for instance. If the infection is not systemic, that is, engulfing the whole animal, you throw out the head and pass the body. Another animal comes along with a liver disease but the rest of the carcass is OK. You throw out the liver and pass the body. Another animal may be suffering from tuberculosis or cancer and the illness is systemic. In that case the whole animal is condemned.

Condemned parts and animals that are rejected for human consumption are commonly used in commercial pet foods. So-called "4-Ds," meaning dead, dying, diseased, or disabled animals, are also used for pet foods.

Shocking, isn't it? The buying public hasn't got the foggiest notion that 4-D animals are used in pet foods. Do you expect the TV commercials to boast that product X uses the finest of diseased meat? One USDA official made this comment to me: "Some of these companies claim all beef in their cans and this is true. But they don't tell you the source is a 4-D animal. Most people think they are getting sirloin steak. If they think the healthiest animals in the world are going into those products, they are sadly mistaken."

Let me give you an idea of what goes on. If an animal dies in winter and freezes up or is placed in refrigeration pretty soon after death, it doesn't go through much decomposition. This kind of animal can be boned out and sold as muscle meat or various other fleshy constituents, primarily for canning operations. It will be put through a heat and pressure process that will make the meat commercially sterile. On the other hand, if the animal dies in the middle of summer and is pretty rank, it is sterilized and then rendered and made into meat and bone meal, the two major ingredients of dry dog food.

Some might argue that meat is meat and dogs will eat it even if it is not fit for human consumption. I have always wondered if there is any effect on the animals eating diseased meat, even if it is sterile. Remember that pets are being fed this on a daily basis.

Range death is not always due to disease. In this age of chemical pollution, there is a significant loss of animals due to chemical poisoning. And where do those animals wind up? You guessed it. Many are processed into pet food, toxins and all.

One veterinarian toxicologist at the FDA, whom I asked about this problem, expressed concern about the potential health hazard for the consuming pet:

There are many things that are going into pet foods that are questionable in nature, and among them are the toxic agricultural chemicals—the pesticides and herbicides—that are killing numbers of livestock every day. These animals are then processed for pet food or livestock and poultry feed.

Nobody knows how much of the toxins are coming through the processing. We don't have the adequate means for evaluation. The sterilization will take care of the microbes and nothing else, but most agricultural chemicals will survive the high temperature involved in processing.

Even if the toxins are not present in appreciable amounts in the muscle tissue, and we are not sure of that, I have a great deal of concern about the visceral parts where larger amounts of the toxins may be present. These internal organs accumulate toxins that the body had been unable to excrete and thus contain the actual chemicals that cause the death of thousands of animals.

Certainly these are not the type of ingredients that should be in animal feeds.

One pet food producer who makes a quality product I have been using for years told me that many companies use 4-D animals. He feels, as I do, that some government agency should pass a law requiring the manufacturer to identify the source of the meat. A consumer should know what he or she is giving to an animal that in many cases is a family fixture.

The question is who should call the pet food industry to task?

The FDA has the obvious priority to protect food used by humans and as the toxicologist pointed out to me, the appropriations that do exist are inadequate for the mandated actions of the agency.

"We just don't have enough funds to do as much as we are supposed to do," he said. "So we have to make a choice."

What about the U. S. Department of Agriculture?

The USDA is only concerned about meat for human consumption. It has no federal standards for animal foods. Only one national producer of dog food (Quaker Oats) claims "government inspection" on the label, and it is entitled to the claim because it has voluntarily paid for an inspection service provided by the USDA. The inspection covers only the company's canned and semimoist product and not its dry pet food. Three plants are involved and they are required to meet the same standards as any meat processing plant for human food under the jurisdiction of U. S. Department of Agriculture inspection, according to a spokesman for the USDA's Food Safety and Quality Service. The products must meet NRC requirements, the spokesman said, and what's more, "the raw meat materials must have originated from U.S. inspected and passed carcasses. Lungs from approved animals are not eligible for human food but are considered wholesome for dogs and are permitted to be used here. We know what is going into that product. This company could not be using 4-D animals for its canned and semimoist products."

The spokesman said that only one other canned food producer, Florida's Winn Dixie Stores, operates under the USDA inspection service.

Thus, there are no dry products and, with the smallest of exceptions, no canned or semimoist products with any kind of federal inspection. Good or bad, the standards are a matter of company individuality, and whatever policing the overworked FDA can manage.

Here in California, no 4-D animals can be slaughtered for pet food. That's a state regulation. But, as one state meat and poultry inspection official told me, "it is conceivable that canned pet food from other places might have such in it. We'd have no control over that."

The truth is that control over product ingredients and quality is feeble at best and that much of the commercial dog food is based on diseased material. Even if it is denatured and sterilized, I still have to ask the question: What's happening to the digestive systems and internal organs of the pets that have to eat and process this inferior, impure food on a long-term daily basis?

For years it has been common knowledge among the veterinarians of the San Jose area—and probably elsewhere as well—that one of the popular brands of canned dog food is a notorious contributor to kidney disease. A client comes in complaining that the dog is listless, has no appetite, and its breath smells of urine. Older dogs are usually affected after eating this brand for years. The symptoms were so well-defined and the product incriminated so many times that the condition was called by the brand name.

This product has been extremely popular over the years because it sells very cheap. People buy it by the case. I opened up a can once and it really looked like the cheap product it was. It was obviously not muscle meat but seemed to be comprised of tendons, ligaments, and gristle, which are poor-quality protein.

In all fairness, not all the meat and meat meal is of questionable origin. Some of the rendering plants pick up supermarket and restaurant scraps and process these into meat or bone meal for pet food companies. It would be impossible to tell if the meal in any given bag of dry food came from diseased or approved sources. Only the manufacturers know the source of their ingredients and they aren't talking.

A Chemical Feast

Commercial dog food, like the master's food, has its ungodly array of chemical additives. Many of the same additives that are used in processed people's food are used in pet food. The standard daily menu of synthetic and manufactured nutrition that we place into our gullets has little or no resemblance to the food that nurtured the evolution of mankind. The same can be said for the dog. The only difference is that we can read labels and choose what we eat. The dog takes what we give him.

Dr. Benjamin Feingold, the well-known expert on the relationship of food additives to hyperactivity, says that additives affect every part of the body. From him we have learned that two commonly used additives cause behavioral difficulties in sensitive children and impair their learning ability. The two additives are butylated hydroxyanisole (BHA) and butylated hydroxytoluene (BHT). They are found in the vast majority of commercial pet foods. BHA and BHT are chemical antioxidants. They are added to prevent the fatty contents of the food from becoming rancid as they sit in warehouses, on store shelves, or in your garage. The fats are highly subject to oxidation and when this happens substances called peroxides are formed and can be very harmful to an animal.

BHA and BHT are under present inquiry following animal tests showing adverse kidney, liver, reproductive, brain, behavioral, and allergic reactions to the additives. BHT is banned in Romania, Sweden, and Australia and not permitted in baby food in England. The incriminating evidence has prompted the FDA to remove these preservatives from the GRAS list—Generally Regarded As Safe—however their continued use is permitted pending clarification of their health effects.

Experts whom I have asked about BHT and BHA have told me that this is a damned if you do and damned if you don't situation. If foods containing fatty substances are not eaten fresh, they can be very harmful. With the addition of preservatives, you have removed one possible source of trouble and replaced it with another. Short-term and high-level testing with BHT has produced enlarged livers in dogs. What then is happening over five or ten years? Might the BHA or BHT be causing cancer or setting up the biochemistry for some other disease process? Nobody knows for sure. The long-term tests are too expensive and demanding and so nobody does them. What tests have been done however indicate the probability of significant numbers of animals being unduly sensitive or allergic to preservatives.

The list of chemical additives in pet foods only begins with BHA and BHT. *Consumers Digest* says, "As a category, few foods are so liberally laced with artificial flavors as pet foods." The magazine quotes a source in the additive industry as saying that the addition of phony flavors such as bacon, garlic, lamb chop, blue cheese, and chicken is the only way to get pets to eat the poor-quality food.[8]

In a 1960 survey of packaged dog foods, *Consumer Reports* magazine commented that the products "are rigged for more than culinary and nutritional appeal to the dog; many of their most highly advertised characteristics are incorporated to appeal to the master."

Why were "meat red" colors or multicolored biscuits necessary, the magazine asked. "It seems incongruous when you realize that dogs are color blind."

As for the garlic added to many canned products, this addition only serves "to mask odors unpleasant to the master," the magazine said.[9]

Paul Newberne states "there is no evidence that any of the other flavors that are so widely used today have any influence on the acceptability or palatability of the dog food. In fact, it seems clear that most, if not all flavors, simply reflect the preferences of the dog's owner rather than the dog."[10]

Whether these kinds of additives are in there as enticement for the animals or perfume for the owner is not important to me. The fact is that they serve a questionable if not deceitful role. Company profit, not pet health, is the obvious purpose.

I am incensed at the presence of coloring additives that are purely for cosmetic appeal to the owner at the clear risk to the animal's health. Writing on food additives in *FDA Consumer* magazine, Phyllis Lehmann explains that coloring agents are used solely to improve appearances. "They contribute nothing to nutrition, taste, safety, or ease of processing," she writes. "And some consumer advocates argue that food is often made to look more appetizing at the risk of increasing health hazards."[11]

To me a prime case in point is the addition of sodium nitrite to many canned meat products. This chemical ingredient is used to make the product look bloodred. As the label euphemistically says, "to retain color." Since 1962, scientists have known that nitrite can combine with digestive, food, and agricultural chemicals to form nitroso compounds, many of which cause cancer in laboratory animals.

One of the world's leading experts on these compounds is Dr. William Lijinsky, director of the Chemical Carcinogenesis Program at the Frederick Cancer Research Center in Maryland. I asked Dr. Lijinsky about the risk to dogs eating products with sodium nitrite, even if the level of the additive is based on industry-accepted standards.

"My feeling is that sodium nitrite in food poses some risk," he said. "There is a risk to people and there is a risk to animals. Some pets live almost entirely on canned food and they are being exposed to the sodium nitrite for years.

"It doesn't mean that it would cause cancer but it might increase the risk.

"I have no idea why they put it in dog food since dogs are color-blind. It is apparently put in there for humans, which is absolutely ludicrous."

Israeli scientists have shown that sodium nitrite produced epileptic-like changes in the brain activity of rats who ate it regularly. The brain abnormalities appeared and persisted even in rats fed low doses of nitrite—not much more than what a heavy eater of cured meat might consume.[12] Convulsive seizures are not uncommon in dogs and veterinarians are often stumped in finding the cause. Could sodium nitrite be a factor?

Anne Rogers Clark, proprietor of the Surrey-Rimskittle Kennel in Cecilton, Maryland, has long been concerned about the chemical additives. She told me about a problem she had with commercial dog food:

In the beginning I was going like a grasshopper from one product to another until I found one that was palatable and

*didn't cost the earth and that the dogs did well on. I have
stayed with that commercial product for years but they have
done me dirt on several occasions, changing the formula
without having the kindness of telling people.*

*About four years ago, I suddenly had a kennel going
down the drain because all the dogs had diarrhea. I was
feeding twice the amount of food in order to maintain condition. But in the meantime, I was picking up four times as
much stool on the kennel runs. Finally I realized that the
problem was the dry food. The product had changed somewhat. The color was lighter and the flakes were larger.*

*I called the company to complain and they said, "Oh, oh,
we should have said something."*

*I really had a serious problem. And I wasn't alone. I
travel all the time and I talk to many dog people. When I
was having my problems I heard that a lot of other people
around the country using this same brand were having
problems as well. There was an extraordinary number of
cases of bloat with that particular food, as well as diarrhea.*

*The company settled a lot of cases out of court and went
back to its original formula. All of this, of course, was
hushed up.*

*The fact of the matter is that breeders are aware of the
impurities. You know from the change of color and texture
they are tampering with the product. But you have no other
place to go when feeding your dog is just a part of your life
and not your whole life.*

If ever there was a chemical feast, it is the semimoist food
products that have become popular over the last several years.
They are loaded with all kinds of artificial flavors, artificial coloring agents, and strange-looking additives with unpronounceable
names. One of these is ammoniated glycyrrhizin. Try pro-
nouncing that. According to Ruth Winter's *A Consumer's Dictionary of Food Additives,* this tongue twister is a product of the
licorice root and is found on the Food and Drug Administration's
top priority list for "short-term testing of mutagenic, teratogenic,
subacute and reproductive effects."[13] What that means is that it

is suspect of being able to create genetic and reproductive disturbances and physical deformities in developing embryos.

In addition to an alphabet soup of additives, these delightful products are liberally laced with different kinds of sugar. The sugars are supposed to help maintain a nice soft plastic texture.

Sucrose (white sugar) makes up 22 percent of the typical composition of semimoist food.[14] Are you worried about what sugar may be doing to your children? Start worrying now about what it may be doing to your pet. Sugar depletes the body of vitamins and minerals because it requires considerable amounts of these nutrients for its metabolism.

Paul Newberne has written that some of the additives used in the semimoist foods "are not well tolerated by all dogs." Cats are even more sensitive, he points out.[15]

Consumer polls have revealed that people are becoming increasingly concerned about the addition of chemicals in the food they eat. I certainly share this concern, not only for the food I myself eat but for the food that our pets have to eat. The food manufacturers don't seem to share this concern. More and more their products reflect the modern art of food technology. Resemblance to nature seems purely coincidental and is clearly waning. I have the feeling when looking at labels of commercial food —of both the people and pet kind—that I'm reading a chemical who's who.

Medical science cannot keep up with the whirlwind pace of chemical and food science. Who is to say, let alone prove, seven or eight years down the line when your dog becomes diseased, that the cause is BHA or sodium nitrite or some other specific additive or a combination of them? Your dog is exposed to a lifetime of chemicals not only in the food but in the air, in the environment, in his medicine. A whole multitude of factors can influence the disease process.

Industry usage of additives is inadequately controlled by government. There seem to be as many loopholes as there are additives, and there are thousands of them. In their book, *Eating May Be Hazardous to Your Health,* Jacqueline Verrett and Jean Carper reported that the GRAS additives—those "generally regarded as safe"—are indeed considered "so safe they are unrestricted and can be used in any amount in any food." They said that these additives "were not supposed to have detrimental information [to man or animal] against them in the medical literature, although as it was revealed later, few of the medical authorities consulted by the FDA even made a search to find out."[16]

Safety testing is generally conducted by the individual manufacturers themselves and not by independent researchers. Can objective findings be expected? I have my doubts. Moreover, the tests are usually conducted on a short-term basis and not for a long enough period to determine possible chronic toxicity.

The Lead Danger in Dog Food

In addition to what manufacturers intentionally put into pet food, there are other questionable elements in there as well. The agricultural and industrial chemicals I spoke about are examples of such. Lead is another.

Both humans and animals are exposed to many sources of lead in the environment. Lead forms 5 percent of the particulate matter in the air near large cities, mainly because of the use of lead in gasoline. Contamination from this source is a serious environmental problem. Past use of lead in pesticides has increased the level of lead in agricultural soil. There is an added exposure for people or animals who eat canned food because the lead used to solder the side seam of food cans "leaks" into the contents.

Lead is becoming a major health concern because of the toxic effects of this metal for which there is no known biological requirement. It does no good inside the body—yours or your animal's. The more lead in the body the greater the hazard to health.

Peeling paint and plaster and lead-laden dust in slum-type dwellings has been a frequent source of lead poisoning in children. In small animals, the most common cause of acute lead intoxication has been the licking or chewing of painted surfaces, particularly by puppies.

In both man and animals, the lead affects the nervous system, the kidneys, red blood cells, and the enzyme systems. Tests have shown lead to reduce the resistance of mice, rats, chickens, and rabbits to bacterial and viral challenges. In short, it causes a weakening of the immune system. Prolonged low-level intake of lead from inhaled air or ingestion of contaminated water or food has been singled out as a cause of hyperactivity and mental impairment in children. Lead is also suspected of causing cancer.

In 1975, researchers at the Connecticut Agricultural Experiment Station found that some canned dog food contained nearly ten times the 0.3 milligrams that is considered a hazardous daily level for children. The researchers purchased five samples of canned dog food at local food markets. Based on a typical fifteen ounce serving for the dog, all samples had more lead than the 0.3 level. The range was 0.43 for a chicken liver product up to 2.38 milligrams for a can of horsemeat and meat by-products.

Although the amounts of lead that may cause biochemical changes in an animal's body are not known, the researchers felt that the potentially toxic level of lead would be the same as that for a child. Clearly, they said, there were "potential risks to pets ingesting low levels of lead from pet foods."[17]

The year after the Connecticut revelations, veterinarian researcher James G. Fox of MIT published an analysis of all three types of pet food—dry, semimoist, and canned. He expressed concern that many of the products expose animals to "potentially toxic cumulative lead intakes," adding to the burden of lead they already absorb from the environment.

Fox analyzed thirty-two samples of canine products from eleven different manufacturers. If a twenty-pound dog were to eat his typical daily requirement of food in the form of semimoist food, the amount of lead content, on the basis of seven samples, ran from 0.024 to 0.171 milligrams—the lowest of the three food types. The same dog eating its daily ration in dry food would take in 0.29 to 0.71 milligrams of lead, based on five samples. With canned food, the lead levels ranged from 0.105 to 1.050 milligrams, or, expressed in another way, from one-third to five times the daily level considered hazardous for a child.[18]

Along with these findings came a reminder that nutritionists are concerned about the health of humans who consume pet foods. The prospect of people eating pet food with the high lead and chemical content is rather horrifying. However, I understand that because of economic reasons some older and low-in-come individuals do actually eat it on a regular basis. Perhaps they might be cured of that habit by reading this chapter.

A subsequent study by Fox revealed marked lead contamination in the mineral mixtures that are used to fortify the foodstuffs. Fox urged the commercial food companies to more carefully monitor the mixes in order to reduce this "major source of lead."[19]

The problem is really not so simple. Lead is everywhere as a major component of industrial and agricultural pollutants and as a factor in the processing and canning of products. People, dogs, cats, wild rats and laboratory rats, and all living creatures are continually absorbing it. I am convinced that a significant proportion of health problems in animals have their origins in the constant and excessive absorption of lead and other toxic metal contaminants like cadmium and mercury. Subtoxic levels of lead have been shown to decrease the efficiency of the immune system, affect liver and kidney function, and actually decrease the life-span of experimental animals. I am sure it is doing the same thing in pets.

Working with a California pet foundation, I determined that lead levels in cats suffering from feline leukemia were extremely high. Mercury was also found to be present in abnormally high amounts—supplied probably by dietary fish. Feline leukemia is believed caused solely by a virus. How, I ask, can a cat keep its resistance high when the very food it eats is undermining its immune system?

In a study of lead poisoning in small animals, Dr. E.G.C. Clarke of London's Royal Veterinary College provided some insight on the extent and impact of lead-related problems in dogs:

— A New Zealand veterinarian found that 30 percent of the dogs he autopsied had levels of lead in the liver indicative of poisoning.

— A 1963 study of lead poisoning concluded that "many cases may be overlooked."

— A 1948 study suggested that lead poisoning may often be the cause of "fits" in dogs.

Clarke made this comment about the intake of lead: "It has been estimated that a [grown] man has a daily intake of 0.5 milligrams obtained from food, from water, and from the atmosphere, and that a continuous intake of 1.0 milligrams a day over long periods may result in symptoms of lead poisoning. Although no definite figures are available it is probable that a similar state of affairs exists for domestic animals. In fact, the intake may very well be proportionately higher owing to lower standards of hygiene and less stringent dietary safety levels. Thus there is only a narrow gap between normal and potentially toxic lead intake, and any adventitious source of lead may bridge the gap and give rise to poisoning."[20]

I feel that the gap may be bridged every day. According to Fox's estimates, a 20-pound dog is getting anywhere from 0.29 to 0.71 milligrams a day of lead from his dry food alone. A dog weighing 110 pounds is receiving from 1.0 to 2.5 milligrams of lead! These figures are clearly in the danger zone!

The FDA, concerned about the high level of lead in human food, has asked food processors to reduce the lead content in their products by at least 50 percent. It has not asked the same of the pet food industry. Doesn't anybody care?

An FDA official told me that there is no way to justify the level of lead in pet foods.

"With adequate testing and controls," he said, "it could be eliminated. But these controls cost money and what are people willing to pay to feed their pets? Whatever the cost to the company it would clearly be felt by the consumer in higher prices."

If, when, and how much the pet food industry will move to clean up its lead act is a question that needs answering. Fortunately, lead is a slow poison and you can take some remedial action to prevent your animal from suffering any physical damage from this omnipresent poison. The solution is actually much simpler than the problem. By regularly supplementing your dog's daily diet with vitamins and minerals, including the high doses of vitamin C that I recommend, you can neutralize the effects of lead intake and keep your animal's immune system strong and his vital organs robust.

As I will explain later on, vitamin C is a marvelous detoxifier of harmful metals like lead and cadmium. It handcuffs these metals and escorts them out of the body. Zinc, iron, calcium, and magnesium, taken as supplements, have also been determined to reduce the toxicity of lead.

Bacteria: A Problem of Unknown Proportions

The consumer buying a pet food product isn't concerned about germs and fungi when picking up a product off the shelf and tossing it into the shopping cart. It would probably never enter that person's mind that such a danger exists. And certainly, for the canned products that undergo a heating and pressure sterilization process, there is essentially no problem. However, the risk does exist with the dry foods.

In 1974, two veterinary researchers examined the germ content of ten samples from each of thirteen brands of dry dog food. The samples were bought from local retail markets.

Dr. Warren C. Ladiges and James F. Foster found contamination from several bacteria that are known to cause illness in people and dogs. They didn't know, however, whether the amounts they found could actually cause disease. "The basic question remains whether dry dog foods are a source of sporadic disease in dogs," they said.[21]

More questions were raised in an investigation of dry dog food conducted by the city of Milwaukee. The probe followed a 1975 case of gastrointestinal infection in a hospitalized baby girl. The infection was traced to salmonella, a bacterial food contaminant. The health department investigators found a sick dog in the household. It was tested and found positive for salmonella. Dry dog foods have been incriminated as the source of salmonella infections among laboratory animals as far back as 1952, and now the investigators wanted to know if the sick dog had been contaminated through its diet. Examination of the commercial dry food being eaten by the dog turned up the presence of two types of salmonella bacteria. The question still remained as to whether the dog food became contaminated in the home through unsanitary conditions or was already contaminated upon purchase.

Twenty-five samples, representing four different manufacturers and two retail store brands, were purchased. The products of two of the manufacturers were found to contain bacterial contamination. Eleven samples of the original suspect product were examined and all were found to contain salmonella. As many as eight different strains were isolated in one bag!

The health department officials suggested that the potential hazard of product contamination be investigated because "the possibility that dried dog foods may provide a vehicle to introduce salmonella into the home is not sufficiently recognized by consumers."[22]

Following this incident, the FDA conducted an investigation of plants operated by the large manufacturer that had been so roundly faulted. The source of salmonella contamination was found near the end of the processing line, after the point where the product undergoes routine heat treatment to destroy all such microorganisms.

The pet food industry has tried over the years to prevent this kind of contamination and to a large degree it has succeeded. In 1955, as a point of comparison, researchers found that 26 percent of dry dog food they examined contained salmonella. A recent FDA probe turned up only 2 positive results out of 207 samples. That translates to 1 percent—a sharp drop in the contamination level.

The investigations indicate that pet foods can be produced virtually salmonella-free. Still, if 1 percent of dry food is contaminated during the manufacturing process, that spells potential trouble for a lot of dogs. Probably many dogs are carriers and not showing the signs. They could, of course, pick up salmonella not only from food but from other animals, from fecal matter in the street, or from contamination on the kitchen floor brought in from outside. Salmonella poisoning can cause vomiting and diarrhea within thirty-six hours after contact, however this condition may mistakenly be diagnosed as something other than food poisoning.

As the Milwaukee case showed, salmonella can be transferred from animal to human. We live in very close contact with our pets. It may be a good idea to follow the suggestion written in the Koran, namely that "all those of the Mohammedan faith who handle a dog must wash their hands seven times."

Clearly, sanitary conditions vary from manufacturer to manufacturer, from plant to plant, from worker to worker. *DVM*, the news magazine of veterinary medicine, reported in 1979 that the

FDA had clamped down on one particular pet food canning operation because the company's practices "represented a significant health hazard," specifically the threat of another bacterial contaminant, botulism. Agency officials said this was not the only action underway concerning pet food manufacturers and possible good manufacturing practice violations.[23]

One government observer of the pet food industry told me there is a constant problem with bacterial contamination at rendering plants where employees are not adequately controlled or made adequately aware by management of potential danger.

"Let's be frank about it," he told me. "The people working at rendering plants are not cognizant of the dangers or potential for transmission of bacteria, or they just don't give a damn. They will walk from a dirty area where they are receiving the animals to a clean area where processing is going on. They shouldn't be allowed to do that. Walking from filth to finished product area is very unfortunate but occurring every day of the week."

What You Can Do

As I described earlier, there is inadequate testing of pet foods. More independent studies—away from the influence of the manufacturers—are needed. There are unfortunately too few independent researchers or bodies policing the industry, and this situation should be corrected. Virtually all of the research is funded by the pet food interests themselves. There is an organization of veterinary nutritionists and it receives most of its funding from the companies. Individuals on the dog nutrition subcommittee of the NRC are also supported in their research by the industry. The whole relationship raises the question of independent thinking and bias.

"It's kind of sad but that's the way it is," an FDA spokesman said in regard to this situation. "Otherwise, they can't do the research at all. I would like to have survey information on various toxins and heavy metals. There is no money for it. We just don't have the data on pet foods that we have on human foods. And even with human foods we have gaps all over the place."

The real problem for me and other veterinarians is the cumulative effect of all those additives, toxins, heavy metals, and the very questionable source of the natural ingredients. While these factors can cause acute reactions, most often they simply nibble away at an animal's health, reduce the efficiency of bodily functions and organs, undermine the immune system, and generate nagging allergic reactions such as skin irritation and scratching.

Dr. Alfred Plechner, a West Los Angeles veterinarian who specializes in allergies, says that the reality of the pet food market is "not what food is best to feed but rather what food will cause less problems."[24]

If all this bad news about pet food seems overwhelming, take heart. There are some simple steps you can take to protect your animals.

1. When buying commercial pet food, be choosy.

I tell my clients to try and choose foods that have a minimum of additives or none at all. Read labels. Be on the lookout for BHA, BHT, sodium nitrite, propylene glycol, sugar, artificial color, and artificial flavoring. Your dog doesn't need any of these things. Avoid the semimoist products, which are loaded with chemicals.

Most products have preservatives and other additives, but the fact that they may not be necessary at all is borne out by the presence of preservative-free products on the market. I have seen dog foods with no additives and I have seen others with ten or more. You can choose, so be choosy. Pet shops and health food stores stock pet food products that are free of additives. I suggest you look in these stores if your regular outlet doesn't carry any such items.

Remember that the fewer additives your animal digests, the less risk there is to his health.

Ask your veterinarian for his advice on what products he has found to be the most problem-free.

I feed my hospitalized animals Tyrrell's, a high quality line of canned products made in Seattle. It is totally free of additives. I am convinced that the chemicals in many products are responsible for diarrhea. Often I have taken an animal that has a nonspecific diarrhea and fed it Tyrrell's, and the diarrhea has cleared up.

If you are buying dry dog food, don't purchase large bags unless you have several pets and will be using up the food fast. Saving money on a more economical-size bag is bad nutrition. The longer the bag sits around, the more it is opened, the more it is subjected to the hots and colds of the weather, the more vitamin content is lost.

Buy your dog food from a store that does a big turnover. The longer the package is sitting on a store shelf the more nutrient loss may take place.

2. Feed your dog table scraps.

The dog food industry has tried to discourage people from doing this, probably because they want to sell more of their products. The manufacturers would have you believe your animal is getting all the nutrition it needs out of the bag or can. But I have not been able to accept that. I have seen too much disease and minimal health. As a result, I have always been an advocate of table-scrap feeding.

The breeders don't believe the manufacturers either. They supplement their animals' diets with all kinds of things. Anne Rogers Clark makes a stew of vegetables, kidney suet, wild goose livers and gizzards, every bit of food that's left over from the table, including egg shells, and mixes it with a commercial dog food and feeds the concoction to her kennel of poodles. Doris Wear, a Maryland breeder, feeds her whippets and smooth fox terriers a brimming menu of vegetables, beef and beef by-products, suet, fresh raw milk, bran and raw wheat germ, steamed bone meal, half-raw green tripe, rolled oat flakes, commercial fine grind dry dog food, and, three times a week, a hard-boiled egg complete with shell. Both ladies, in addition, feed an array of vitamin and mineral supplements.

Obviously, the average pet owner can't go to this kind of fuss. I only mention these programs simply to show how breeders, who *must* care about the maximum health and appearance of their dogs, use commercial food as only one part of their feeding regimen.

I know a nutritionist at a major dog food manufacturing company who confided in me that he feeds his dog table scraps in addition to the company product. Obviously, he doesn't believe his own employer's propaganda.

What's wrong with carrots and peas and salads and even fruit and cooked cereals? Nothing that I know of. I know a retired veterinarian in his eighties who has been feeding generations of dogs from table scraps. Meat, vegetables, grains, fruit. His dogs were rarely ill.

The only true carnivores on this planet are cats. Dogs will really eat anything. It is believed that dogs don't digest starches very well, but the Irish have had great success over the centuries feeding their dogs a diet of milk and potatoes. Some of the stronger breeds, like the Irish wolfhound, Irish setter, the Sheltie, and the border collie, thrived on this kind of a diet. I haven't heard of many dogs that will refuse table scraps. They like variety, just as we do.

Avoid sugar and sweet stuff except perhaps for the occasional treat.

You can feed your dog entirely from table scraps or in combination with regular dog food. If you do the latter, then you cut back on the amount of regular dog food in direct relation to the amount of table scraps provided. For instance, if you want to add a half-pound of table scraps and your dog's regular daily ration is a pound of dry food, then simply reduce the dry food by a half-pound.

As far as I am concerned, the more table scraps and less commercial food, the better. That means less impurities and dubious quality of ingredients.

Another way to serve up some variety is to purchase trimmings, tripe, melts (spleen), kidney, or liver at the butcher shop or supermarket. Your dog will love it, raw, or partially cooked.

3. Supplement your animal's diet with vitamins and minerals.

Whether you feed from table scraps or commercial dog food or both, supplements are necessary if you want your animal to be in the best possible health. Vitamins and minerals have the power to neutralize the possible harmful effects of impurities and toxins present in a dog's food or environment. They will also ensure against possible dietary deficiencies and provide extra nutrition in times of stress. As we will see in the following chapters of the book, vitamin and mineral supplements can do many things for your animal. Later, in Part Three, I will advise you on what to supplement and how much.

Part Two

VITAMINS AND MINERALS: THE THINGS THEY DO

Vitamin C and the Dog

Several years ago, a man walked into my hospital and introduced himself as a dogsled racer. He participated in all the big racing events held around the country.

He was worried about one of his dogs, a young female who would collapse after running a couple of miles. He had consulted with veterinarians in San Francisco but they couldn't explain it. He probably felt he had nothing to lose by talking to me since the more orthodox vets hadn't been able to help him. I had the feeling he regarded me as sort of a last resort.

"Tell me about the dog," I said.

"She falls and then can't run again," he said. "She drags herself up and hobbles along very slowly and apparently with great difficulty. She wants to continue but can't. Her tongue appears swollen and she bleeds from the gums."

"It sounds to me like scurvy," I said.

"Scurvy?" he said, his face crinkling up in puzzlement. "But how can that be? It's common knowledge that dogs produce their own vitamin C. Humans get scurvy because they don't make their own, but not so with dogs or other animals."

"That's true in part," I said, "but you are putting your animal under a great deal of stress by running her. Dogs do indeed produce their own vitamin C, like most other animals, but they are comparatively poor producers. Stress can quickly burn up the small amounts that they make. Without enough, an animal will become ill and die. Another consideration is the individuality factor. One dog will have a greater ability to produce vitamin C than the next. Your female is apparently weaker in this respect than the other dogs on the team. Down in the Antarctic cold,

husky sled dogs have been observed to quickly fatigue and develop swollen, bleeding gums when they were worked extremely
hard and given no fresh meat. These are classic signs of scurvy
and they readily cleared up when the dogs were fed fresh seal
meat containing vitamin C."

I suggested to the dogsled racer that he give vitamin C a
chance with his ailing animal. I told him to administer extra
strong daily doses and to rest the dog for about two weeks.

In a month the man returned. He said he had followed my advice and now the dog could run forever. There was no more
swelling or bleeding. And now the man was a believer that dogs
get scurvy and can benefit from extra vitamin C.

The mainstream of veterinary medicine contends that dogs
don't need extra vitamin C because they manufacture a sufficient
amount themselves. In experiments going back to the thirties,
dogs have been kept on vitamin C–free diets for extended periods and have shown no adverse effects, no signs of deficiency.
But dogs living under laboratory conditions, I should point out,
are not subject to the same stresses, environmental pollution, and
human mismanagement as the canine population at large. These
are all factors that deplete vitamin C.

Parallel to the experimental work showing dogs to produce
sufficient vitamin C, there have been a number of scientific reports raising the disturbing possibility of deficiencies and even
forms of canine scurvy. The profession has failed to investigate
these developments vigorously, preferring instead to fall back on
the comfortable concept of vitamin C sufficiency. Untold numbers of dogs have suffered or died as a result of this scientific
lapse.

The attitude of vitamin C self-sufficiency has been adopted by
the Subcommittee on Dog Nutrition (of the NRC), the arbiter
of nutrient requirements for the dog. In its most recent publication (1974), the subcommittee concludes that "there is no adequate evidence to justify recommendation of routine vitamin C
additions to the diet of the normal dog."

Wrong, I say, and one of the aims of this book is to show the
error of that thinking.

Fifteen years of clinical experience, involving over two thousand cases, has told me that dogs definitely benefit from extra

vitamin C. When given supplements, they are much less likely to develop hip dysplasia, spinal myelopathy, ruptured discs, viral diseases, and skin problems. They live healthier and longer. Vitamin C works preventively and therapeutically. I have published a number of papers on my work in professional literature and by now other veterinarians have tried vitamin C and witnessed the same good results.

In the beginning of my courtship with vitamin C, I wasn't too clear about why the vitamin was working so well. I only knew it was working. Later I met Dr. Irwin Stone, who gave me a thoroughgoing education on this remarkable substance.

Stone, a retired biochemist, began a lifetime of work with ascorbic acid—the more precise name for vitamin C—in 1934. Several years later, he patented techniques for the synthesis of ascorbic acid and for its use in stabilizing foodstuffs. For over three decades, he has been a tireless researcher of the medical applications of vitamin C. His 1972 book, *The Healing Factor: Vitamin C Against Disease,* is a comprehensive collection of information on vitamin C as it relates to medicine and health.

To understand vitamin C it is important to back up in time. To Captain James Lind, a naval surgeon in the British Royal Navy, goes the credit of discovering, more than two hundred years ago, that citrus fruit could prevent the scurvy that decimated the ranks of men at sea.

Sometimes galleons would be found floating aimlessly, entire crews dead from scurvy. In 1740, British Admiral George Anson embarked on a round-the-world cruise with six ships and 1,955 men. Four years later, only the flagship and 904 men returned. More than a thousand men had died, mostly from scurvy. This disaster prompted Lind's experiments with citrus fruit in 1747.

To show how effective it was, when Captain James Cook circumnavigated the world between 1772 and 1775, he made it a point to obtain fresh vegetables and fruit when touching land. He lost only one man out of his crew of 118.

Although the plight of sailors dramatized the ravages of scurvy, it was by no means a mariner's disease exclusively. Scurvy is one of the oldest recorded medical conditions. Egyptian hieroglyphs, dating to 1500 B.C., portray the bleeding gums that are typical of the disease. One thousand years later, Hippocrates described conditions that resembled scurvy. Throughout history, armies engaged in long sieges where only dry rations were available suffered from scurvy. And annually, during the long winters in northern climes, where fresh food was unavailable, whole populations were weakened by varying degrees of scurvy and made easy prey for rampant bacterial and viral infections.

The disease runs through a course of typical symptoms starting with a change in complexion, which becomes sallow or muddy. Then follows a chronic and increasing fatigue, breathlessness, and need for sleep. The gums become sore and inflamed and bleed easily. The teeth loosen. The breath becomes foul. The nose bleeds. The eyelids swell. Hemorrhages erupt all over the body. The bones become brittle to the point where they can break at the slightest movement. Pains in the joints render the individual immobile. The slide from apparent health to a miserable death can take only a few months.

It wasn't until this century that scientists discovered why citrus fruit prevented scurvy. The thing doing the job is a chemical molecule called ascorbic acid. The word ascorbic means not having scurvy. The molecule is found in citrus fruit, vegetables, and the internal organs of most animals.

Essential to Life and Biochemical Balance

Ascorbic acid is absolutely essential to the living process and all living forms either produce it themselves or get it in their food, or they perish within three months. No other vitamin deficiency works that fast. Besides preventing scurvy, this substance plays vital roles in immunity, in the growth and maintenance of connective tissue, and in combating stress and toxins. It is the guardian of biochemical balance in the body.

Ascorbic acid is produced in large amounts in most animals through an enzyme system that uses glucose, a naturally occurring sugar, as the raw material for conversion. This conversion is carried out within individual cell membranes, in tiny particles called microsomes. In amphibians and reptiles, this system is located in the kidneys. In mammals, it is found in the liver.

Daily production in the reptiles and amphibians is limited because of the size of their kidneys. These cold-blooded creatures maintain a sluggish metabolism and thus have been able to get along on relatively little ascorbic acid.

But not so in the case of the mammals with their souped-up, warm-blooded physiologies. They require more ascorbic acid in the scheme of things, so the task has been assigned by nature to the liver, the largest gland in the body. Moreover, mammals were equipped with an important accessory, a biochemical feedback mechanism that enables them to produce extra ascorbic acid in times of increased stress. Stress upsets the body's biochemical balance, so more ascorbic acid is needed to restore equilibrium. A rat, for example, can hike its output of ascorbic acid tenfold under stress. This protective mechanism has had tremendous survival value.

Along the evolutionary way, some mammals like humans, apes, guinea pigs, and bats, as well as some birds, were short-changed when it came to the liver enzyme system. One key enzyme is missing in the glucose-to-ascorbic acid chain. Thus they do not produce their own ascorbic acid. They must get it in their food or die.

The following chart shows the relative ability of some animals to produce vitamin C:

Daily Production of Ascorbic Acid in Animals[1]

ANIMAL	MILLIGRAMS PER KILOGRAM OF BODY WEIGHT
Snake	10
Tortoise	7
Mouse	275
Rabbit	226
Goat	190
Rat	150
Dog	40
Cat	40
Ape, Man, Guinea Pig	0

Dogs and cats, as can be seen, are poor producers. They manufacture forty milligrams per kilogram (2.2 pounds) of body weight per day, less than any other mammals except the absolute nonproducers. A goat the same size as a Great Dane or Saint Bernard makes almost five times as much vitamin C.

The veterinary tradition has taught that those animals capable of making their own ascorbic acid produce enough each day to fully satisfy their requirements. But this does not seem to be borne out by the evidence.

Stress, in the case of our household pets, sorely taxes and depletes an already low vitamin C output. I have found that the liver of a dog or cat with a high temperature makes little or no ascorbic acid. Dogs with skin disease have been tested and found to have low blood levels of vitamin C.[2]

The average dog encounters a series of jolting stresses during the first year of life. Stress is separation from the mother and littermates and relocation in a new home. Immunizations, tail docking, ear crops, and deworming are further stresses. Teething is a stress. If the puppy is put through conformation and obedience training, there is added physical and mental stress. And throughout all these episodes, the puppy must also withstand the natural ongoing stresses of growth.

All these stress conditions place a great demand on the dog for ascorbic acid that it seems unable to meet. This inability to produce more to meet internal or external challenges suggests a failure of the stress-triggered feedback mechanism or a sluggish liver enzyme system. Perhaps long-term inbreeding or the early domestication by man may have affected this ability.

When less than optimal levels of ascorbic acid are available to the animal, whether it is produced inside or provided from the outside, the stage is set for a condition that Irwin Stone has named chronic subclinical scurvy. The body as a whole or some of its organs, systems, or parts are weakened enough to open the door to virus, bacteria, deformities, and disease. Chronic means that the condition is always there. Subclinical means that the symptoms are less severe and identifiable than the acute signs of terminal scurvy.

Among animals there is also the individuality factor, as I explained to the dogsled racer. For instance, within one group of

104 dogs, the scale of vitamin C levels in their blood measured from .02 milligrams up to .84 milligrams for each 100 cubic centimeters of blood. That's a 42-fold difference.[3]

The situation is essentially the same with humans, except that they have to get their vitamin C from food or supplements. Why are some people subject to more colds, flus, and infections than others? Some are more robust than others of course, but there is more to it than that. I feel the answer has something to do also with the individual amounts of vitamin C people take and the amount of stress they confront in their lives. Smoking and taking lots of aspirin and medication are forms of chemical stress on the body. Physical, emotional, and mental strain are also forms of stress. These things burn up the body's vitamin C stores and if there isn't much in there to burn up then you start running into a deficit. The condition of chronic subclinical scurvy is created. The immune system weakens and the body becomes vulnerable to the same kind of germs that it may have successfully resisted if there were enough vitamin C on hand.

The Antigerm Factor

If a dog is low on C, he is wide-open to disease. Remember, he constantly has his nose and mouth in places where germs abound.

In my practice I have seen the dramatic results of treating distemper, a virus, with vitamin C. When used at high, or what we call megadose levels, vitamin C is a therapeutic virucidal (antivirus) agent. It is also nontoxic.

When we put the animal on a lesser, what we call maintenance, dose of C, then we are attempting to prevent the decline into chronic subclinical scurvy. We are shutting the door on an insidious disease process. We are keeping the immune system strong.

Within this system are the white blood cells. They are responsible, among other things, for engulfing and destroying bacteria. One consequence of low vitamin C levels is an increased susceptibility to bacterial infections. The ability to destroy these germs is directly related to the ascorbic acid content in the blood. I have found supplementation of vitamin C a good way to keep this defense mechanism high.

Vitamin C is so effective that I have been able to cut my usage of antibiotics in half. I routinely see animals brought in with temperatures, and in many cases the clients are unwilling to spend the money for blood tests to find out what the problem is. In these cases, I administer ascorbic acid intravenously and usually in short order the animal is back to normal. Upon discharge, I prescribe oral supplements of vitamin C. A dog thus treated recovers quickly. The treatment is inexpensive. The client is happy.

I have used vitamin C quite effectively to deal with tonsilitis, a common bacterial infection in dogs. Most often veterinarians use antibiotic and steroid drugs to treat this condition. Once the dog is healed and the drugs removed, the tonsils frequently become inflamed again and the dog is back in the hospital for another round of treatment. Maintaining the animal on vitamin C after treatment solves this nagging problem.

C for Collagen

Vitamin C in ample quantity is necessary for the production, formation, and maintenance of collagen, the intercellular protein cement of connective tissue. Collagen is the substance that binds the muscles, the blood vessels, the ligaments, tendons, and cartilage, giving them all strength and structure. Collagen is the honeycomb into which minerals are deposited to form bone. Without collagen, the body would come unglued and collapse. Scurvy.

I have come to regard the crippling canine condition known as hip dysplasia as a symbol of chronic subclinical scurvy. Large breed puppies are particularly susceptible. The first year or two of life is an extremely high-growth and high-stress period for them. The demands on the body are great; the demands for large quantities of ascorbic acid are great. But because there is insufficient ascorbic acid, the production of collagen suffers. Weak collagen means weak parts. A frequent result of this insufficiency is hip dysplasia, a painful, crippling condition that leaves the young dog arthritic and hunched up in the hind quarters, favoring one leg.

Two centuries ago, James Lind observed that the cadavers of scurvy victims had loose ligaments of the joints. Hip dysplasia is also a loose joint problem.

Hip dysplasia has generally been considered to be a genetic problem. But I consider it an easily controlled biochemical condition. In a study I did of eight litters from dysplastic German shepherd parents or parents that produced dysplastic offspring, there were no signs of hip dysplasia when the bitches were given megadoses of vitamin C during pregnancy and the pups kept on a maintenance regimen throughout puppyhood.

Strong collagen is a lifetime necessity. The proper functioning of organs and limbs depends on it. It is as important to an older dog as to a growing puppy. In later years, in fact, an animal's ability to produce vitamin C deteriorates. As it does, the quality and strength of collagen deteriorates as well, leading to the physiological breakdowns associated with aging. Supplementation of vitamin C slows down the aging process by keeping the collagen strong.

The Great Detoxifier

Vitamin C is one of nature's most competent general detoxifiers. It takes on any foreign substance reaching the blood and, if in abundant supply, can nullify the toxicity. Most mammals, when facing a toxic challenge, will produce more ascorbic acid than usual. This is the body's response, to maintain the normal biochemical balance that is being threatened by the toxic invaders. If the toxins overwhelm the animal's ability to detoxify them, the result is sickness or death.

Toxins enter through many doors and come in different shapes. They are encountered through simple contact, breathing, eating, poisonous insects and reptiles, drugs, allergies, bacteria, virus, fungi, parasites, and infections. In the last chapter I examined the role of toxic chemicals in food and how these constitute a steady stream of stress and potential risk to the health of animals.

Regularly encountered chemical stress will severely tax an animal's natural supply of ascorbic acid. But when they get vitamin supplements, animals have been consistently found to benefit from the detoxifying powers of extra vitamin C. Dr. I. B. Chatterjee, an Indian biochemist and authority on vitamin C production in animals, found that exposing rats to toxic metals like cadmium, lead, or mercury reduced the liver level of ascorbic acid. Remember that the liver is where the vitamin is made. Low levels mean low resistance. The C apparently was being used up to combat and nullify the toxicity of the metals. Chatterjee then fortified the diets of these rats with ascorbic acid and the liver levels returned to normal.[4] Keep in mind that rats are much better producers of their own ascorbic acid than dogs. So if rats benefit from the extra vitamin C, dogs presumably would benefit at least as much if not more.

In *The Healing Factor: Vitamin C Against Disease,* Irwin Stone cites an interesting Chinese experiment involving tadpoles and lead. The researchers placed one hundred tadpoles in water with high lead content. In twenty-four hours, eight of the baby toads died. The remaining tadpoles were then divided up, half of them placed in a tank containing plain water and the others in a tank with plain water and ascorbic acid. Six days later, 88 percent of the tadpoles placed in the plain water had died, while all of the tadpoles in the ascorbic acid–treated water were alive. Stone also mentions work done in the Soviet Union where ascorbic acid and cysteine, an amino acid, were successfully used as an antidote on rabbits suffering from lead poisoning.[5]

Over the years, vitamin C has been found effective against acute and chronic lead poisoning in humans. Industrial workers exposed to lead have benefited from the protection of supplemental vitamin C. As long ago as 1939, laborers complaining of lead poisoning symptoms were successfully treated with the vitamin. More recently, Dr. Carl C. Pfeiffer at the Brain Bio Center in Princeton, New Jersey, dramatically improved the health of lead workers by using a daily dietary supplement of two grams of vitamin C in combination with thirty milligrams of zinc gluconate.

The vitamin C and zinc approach, says Pfeiffer, is safer,

simpler, and cheaper than the current treatments of lead poisoning involving chelation therapy with agents such as EDTA or penicillamine.

Pfeiffer believes that an abnormal burden of lead and other toxic metals will hasten aging and shorten human life.[6] His opinion is shared by a number of scientists who have found that even subtoxic amounts of lead can decrease the life-span of laboratory animals. This kind of scientific opinion makes a strong case for vitamin C supplementation. I am worried that our pets are fighting a daily battle against the lead and other toxins they encounter in their food and environment. The result, I feel, is a weakened, disease-prone animal that is unable to cope with the otherwise natural stresses in his life.

Cadmium is another toxic mineral that pets have to contend with. Animals—and humans as well—commonly get it in their food in small amounts, and in drinking water, the air, from car exhaust fumes, and from cigarettes and even cigarette smoke. Cadmium, like lead, is a ubiquitous by-product of the commercial and industrial era.

Health officials are alarmed about possible harmful effects to health over long periods of exposure. In experimental animals, even low dietary concentrations of cadmium have impaired growth, caused hypertension, disturbed enzyme function and the utilization of essential mineral nutrients, and interfered with reproductive cycles.

A U. S. Department of Agriculture review on cadmium notes that some of the toxic effects may be prevented by supplementary levels of iron, copper, zinc, selenium, and manganese in the diet.[7] The FDA's Department of Nutrition showed that vitamin C is also a cadmium stopper. Japanese quail were given a high dose of cadmium in an otherwise normal diet. These birds were chosen because they are extremely sensitive to environmental pollution. The feeding of cadmium caused an iron-deficiency anemia and depressed growth rate. Vitamin C supplementation provided a "marked protective effect" against these conditions, the researchers found.[8] Quail make their own vitamin C and still they benefited from supplementation. Surely our domesticated animals will benefit as well.

In the last chapter I talked about sodium nitrite, the chemical additive used cosmetically to give dog food products a fresh, reddish appearance. Sodium nitrite is one of many nitrite compounds found in food, food additives, drugs, and pesticides that can reach an animal's digestive tract. There, they can react with nitrogen to form so-called nitroso compounds. More than one hundred different nitroso compounds have been found to cause animal tumors. Sodium nitrite alone has been linked to cancer in over twenty different species of test animals. The effect of routine commercial levels of sodium nitrite eaten over a number of years is not known. Nevertheless it is a risk factor for cancer.

Once again, vitamin C, the great detoxifier, can reduce the risk. Research conducted with vitamin C has shown that at high levels it blocks the formation of nitroso compounds in test animals.[9]

Vitamin E has also been shown to block these compounds. Dr. Steven R. Tannenbaum, an MIT food scientist, suggests the routine use of vitamins C and E since exposure to the potentially dangerous nitroso compounds seems unavoidable.[10]

I have read accounts of vitamin C bringing off rapid recovery from rattlesnake bite in dogs and, by a single injection of one gram, similar speedy recovery from a scorpion sting.[11]

Space does not permit listing all the specific toxins that vitamin C can counteract. But I will mention just one more—one of the body's very own toxins. Histamine. The name is familiar to most people. Most commonly it is associated with allergic reactions. It is an irritating chemical released by body cells in stress situations. Histamine reacts dramatically in capillaries making them more permeable and permitting excess waste material from the blood to enter the tissues. This causes swelling and a discomfort well known to any hay fever sufferer. Likewise in animals, a constant itching problem may be due to the effect of histamine from an allergic reaction. Not only allergy, but infections, burns, cold, and a whole host of nonspecific stresses can result in the release of histamine into the bloodstream. Ascorbic acid has been shown in a number of studies to be able to inhibit the release of histamines.[12] Thus it is a natural antihistamine.

The manner in which vitamin C detoxifies is a highly complex biochemical process not clearly understood. The simple fact is that it works.

C Kills Pain

I have found that vitamin C acts as a good analgesic. I always recommend it in cases of neuralgialike problems that animals seem to develop with the onset of winter. Similarly, animals with joint pain seem to experience more comfort if they take vitamin C. The dogs can't talk and tell me they are in less pain but I have found their behavior and activity indicative of reduced pain.

From the human experience, there is good evidence of vitamin C's analgesic powers. We know from the work of Dr. Ewan Cameron in Scotland that cancer patients given megadoses of vitamin C report an improved state of well-being. They feel less pain and require less pain-killing drugs.[13]

Dr. Fred Klenner also reported the pain-relieving effect of high doses of C in the treatment of severe burns and snakebite.

For years, Dr. James Greenwood, Jr., professor of neurosurgery at the Baylor College of Medicine, has been recommending high doses—normally two grams a day, but as high as ten in some cases—to diminish the pain and swelling of osteoarthritis.

I personally have had very positive results using vitamin C to deal with pain. Several years ago I developed a case of tennis elbow—not from playing tennis but from the routine lifting of heavy dogs in my practice. I suffered excruciating pain in my right elbow. It became difficult for me even to lift a glass of water. I began taking as much as ten grams of vitamin C daily and in two weeks the pain was gone and never returned. Since that time I take six grams every day. If I ever have a headache, I treat it with five grams and in ten or fifteen minutes the pain is gone.

I don't think scientists know how vitamin C actually eliminates pain. Again, all we know is that it works.

Many veterinarians, like M.D.s, will prescribe aspirin for pain. This is a case of robbing Peter to pay Paul. Aspirin has been found to deplete the body of vitamin C. In one experiment, some Irish students were given average amounts of aspirin over a four or five day period. Then their blood was tested for vitamin C content. The aspirin had caused such a stampede of vitamin C out the body through the urine that the levels measured out "just in excess of those associated with scurvy."[14] Individuals who take aspirin on a regular basis, such as arthritis patients, would be well advised to take plenty of vitamin C as well.

In my practice I caution clients against using aspirin for their animals. I never prescribe it.

How many times have you taken your pet to the veterinarian and the animal was treated with antibiotics and steroid drugs? And how many times did the animal show some temporary improvement before the symptoms returned again? Often, I'll bet.

These drugs eliminate certain symptoms. But what they also do is suppress the immune system. It's another example of robbing Peter to pay Paul. Of course the symptoms will return when the drugs wear out or are used up. The immune system, weak in the first place, has been further weakened by the drug.

Steroids are anti-inflammatory drugs commonly used in both human and animal medicine. Extended treatment with these drugs not only interferes with the immune system but can also disturb the formation of collagen, cause a thinning of bone tissue, and lead to skin problems. Adequate supplementation with vitamin C will reverse or prevent the harmful side effects of steroid therapy.[15]

I am not opposed to the use of these drugs. I use them in my practice. But I combine them with protective doses of vitamin C and other vitamins and minerals. One additional benefit of vitamin C is that it makes a drug more effective. Thus, less of the drug is needed. I have been able to greatly reduce the dosage of drugs when I incorporate vitamin C in my treatment.

Toxicity and the Kidney Stone Myth

Sometimes I am asked about the toxicity of vitamin C. Isn't too much dangerous for my dog? people want to know. The question is a fair one. Too much of anything can have adverse effects.

Actually we find that medical science has described ascorbic acid as one of the least toxic substances known. People have ingested 125 grams (over a quarter of a pound) at one time without harm, and an equal amount has been injected into a human without harm.[16]

In 1977 I conducted a toxicity study with extremely high levels of vitamin C: twenty times more than the preventive dose I would normally recommend for an animal. For five days I administered intravenously two grams daily per pound of body weight into three small dogs. The animals weighed about ten pounds each, so I was injecting about twenty grams into each dog. I should point out that intravenous injections are much more potent than oral administration of powder or tablets. This is because the substance is placed directly into the bloodstream while anything taken through the mouth suffers some degree of degradation because of chemical reactions in the digestive tract.

There were no side effects from these high doses. On the contrary, one dog had had bad cystitis and was urinating blood, and after the second injection the condition cleared up.

One of the most widely held myths involving vitamin C is that large amounts of it will cause urinary tract stones. Linus Pauling, who has thoroughly researched this question, states that "not a single case has been reported in the medical literature."[17] Just the contrary, there is medical evidence that points to a deficiency —not an excess—of vitamin C as the cause of stones, and when corrective amounts of ascorbic acid are administered, the conditions have been shown to improve.[18]

Personally, I have never encountered a single case of urinary tract stones when a dog was kept on a maintenance dose of the vitamin. I do know of two cases where vitamin C has actually been used to dissolve the stones in dogs.

To go into all the roles of vitamin C could involve volumes. I have tried to spotlight some of the main functions and how they relate to the dog.

The main point I want to make here is that although the dog has not been shortchanged like the human, who produces no vitamin C at all, the canine apparently doesn't make enough to give him optimal health and protect him from the stresses of life and the battering of modern environmental pollution—including the pollution in his very own food.

I have come to the conclusion that the incidence and death rate involving chronic subclinical scurvy among dogs and cats is extremely high. In fact, it amounts to a condition afflicting most of these animals throughout their entire lives.

When dog food manufacturers fortify their products with vitamins, they add no vitamin C. The reason is the widely held belief that the dog produces all the vitamin C he needs and that therefore putting any extra in the food is superfluous. In the wilds on his own, beyond the reach and "wisdom" of food processors, the dog does indeed seek out vitamin C sources in his food. He eats the ingested material of the prey, which is rich in vitamin C. He eats the liver where the ascorbic acid is produced, and the adrenal glands, a storehouse of vitamin C, and even the muscle tissue, which has some C. He eats it raw, while man gives it to him cooked. Cooking destroys vitamin C. In the wilds, the dog also eats vegetables, fruit, and berries, additional sources of vitamin C. People say that the dog makes enough and doesn't need more. On his own, in nature, the dog acts like he needs more.

I believe that supplementation of vitamin C is perhaps the single most important thing you can do for the health of your pet.

5

The Vitamin Team

I like to think of vitamins and minerals working together like a football team. On the team you have a player who specializes in running the ball, another who catches passes, another who kicks the extra point after touchdown, and a whole line of them who protect the quarterback, the playmaker of the team.

Along with these primary assignments, players make numerous other contributions to the team. Perhaps the player who runs can also block well. Another player who blocks well can also catch passes.

So it is with vitamins and minerals. Each nutrient generally has a celebrated function but also contributes to the total picture in any number of ways. Big and little. Known and unknown. Together they make each other work better. E protects A and together they protect the lungs against damage from pollution. Selenium makes E more efficient. D ensures proper utilization of calcium and phosphorus, two major components of bone tissue. Vitamins and minerals are said to work synergistically. This means that together they have a greater total effect than the sum of their individual effects. This is the basis of every good team.

In my opinion, vitamin C is the star of the team. Before I began using other vitamins and minerals, I found vitamin C by itself was a real do-it-all. It protected the bitch during pregnancy and the offspring during puppyhood. It cleared up skin problems you might normally associate with a deficiency of vitamin A. It improved spinal problems. It prevented and cured so many conditions that indeed I began regarding it as a panacea even though all my medical training told me there is no such thing.

Prevention magazine's *The Complete Book of Vitamins* describes C as "the most versatile of vitamins with functions and effects so far-reaching that it can actually replace any other vitamin for a limited period of time and keep the body functioning and healthy."[1]

Still, as good and varied as the benefits of vitamin C seemed, I discovered that when I added the full spectrum of nutrients into my program the results were even better. It was like going from fine to finer, from good to excellent.

As far as I am concerned the vitamins and minerals available to dogs in commercial pet food can be equated with a second-rate team. You might have a few good players in there, but for the most part the lineup is lacking. When you add vitamin C, the animal perks up. There is new zest and increased health. When you add other nutrients, the picture improves even more. In football or any sport, when you supplement a so-so team with better players, you are going to have a better team. When all the vitamins and minerals are operating in strength, they will bolster your dog in the fight he wages on a daily basis against stress, viruses, bacteria, and degenerative disease.

In the second chapter I explained the orthomolecular medical philosophy to you, namely that you can both prevent and treat disease by providing the whole body with vitamins and minerals. This is medicine at the cellular level, where problems begin. By supplementing with the wide range of vitamins and minerals you are attempting to bring an optimal payload of nutrition to all the cells in the body. A typical commercial diet provides only a minimum of nourishment and the quantity, quality, and balance of nutrients differs not only from product to product, but likely from week to week in the same product.

Down at the level of the cells there may be a condition of insufficiency involving any one or more vitamins and minerals that are required by the cells to function well. Any degree of insufficiency can cause any degree of malfunction among the cells, and that spells trouble.

Dr. Roger J. Williams, a brilliant contemporary biochemist, coined the term "cytopathy." He describes this condition as one in which there is a generalized state of cellular malnutrition. Something is missing. The cells are being shortchanged of some of the nutrients they need. When this situation exists you get malfunction, then symptoms. The symptoms are indications of a general malaise deep down at the basic level of life—the cells.

The symptoms, says Williams, show up first in that area of the body where the cells are the weakest and most susceptible to insufficient nutrition. A prime target area in both humans and animals is the skin. The skin is the largest organ in the body and is ultrasensitive to nutritional deficiencies, in part because the circulation does not provide it with abundant nourishment.[2]

One cause of skin problems may be inadequate vitamin A. So you give the dog extra vitamin A and the skin condition heals up. Since there is a general cellular deficiency of this vitamin you find that not only does the skin benefit but the appetite improves and the animal also becomes less susceptible to infections. These are other aspects of vitamin A deficiency. The whole body is using the vitamin, not just the skin. Other systems, short on this nutrient, have been reinforced and now show the benefit. You often see unexpected side benefits with supplements. The reason is because you have supplied the whole body rather than treated one specific symptom. Nutrients work this way. Drugs don't. They are targeted to specific symptoms alone.

Remember what I said about the whole team. Vitamins and minerals perform more efficiently in a team context than as separate individuals. If a team is going to be a winner, it has to be solid at every position, not just at one or two. If you want your dog to be optimally healthy, then he will need to be solid in all the vitamins and minerals.

A San Francisco area woman came to me with her elderly boxer dog that was suffering from a spinal degeneration problem. She had been to a university school of veterinary medicine but they said they couldn't do anything for the animal. She had heard about my work and thought that vitamins might be worth a try. Again, a case of last resort.

I gave the dog vitamin C injections and put it on a good multivitamin and mineral supplement.

The dog also had colitis—an inflammation of the lining of the large intestine—which is a common disorder among boxers. The animal required a bland diet and couldn't eat anything even vaguely acidic. After a couple of months on the supplements, the dog started eating tomatoes in the woman's backyard. Previously, this would have caused tremendous problems, such as hemorrhage and a bloody diarrhea. The woman began feeding the dog vegetables and fruit and found that he now tolerated all this very well. The colitis seemingly had been reversed. We noted too that the spinal condition improved. The animal had been confined and after a few months the owners were able to take it walking. The last I heard they had just begun jogging with the dog.

By treating the whole body with nutrients we were able to strengthen the animal. At least two known problems were improved. We were covering some nutritional cracks in his diet that had led to a cytopathic condition. This boxer was being healed and rejuvenated at the cellular level.

While the animal's commercial diet was based on formulas designed to supply adequate nutrition, this dog obviously wasn't getting all he needed. The fact that he benefited in both general and specific ways showed that he needed more. It could be that he needed more of one particular vitamin or mineral, or two or three. Finding the precise needs is a difficult task, maybe even impossible, because nutrient needs change throughout life. Medical science has not yet devised a technique to determine specific nutrient needs for each individual; not for humans, not for dogs. Instead there are averages. But the need for specific nutrients can vary greatly from what is regarded as average. One dog might need ten milligrams of vitamin X. Another dog of the same size and breed might need a hundred milligrams. And they both might need more, or less, when they are pregnant, working, idle, or old.

The recommendations of the NRC's Subcommittee on Dog Nutrition are designed to provide levels that research with dogs and other species have proven satisfactory in practice. Just like the RDAs for humans, these recommendations are by no means sacred numbers. They change as science uncovers more information.

My interest is not in satisfactory or RDA levels but in optimal levels. For me the questions remain: Are even adequate levels available in commercial dog food? Just how much do the additives and impurities in the food detract from the existing nutrient values? Supplementation is my answer to these questions.

Very little research has been done with supplemental levels of nutrients for dogs except to determine what levels are toxic. In searching for the effects of supplementation I have frequently had to turn to work done with laboratory animals like rats and mice. These creatures are chosen for scientific experiments because of short life-spans and the obvious economics of their small size. Furthermore, effects are more readily visible and measurable. They are mammals, like the dog, and will react similarly to chemicals and nutrients. Mouse and rat studies are commonly used to evaluate possible effects in humans.

I want to look now at the roles of some of the major vitamins and minerals and show what they can do on a supplemental basis.

Vitamin A

Vitamin A is sometimes called the growth vitamin because of experiments conducted in the 1920s that showed this food factor to play a key role in the achievement of optimal growth in laboratory test animals.

It is also known as the skin vitamin because it maintains the integrity of the epithelium, a tightly knit top layer of cells that forms a continuous sheet over every surface of the body that comes in contact with foreign substances. With different shapes and accessories, in dry form or wet, the epithelium covers the teeth and gums, the eyeballs, the top-to-bottom digestive tract, the mucous membrane of the respiratory tract and the air sacs of the lungs, the lining of the bladder, and the living, growing layer of skin. Everything, in short. It is literally both inner and outer armor, protecting against infection.

When there is even a mild deficiency of vitamin A, the epithelium suffers. Often it is most readily seen, in both humans and animals, in a dryness, hardening, and itching of the skin.

Veterinarians probably see more skin problems than any other canine condition. In my own practice, whenever I see a dog with a chronic skin disorder, I often turn to vitamin A for relief. The vitamin acts to lubricate the skin just like oil in your automobile engine.

But vitamin A is many more things. Dr. Erwin DiCyan, a drug and vitamin expert, says vitamin A "can just as well be called the hair vitamin, or eye and sight vitamin, the glandular, or teeth and gums vitamin, since it has a profound effect upon the development and well-being of all these structures."[3]

Like vitamin C, A provides protection against infection and toxic chemicals. In one experiment, mice that were injected with bacteria and fungus showed more resistance to infection when they were supplemented with vitamin A.[4] Likewise, rats that were supplemented with the vitamin suffered less harm than nonsupplemented animals when highly toxic polychlorobiphenyls (PCBs) were placed in their diet.[5] The finding that vitamin A and perhaps other nutrients as well may counteract the poison of PCBs is highly significant. PCBs are industrial chemicals that have reached the food chain through seepage into waterways or through industrial accidents. People who have eaten contaminated food have suffered health problems ranging from skin eruptions to irregularities at childbirth. Cattle have been poisoned by exposure to PCBs, and, as I mentioned in Chapter 3, the possibility exists that such cattle may be slaughtered for pet foods with the chemical toxins coming through intact and winding up in the food you give your animal. It is worth emphasizing the point that supplementation enhances an animal's ability to detoxify any of these poisons that may reach his food supply. The investment for this kind of protection is cheap when you consider the risk to the health of your pet.

Vitamin A is a fat-soluble vitamin and excess amounts are stored in the liver. This stay-put action is unlike the action of water-soluble vitamins, such as C and B complex, where excesses are excreted through the urine. Many people—doctors included— are haunted with specters of vitamin A toxicity, of too much vitamin A damaging the liver and nervous system. This fear is prevalent despite infrequent cases of vitamin A overdose. The problem as I see it is not one of too much but too little. I feel commercial dog foods contain marginal amounts of this important nutrient. The commercial dosage may in part account for the overwhelming number of skin cases seen by veterinarians. A

25-pound dog on my prevention program will get about 3,000 IUs supplementally in addition to the approximately 1,000 IUs he may—or may not—be getting in his commercial food. I will put a dog with a bad skin problem on 10,000 to 20,000 IUs of vitamin A daily. I have never had any problems with these doses. Only good results.

Puppies have been fed 10,000 IUs *per kilogram of body weight* daily for 10 months without any adverse effects. It was only when researchers reached levels of over 100,000 IUs *per kilogram of body weight* that they began to run into toxicity problems.[6] These are exceptionally high doses and it is unlikely an animal will ever be exposed to them.

Nitrite compounds, among their many dubious distinctions, can deplete the vitamin A stores in the body. Remember that one such compound is sodium nitrite, a common additive in dog foods. Buyer beware!

In addition to increased susceptibility to infections and skin problems, some other signs of vitamin A deficiency are nerve degeneration, reproductive failure, night blindness, muscular incoordination, convulsive seizures, lack of weight gain, and deafness. Progeny can suffer severely if the vitamin is in short supply. This was dramatically demonstrated fifty years ago in a Texas agricultural experiment. A deficient sow delivered eleven piglets all minus their eyeballs. Other pigs fed poor vitamin A diets produced offspring with extra ears, cleft palates, and irregular kidneys. Later, with vitamin A reinstated in their diets, the same sows delivered normal young.[7]

The B Complex Vitamins

The B complex vitamins are vital to the health of the nervous system and are sometimes referred to as the "nerve vitamins." When deficiencies develop, problems can occur anywhere. Mouth, eye, skin, and reproductive organs are typical trouble spots. Stress is a B killer, quickly using up the body's supply and necessitating quick reinforcements. As we have already seen, dogs face considerable stress in their lifetimes. The stress of winter and cold temperatures may be cushioned by supplementation of the B complex, since these vitamins take part in the heat generating processes of the body. The B complex vitamins provide necessary chemical partners for the proper metabolism of fats, carbohydrates, and proteins.

The vitamins in the B family have both names and numbers. The main components we will be looking at are B_1 (thiamine), B_2 (riboflavin), B_3 (niacin or niacinamide), B_5 (pantothenic acid), B_6 (pyridoxine), B_9 (folic acid), B_{12} (cobalamin), and biotin (sometimes referred to as vitamin H).

It is important to keep in mind that the B factors are a close-knit family, a team within a team. When a deficiency occurs of any one B complex vitamin, there is usually a shortage of another B vitamin to some degree as well. This is why supplementation and treatment usually includes several factors of the complex, if not all.

Vitamin B₁, Thiamine

This nutrient can be described as the first vitamin. Way back around the turn of the century, a missing dietary factor, later identified as thiamine, was implicated as the cause of beriberi, a widespread and often fatal Asiatic disease. Beriberi, in Sinhalese, means extreme weakness.

In 1897, a Dutch doctor produced a polyneuritis in chickens by feeding them a diet of refined white rice. The polyneuritis in the animals was the same condition as beriberi in humans: lesions (damage) in the nerve tissue of various parts of the body with consequent pain and loss of muscular control. British researchers pinpointed the human beriberi to a diet of the same white rice.

White rice is the commercial result of the mass-production milling method that became the industrial standard in the nineteenth century. In this method, the grain's hull, embryo, and outer layers are lost. These parts contain B vitamins and protein. Until the introduction of milling machinery, rice was hand-milled and retained much of its nutrient content. While the natural, unprocessed whole brown rice was the traditional staple for people in many parts of the world, and particularly Asia, it did not have a long shelf life and quickly grew rancid in the mass-distribution scheme of modern commerce. Processed white rice was the solution. It could live on the shelf forever. But at what cost?

The early workers found that if the whole brown rice was substituted for the processed white rice, the beriberi condition could be prevented and even reversed. At the time there existed only scientific suspicion that unknown elements, so-called protective substances, had been removed from the rice by the mechanical milling.

In 1912, Casimir Funk, a Polish-born chemist, cured diseased pigeons by feeding them rice polishings (the discards of milling). He concluded that beriberi, along with rickets, pellagra, and scurvy were caused by diets deficient in the "protective substances." He then named these substances "vitamines."

The word comes from *vita*—Latin for life—and amines, a group of chemical compounds to which all vitamins at this early time were thought to belong. Thiamine itself was not chemically isolated until 1926.

Clients who follow a good preventive program tell me their dogs appear more alert, more intelligent. This is especially true of puppies coming from supplemented mothers. My assumption is that the extra vitamins and minerals are working together to improve animal brain power. The brain is really just another branch of the total physical and biochemical picture. If the animal is optimally healthy then he should also be optimally intelligent for the breed.

The B complex group of vitamins must be present in the body in liberal quantities for the proper growth and function of nervous system tissue. Back in the thirties, researchers began to probe the importance of these nutrients in brain function. Rats were the most frequent choice for animal studies and scientists fed them diets either sufficient or lacking in B complex. The animals were then put through a series of maze trials to determine mental performance, choice-making ability, and efficiency; in other words, a test of their learning ability and intelligence. Their findings revealed that vitamin deficient rats showed a lesser learning ability than animals on a sufficient diet. Taking the inquiry one step further, scientists began to look at supplementation and its effect on intelligence. What happened when you added nutrients to the diet above the normal levels?

For some time it had been suspected that B_1 in particular had a major influence on intelligence. In 1949, Philip O'Neill of Fordham University examined how graded amounts of B_1 in the diet of young rats affected their ability to learn a water maze. "Larger amounts of thiamine led to better maze performance," he concluded.[8]

While B_1 may be beneficial to mammals, it may not be so nice for lesser forms of life such as fleas and other parasitic insects. These worst enemies of man's best friend don't like B_1 at all. It apparently leaves a particular aroma in a dog's skin that repels bugs. Brewers' yeast is a rich source of all the B complex vitamins, including B_1, and when dogs are given a good healthy dose of this powdery stuff routinely in their supper bowl they seem to have fewer problems with parasites.

If you supplement with brewers' yeast and/or a vitamin tablet, you don't have to worry about your dog getting too much of the Bs. Unused quantities are passed out through the urine. You get into toxic levels only when doses measured in the hundreds of milligrams per kilogram of body weight are involved. A tablespoon of brewers' yeast, a typical serving for a dog, carries about 1.25 milligrams of B_1. A high potency B complex tablet will contain 100 milligrams.

Some noticeable signs of B_1 deficiency are lack of appetite, vomiting, unsteadiness, and moderate spasticity of the hind legs.

Vitamin B₂, Riboflavin

This nutrient is vital to a dog's health because of its major involvement in protein and fat metabolism. It helps the body transform these foods into energy and new tissue.

B_2 is essential for healthy eyes and may prevent the formation of cataracts, a problem encountered in many older dogs. Bloodshot eyes and conjunctivitises are often symptoms of a deficiency. Dogs on a good supplementation program that includes B_2 don't seem to suffer from these eye conditions.

Vitamin B₃

Two different compounds having similar properties are interchangeably called B_3. One is niacin. The other is niacinamide. The latter is often preferred in treatment because niacin causes a discomforting flushing and burning sensation in the skin. For the sake of simplicity, I will refer only to B_3.

This vitamin is known as the antipellagra vitamin. In the early years of this century, pellagra swept through the United States. In one year alone, it killed more than 10,000 persons. Pellagra is a disease that strikes the skin, the gastrointestinal tract, and the nervous system simultaneously. Poor field hands working the cotton plantations of the South were chronic victims. Their diets were loaded with foodstuffs like corn, degerminated cornmeal, soda biscuits, grits, corn syrup, and fatty salt pork, all of which are poor sources of B_3 and other B complex vitamins as well. The same one tablespoon of brewers' yeast that contains 1.25 milligrams of B_1 also contains 3 milligrams of B_3. A whole ear of cooked corn carries only 1.1 milligram of B_3.

The addition of lean meats, eggs, canned salmon, peanuts, and vegetables to the food of the corn-eating laborers led to a greater control over pellagra.

It was not until 1937 however that B_3 was chemically isolated as the primary factor in the prevention of pellagra. And in this scientific advance, the canine played a starring role.

Along with the families that were suffering from pellagra, medical investigators noticed that the dogs they kept as pets often appeared emaciated and weak with their heads held low. Further examination revealed inflammation and ulceration of the oral and throat cavities, profuse salivation with ropy, blood-stained saliva drooling from the mouth, foul breath, and bloody diarrhea. The condition was called "blacktongue"—the canine equivalent of human pellagra. The dogs were eating their masters' food.

Dr. Conrad Elvehjem, a specialist in animal nutrition at the University of Wisconsin, isolated the B_3 factor from liver and injected it into a dog suffering from blacktongue. Within minutes of the injection, the miserable animal began to show improvement.

The B_3 connection was clinched in 1938 when the vitamin was used on several cases of classic human pellagra with a resultant rapid improvement. Other doctors found that where there was a B_3 deficiency there was also a general B complex deficiency, and in some cases B_1 and B_2 were also needed to make treatment successful. This is a good case in point of how vitamins work as a team.

During the forties, Dr. Tom D. Spies, a noted Southern physician, came across frequent cases of dogs ailing from more than one nutritional deficiency. While the symptoms of blacktongue were cleared up by injections of B_3, the dogs often had excessive tearing, sensitivity to light, and dilation of the blood vessels in the eye as independent symptoms, and these did not respond to B_3. They were typical of B_2 deficiency in humans and when Spies added an injection of B_2, these conditions cleared up. "The simultaneous occurrence . . . is evidence that such deficiencies occur as mixed diseases rather than as single entities," Spies reported.[9]

B_3 is important to the dog in converting food to energy and metabolizing fat and protein. In my practice, I have found the vitamin effective in controlling convulsive seizures in dogs.

Vitamin B₅, Pantothenic Acid

Unheralded, but very important. That's pantothenic acid. Dr. Roger J. Williams, the great biochemist, discovered this vitamin in 1933, naming it for the Greek word for everything, *pantos*. This natural chemical, it seems, occurs in all living cells.

One of Williams's experiments showed pantothenic acid to have a positive influence on longevity. Initially, the scientist had become intrigued with the possibility that royal jelly, a secretion of the honeybee, vastly prolonged the life of queen bees. Queen bees produce it. The short-lived worker bees don't. Royal jelly is the richest known natural source of pantothenic acid.

Williams set up a test to see if the vitamin would have a simi-

lar life-stretching effect on mammals. He took two groups of
mice and fed them all a standard diet for their entire lives. The
diet was determined to have all the necessary nutrients—including pantothenic acid—for a normal and healthy mouse life. Both
groups of rodents were treated alike with one exception: one
group received an extra 0.3 milligrams of pantothenic acid in its
daily drinking water, an amount several times more than mice
are believed to require.

The results were dramatic. The supplemented group of 33
mice lived an average of 653 days. The 41 in the control group
lived an average of 550 days. The difference was a 19 percent
longer life-span.

Williams translated this to a human life-span of 89 years as
compared to 75. In dog terms, that would mean something like
13 years instead of 11.

Williams, an objective scientist, warned against regarding pantothenic acid as a "miracle food." But on the other hand he was
so impressed by the findings that he said he was "willing to bet"
that if people were to take 25 milligrams of extra pantothenic
acid daily during their lifetimes, they could have an increased
life expectancy of at least 10 years.[10]

Pantothenic acid is sometimes referred to as the antistress vitamin because it is required for the production of good antibodies
that are involved in protection against physical stresses, infections, and toxins. Dogs deficient in this nutrient exhibit reduced
antibody response to infection. Pantothenic acid is one of three B
complex members that have been linked to antibody production.
The others are B_6 and B_9.

Pantothenic acid is required by the adrenal glands in the making of cortisone and other hormones involved in numerous metabolic functions and in anti-inflammatory roles against disease,
germ processes, and allergies. Pantothenic acid thus bears a simi-
larity to vitamin C in that both are adrenal feeders important in
the body's reaction to stress.

Dogs, like humans, are plagued by a bewildering array of allergies, the causes of which seem to grow day by day as we introduce new chemical combinations into our environment.

One of the conditions that set the stage for increased susceptibility to allergens is an inadequate supply of vitamin C and

pantothenic acid to the adrenal glands. One function of cortisone is to combat the toxins, or histamines, produced by dying cells in the allergic process. Synthetic cortisone is used in allergy control.

Adelle Davis, the late nutritionist and author, declared that "allergies have been repeatedly produced in animals by injections of numerous foreign substances, and invariably the allergic reaction is particularly severe or fatal when pantothenic acid is deficient; the lack of no other nutrient has a comparable effect."[11]

An East European doctor found that supplementation of pantothenic acid reduced the histamine output and resultant skin reactions by 20 to 50 percent in four groups of children exposed to allergy-provoking substances.[12]

The NRC points out that there have been too few studies conducted with dogs to enable the setting of minimum requirements. Given this state of uncertainty, and the knowledge that pantothenic acid does so much, I feel very positive about supplementing with this nutrient. It should have a marked beneficial effect on many dogs.

Vitamin B₆, Pyridoxine

This nutrient is a workhorse essential to an enormous number of chemical reactions in the body, the most important of which relate to the metabolism of protein. A big intake of protein calls for an increased intake of B_6.

Like its B complex brothers, it too contributes to the functioning of a healthy nervous system. The proper utilization by the body of minerals like potassium and sodium and iron depends on good availability of B_6.

B_6 has a close working relationship with pantothenic acid in maintaining a strong immune system.

Dr. John M. Ellis, M.D., of Mount Pleasant, Texas, is one of the country's leading authorities on vitamin B_6. He has written two books about his clinical experiences with B_6. In a personal letter to me, he indicated the importance of dietary sufficiency of B_6, especially for animals as they get up in years. His remarks:

Pyridoxine (B₆) has been under observation by the scientific community since 1934. Since that time animal experiments have provided a great deal of information about this vitamin, first with rats, then monkeys, followed by dogs, and even chickens. The vitamin is essential for the metabolism and breakdown of all protein eaten by animals and fowl.

In more recent years it has been shown that blood vessel disease, that of arteries in particular, is a result of vitamin B₆ deficiency. This blood disease was first shown by Drs. J. F. Rinehart and Louis Greenberg at the University of California, San Francisco, while working with monkeys. The longer the monkeys lived the more nearly did their blood vessels appear as that of humans having arteriosclerosis (hardening of the arteries). It has since been shown by different investigators that in the human, arteriosclerosis develops in the presence of vitamin B₆ deficiency because the vitamin is necessary for breaking down of methionine, one of the amino acids in meat and fish.

The scientific community is indebted to the animals for providing this valuable information about vascular disease. It should be remembered that dogs and monkeys on B₆ deficient diets became very ill, were listless and couldn't walk, whereas control animals on vitamin-enriched diets were unaffected.[13]

Vitamin B₉, Folic Acid

The requirement of folic acid for dogs has not been precisely defined. Signs of deficiency include erratic appetite, retarded weight gain, a watery secretion from the eyes, a type of anemia, and a decreased antibody response to microorganisms.

This vitamin is essential for the formation of red blood cells in the bone marrow. It aids in protein metabolism. It also teams up with pantothenic acid and B₆ in the maintenance of a strong immune system.

Pregnancies are times of tremendous stress and increased nutrient need. Pregnant women are believed to need four times as much folic acid as nonpregnant women.

Although folic acid is a rather unsung member of the B complex family, experimental deficiencies of it with the laboratory rat have caused a whole gamut of abnormalities, including headless offspring, underdeveloped kidneys and lungs, and missing glands.

Dr. Roger Williams points out that this is just another example of how a single nutritional deficiency can leave its mark anywhere in the body.

"The old idea that certain nutrients are valuable for certain parts of the body—calcium for bones, iron for blood, B vitamins for nerves—is quite misleading," he says. "Folic acid is one of the B vitamins, but it is evidently needed for the development of every part of the body."[14]

This is because all nutrients are related and needed by the cells throughout the entire body. They work as a team. If one member is missing or not playing up to par, the whole team is thrown off balance.

Vitamin B12, Cobalamin

Because of its characteristic color and its importance (along with folic acid) to the production and regeneration of red blood cells, this nutrient is known as the "red vitamin." A deficiency of this minuscule but powerful nutrient produces anemia and a poor general condition.

Dogs figured prominently in the discovery of B_{12}, as with a number of other vitamins.

Up until the second quarter of this century, pernicious anemia was a dreaded and fatal disease caused by the inability of the body to produce enough red blood cells. In 1922, a University of Rochester pathologist, Dr. George Whipple, fed large amounts of raw beef liver to dogs suffering from an anemic condition. The dogs recovered. Then in 1926, two other doctors, George Minot and William Murphy, tried the same thing on humans and found that liver cured people too.

The three medical scientists were awarded a Nobel Prize for

their work, but it was not until twenty-two years later, in 1948, that the precise antianemia factor in liver was isolated. The red crystalline substance that was extracted was called B_{12}.

Like folic acid, B_{12} is required only in minuscule amounts in the body, amounts that are measured in micrograms rather than milligrams. One microgram is 1/1000 of a milligram, and a milligram is 1/1000 of a gram.

B_{12} is an important vitamin to puppies in that it stimulates appetite, weight gain, and growth.

A large number of papers have dealt with vitamin B_{12} absorption in dogs but the 1974 edition of the NRC's *Nutrient Requirements of Dogs* says "no definitive data on dietary requirements are available." Because of this situation, the NRC recommends that the B_{12} requirement for the baby pig would be sufficient for the dog.

In my practice, I have always had seemingly good results supplementing animals' diets with B_{12}. For instance, supplementing a pregnant bitch may contribute to bigger and stronger young. An interesting study conducted with rats also strongly suggested this possibility.

Dr. Paul Newberne and Dr. Vernon Young at MIT experimented with two groups of pregnant female rats. One group received a somewhat better than standard diet and the other received the same diet but with a thousand times more B_{12} than what is considered normal. The higher levels of dietary B_{12} were supplied only during gestation. When the young were born to the supplement-fed mothers, they received standard, non-supplemented rat chow identical to that fed the offspring of the mothers who got no supplements.

The researchers found that the B_{12} supplementation had both a short and long term effect on the young. These young were larger than their counterparts at birth and continued to be so a year later. They had more muscle and less fat on their bodies. Most importantly, when challenged with a bacterial infection, they demonstrated better resistance. The researchers concluded that the standard diet fed to the one group of pregnant rats was totally adequate to achieve normal birth weight in the newborn and a normal post-natal growth. However, they were impressed with the long-term benefits of a supplemented maternal diet and particularly the enhanced ability of the young to withstand stress in later life.[15]

Biotin

This nutrient, sometimes referred to as vitamin H, is one of the lesser known members of the B complex family. It too is necessary for synthesizing fat and breaking down protein and carbohydrate molecules so that the body can use them.

Biotin is also involved in the maintenance of the thyroid and adrenal glands, the nervous system, and in healthy skin and reproduction.

The biotin requirement for dogs—and humans as well—has not been established because there is evidence that this food factor is manufactured by intestinal bacteria. Antibiotics used to treat infections destroy these beneficial bacteria along with the harmful bacteria causing the illness. Sulfa drugs also decimate the good bacteria. Supplementation is a particularly good idea when an animal is under treatment with an antibiotic.

According to pet food industry sources, biotin is recommended as a supplement in dog food because it helps to prevent coprophagy—the animal eating his own excrement—and reduces the incidence of skin disorders.[16]

There is no evidence however that biotin is supplemented in dog food, thus it is a good idea to ensure that this nutrient is included in your program. Manufacturers may not add biotin into their products because they consider it too expensive.

Some people like to supplement their dog's food with raw eggs. This is probably not a good idea. Nutritionists believe that raw eggs contain an enzyme that interferes with the body's utilization of biotin. *Cooked* eggs, however, are OK to give your pet. Eggs are an excellent source of protein and dogs usually enjoy them.

Vitamin D

This is the "sunshine vitamin." It has long been recognized as a key element in calcium and phosphorus metabolism in the dog. Strong bones and strong teeth depend on it.

Rickets, the crippling crooked-bone disease, is one result of a vitamin D and calcium deficiency.

Back in 1918, a British researcher working with puppies came up with the first proof that rickets was a deficiency disease. He cured the animals with cod liver oil. A few years later, other investigators found that in addition to the vitamin A present in fish liver oil, there was another factor present, and this was what prevented rickets. This substance, later named vitamin D, was eventually synthesized in 1931.

Vitamin D is not found in significant amounts in food other than in fish liver oils. Commercial milk is fortified with vitamin D. Most animals and humans get what they need from the sunlight, which triggers a chain of chemical reactions in the skin that produces vitamin D. But in northern climates, and especially in the winter, when the sun is weak, deficiencies of vitamin D can take place if individuals do not receive the vitamin supplementally. In the London Zoo, reptiles, birds, and mammals from tropic origins are subject to vitamin D deficiency during the cold months and need supplements for maintenance of good health.

Vitamin E

Here is a genuine all-star that contributes many services to the body of both man and beast. Just to name a few:

— It boosts the efficiency of the heart and the circulatory system. It promotes dilation of small blood vessels, thus increasing the supply of blood and nutrients to distant cells and tissues of the body.

— It improves the immune system.

— It improves muscle power and stamina in dogs.

— It protects against the damaging effects of air pollution.

— It helps heal nagging skin problems.

— It rejuvenates ailing and tired old dogs.

— It makes other vitamins and minerals work more efficiently. The list could go on and on.

Dr. Wilfrid E. Shute, a retired Canadian cardiologist, has been an outspoken champion of vitamin E for forty years. He and his late physician brother, Evan, used vitamin E extensively in their practices.

Shute knows better than any man living just how this vitamin enhances the function of heart and circulation not only in humans but also in dogs. In addition to his professional career, he has long maintained an active interest in the breeding, showing, and judging of dogs. He is a former president of the Doberman Pinscher Club of America. He has been personally responsible for the widespread use of vitamin E among dog enthusiasts.

According to the NRC, there has not been sufficient research conducted to set a minimum vitamin E requirement for dogs. The recommendation therefore is based on work with other species. The NRC suggests 1.1 IU per kilogram of body weight as adequate. This would mean about 30 IUs for a 50-pound dog.

These kind of numbers are being blown right out by Shute and some of the other breeders I have talked to. They use 200, 300, and even more units of vitamin E without any problems. What the NRC considers adequate may indeed prevent such vitamin E deficiency disorders as heart failure, muscular dystrophy, brain and neurological complications, and reproductive failures. What the higher doses do is to help create an optimal physiology where internal organs work at maximum efficiency. Old dogs are renewed. Aging processes are seemingly reversed. You remember the story of Rusty, the old Irish setter, in the opening chapter? That was just one of a number of dramatic vitamin E reversals I have witnessed.

Shute says he gives his Dobermans daily doses of 300 to 400 IUs. "I have a nine-year-old champion male right now," he told me, "who is siring the best litters on the West Coast and he has only been at it for two or three years. Every litter has champions. We have the dog on 300 IUs a day."

Fred Heying, a now retired Southern California breeder of champion dachshunds, talks about miniature dachshunds—ten- or eleven-pounders—getting 1,200 IUs for several days at a time with no ill effects. Breeder friends of his have successfully used that kind of dosage to cure the little dachshunds of posterior paralysis, the disc disease that is the most common problem with the breed.

Heying told me that he has his animals routinely on 200 IUs of vitamin E a day and they just don't seem to have any back problems. It also makes his animals more potent and fertile.

Years ago, before he knew about vitamin E, his Favorite v. Marienlust, the all-time champion sire for the breed, was losing some of his steam. Too much sex probably, he thought. By coincidence, Heying met Shute at a dog show and told him about the problem. Shute paid a visit to the kennel, saw the dog, and suggested vitamin E.

"It helped a great deal," said Heying. "Favorite," on the vitamin E program, sired until he was twelve years old, producing ninety-five champions. He died at the age of fourteen, in 1959. One of his offspring sired eighty-two champions.

The experience with "Favorite" prompted Heying to buy up gallons of wheat germ oil—a source of vitamin E—and douse it liberally on his animals' food. Later, he converted to vitamin E capsules, snipping the ends and squeezing the contents onto the food. This latter method is much simpler and more reliable and I will have more to say about it in Chapter 14.

Much scientific work has been done with vitamin E and animals. The U. S. Air Force supplemented the diets of rats and found these animals had more endurance and stamina in swimming and treadmill exercises and greater ability to withstand high altitudes. Autopsy showed that the vitamin-supplemented rodents didn't suffer the same damaging effects on vital organs as did their littermates who went through the same grueling experiences but without vitamin E supplementation.[17]

From rats to race horses. At two of Canada's leading thoroughbred farms—the National Stud Farm and Windfields Farm, both in Ontario—experiments were begun twenty-five years ago with vitamin E supplementation in large doses. The project was a big winner. Total earnings jumped from $88,260 in 1955 to $196,685 the following year.

In 1960, after five years, a report was issued stating that the performance of race horses in the stable "reached a new high in Canada." The massive doses of vitamin E "will bring horses close to their best effort," it said. "The vitamin enables the tissues of the body to do the same job on less oxygen. It is as if one strapped an aqua-lung on the horse's back. It opens up huge reserves of capillary circulation, sets of vessels not ordinarily used but waiting there for emergency demands." The fertility of mares and potency of stallions were increased, meaning more foals and more sales. The vitamin had a rejuvenating effect on older horses. Out of this unique vitamin project came Victoria Park, the Horse of the Year in Canada in 1960, Northern Dancer, the 1964 winner of the Kentucky Derby and Preakness Stakes, and other top Canadian horses.[18]

Dr. N. H. Lambert, formerly the president of the Irish Veterinary Association, used comparatively large doses of vitamin E in treating dogs and cats. He used the vitamin on old dogs and rejuvenated them. He used it on both racing greyhounds and apparently healthy dogs and found that "the athletic ability" of some of these animals "improved rapidly and markedly after they had been given large doses" of vitamin E. He used it for hunting dogs who had suffered heart failure and put them back in the field for a hard hunting season. He used it to clear up chronic skin ulcers, improve reproduction and whelping in female dogs, and restore lost libidos in males.[19]

Along with its rejuvenating action on the cardiovascular system, vitamin E has another unique quality that appears to slow down aging. It is a natural antioxidant. You will recall that in Chapter 3 I mentioned two synthetic antioxidants, BHA and BHT, that are used in both human and pet food to retard the oxidation—and resultant rancidity—of fats. Vitamin E does the same inside the body. It protects against excessive oxidation of fatty substances that are contained in all cells of the body. Paradoxically, it is the same oxygen that sustains life and is required by all the cells that can also cause unwanted reactions, damaging membranes and enzymes and contributing to the general aging of the body. Vitamin E slows down this aging effect of oxygen.

As if the oxygen we breathe were not enough, mankind has now put synthetic oxidants into the air that similarly damage the fatty components of cells. This is air pollution. If you and your pet live in an urban area blighted with pollution, you should be interested in how vitamin E can provide protection. There is considerable concern among scientists over the health effects of ozone, the main oxidant of photochemical smog. Even at weak concentrations, ozone can damage the fatty content of respiratory tract cells and increase susceptibility to pulmonary infection. This pollutant is already suspected as a factor in the soaring incidence of bronchitis, emphysema, and lung cancer. With vitamin E in abundance, scientists say, the cellular membranes are strengthened, making the fatty contents less vulnerable to oxidation, virus, and bacteria. It is thought also that vitamin E acts like a bodyguard for vitamin A, which is essential for the health of the mucous membrane of the respiratory tract. This is another example of how the nutrients work as a team.

Dr. Mohammad G. Mustafa, of the University of California at Davis, demonstrated in 1974 the protective effect of vitamin E on lung tissue. Mustafa divided 60 healthy rats into 2 groups, feeding one group a standard diet containing 11 parts per 1,000,000 of vitamin E and feeding the other group a diet supplemented with 66 parts per 1,000,000 of vitamin E. After five weeks animals from both groups were exposed to either 0.1 or 0.2 parts per 1,000,000 ozone for seven days. The 0.2 concentration is equal to half the normal ozone content found in smoggy Los Angeles air.

When the lung tissues were examined, Mustafa found that the rats on the higher level of vitamin E had suffered significantly less injury than the others. An increased supply of this vitamin is likely to slow down harmful cellular reactions that may occur because of ozone, he wrote.

Mustafa pointed out that the higher levels of vitamin E he used were approximately twice the recommended daily allowance for rats. The lower rate, of 11 parts per 1,000,000 he added, is like "the average concentration in American diets."

He went on to say that "the findings may be of relevance to human populations exposed to photochemical smog."[20] I would second that motion and add that it would certainly be relevant to the respiratory health of dogs as well.

Other researchers have shown that the ozone in smog has a harmful effect beyond the lungs. Studies reveal damage to red blood cells after ozone exposure. In one 1978 study, researchers found increased susceptibility to biochemical damage in the red blood cells of rats fed a diet deficient in vitamin E, but not of animals given dietary supplements of 45 parts per 1,000,000 of the vitamin. Thus, they said, "Vitamin E appears to occupy a unique place in the antioxidant defense of the red cells."[21]

There is good evidence also that extra vitamin E protects animals against encounters of another kind. Cheryl F. Nockels of Colorado State University fed vitamin E in excess of normal requirements to a number of different types of animals and found that it "significantly increased" immune response and resistance to disease. Mice, chicks, guinea pigs, turkeys, and lambs were challenged with an array of harmful microorganisms and the animals given extra vitamin E emerged from the trials the least damaged.[22]

Research done at Cornell University School of Veterinary Medicine has shown that dogs deficient in vitamin E have inferior immunity.[23]

The scientific evidence makes a strong case for supplementation. A dog clearly has much to gain from extra vitamin E.

The Mineral Team

Minerals are the teammates of vitamins, and they are just as important. But because good ways to study minerals have been developed only recently, they have been largely neglected, and the nutritional spotlight has been dominated by vitamins.

There are, in fact, ninety-six times more minerals by weight in an animal's body than vitamins. There could be no life without minerals and any cell lacking in a single mineral nutrient cannot perform as well as it should.

Minerals are involved in nearly every physiological reaction. They associate with vitamins in the formation of enzymes. They are involved in the transportation of oxygen in the bloodstream. They are essential to the growth of strong bones, tissue, teeth, nails, and hair coat. Bones, for example, are principally composed of minerals.

Vitamins are produced in animals and plants. Minerals are found in the soil, in seawater and fresh water, even in the air. In minute amounts they are absorbed from the soil by plants. Animals get the bulk of their minerals from the water they drink and the food they eat.

Dogs require calcium, phosphorus, iron, copper, potassium, magnesium, sodium, chlorine, iodine, manganese, zinc, selenium, and perhaps molybdenum, fluorine, tin, silicon, cobalt, nickel, vanadium, and chromium.

Some minerals, like aluminum, silver, and gold are thought to be nonessential, while minerals like arsenic, lead, cadmium, and mercury are downright toxic. The latter actually interfere with the absorption and utilization of necessary minerals.

According to the NRC, there is insufficient experimental evidence in regard to many minerals, and so requirements cannot be stated precisely. Thus many of the guidelines for formulating diets adequate in minerals for dogs are based on estimates and information taken from other species.

Calcium and Phosphorus

These two minerals are usually considered in tandem because their utilization in the body depends on certain similar endocrine glands. They are both needed for the formation of bones and teeth, thus it is important for growing puppies to have an adequate supply. Let me emphasize the word adequate. Adequate does not mean excess. Many dog owners cause problems because they pump their young dogs full of calcium. I'll have more to say about that in a moment.

It is vital for bitches in gestation to have some extra calcium and phosphorus to pass on in their milk. A lactating bitch also needs extra amounts. A shortage of calcium can bring on eclampsia, or milk fever, a condition in which the mother's milk stops flowing. Bitches on moderate supplementation don't have this problem.

Calcium and phosphorus are essential for a normal nervous system. Calcium plays a role in proper blood clotting and phosphorus is involved in the metabolism of carbohydrates.

The requirements of these two minerals are closely related, and a dietary calcium to phosphorus ratio between 1.2 to 1 and 1.4 to 1 (by weight) is considered optimal for proper utilization by dogs. This means that there should be from 1.2 to 1.4 parts of calcium to 1 part of phosphorus. Both calcium and phosphorus require an adequate amount of vitamin D to be present in order to be utilized properly by the dog's body.

Deficiencies of phosphorus are believed to be rare in the dog. Calcium is another matter. Bone loss and osteoporosis, a condition of weak, porous bone tissue, are symptomatic of deficiency. Jawbones show the earliest signs of degeneration, followed by gum erosion and the detachment of teeth. Other signs are milk fever, convulsions, hemorrhage, reproductive failures, and spontaneous fractures.

But it's too much, not too little, that bothers me most in regard to calcium. Dog owners have this great urge to oversupplement calcium. A balanced vitamin and mineral supplement should contain all the extra calcium a growing dog or a pregnant or lactating bitch needs. But many people will supplement the supplement with a separate calcium compound such as dicalcium phosphate. Some large dogs may need such high levels, but I would provide it only on the advice of a veterinarian.

If you are one of those calcium enthusiasts, here is a true story that may temper your habit:

A friend and client once bred her Great Dane bitch. When the dog came due I went over to the house and helped with the whelping. Later the puppies were sold. One went to a woman who was a devotee of calcium. She apparently was seeing a veterinarian who encouraged her.

Two years went by and one day the woman came into my office with the dog. It had a kidney problem, she said. I told her to give me a list of everything she had been giving the dog on a daily basis for the two years of its life.

I read the list and immediately became suspicious of the calcium level. The dog was getting calcium in its food, calcium in its water, calcium in a multivitamin and mineral supplement, and more calcium in a separate supplement. It was too much. I did a blood-urea-nitrogen test on the dog, which revealed that it had little or no kidney function. I told her the dog probably had very bad kidney stones. There was so much damage done that I felt I could not help the animal. I suggested she take it to the veterinary school at the University of California at Davis. She did. They made the same diagnosis and told her the animal would have to be put to sleep.

The woman's case was typical of others I have seen. The excess calcium cannot be used by the body. It will wind up as kidney or bladder stones or as painful and crippling calcified joints.

People who use the big doses of calcium usually do it for the first two or three years. Don't! If you are going to do it at all, it is really not necessary to go beyond a year. During the first year in the big breeds the skeletal system is growing. After that there is absolutely no need for massive calcium. You are running a risk if you continue.

It is hard to say what a top limit should be. Individual animals have individual needs. Your own veterinarian should give you the proper information on how much calcium to supplement.

When asked, my usual advice on this question is as follows:

A good multivitamin and mineral supplement, along with the food and water, should satisfy a dog's calcium needs. Deficiencies of calcium usually occur because there is a deficiency of vitamin D. Vitamin D is a catalyst that enhances the body's utilization of calcium. Thus a good multi will usually take good care of the vitamin D–calcium requirement without any need for still additional calcium. Moreover, if you administer the kind of program I suggest, one with plenty of vitamin C and E in it, you have another dimension of protection. Both these factors increase the body's uptake of other vitamins and minerals. There is really no need to take any chances.

Iodine

Iodine is a vital mineral because it is necessary for the production of the thyroid hormone that helps regulate the body's metabolism. Goiter, the condition characterized by an enlarged thyroid, is the main sign of iodine deficiency.

Many years ago, goiter was a major problem in the Midwest and Great Lakes regions, where the soil is deficient in iodine. Millions of Americans suffered from malfunctioning and swollen thyroids. So too did the dogs of the area. Between 1918 and 1925, one Chicago scientist autopsied some two thousand adult dogs and found the incidence of goiter to be 98 percent. This phenomenon completely disappeared in Chicago after 1925, he reported, following the introduction of iodized salt as a general grocery store commodity.[1]

Iodized salt is generally considered effective in preventing iodine deficiency and standard incorporation of 1 percent iodized salt in pet food preparations has apparently eliminated deficiency problems. I have never encountered an iodine-related nutritional problem in dogs.

Iron

Most people think of iron as something that women need. The truth is that everybody needs iron, and so do dogs. Both male and female dogs. One of the most important functions of iron is its partnership with copper, B_{12}, and protein to form hemoglobin, the red-coloring matter of the red blood cells that transports oxygen through the blood to the tissues. The hemoglobin molecules contain most of the iron in the body.

Iron-deficient dogs, like humans, suffer from anemia. On diets containing low iron and low protein, dogs tend to have severely lowered resistance to hookworm infestation. Restoration of good iron and protein levels strengthens the resistance.

Supplemental iron may be another useful weapon in the battle against runaway lead in food and the environment. Japanese researchers, working with rats, found that lead-induced growth retardation and anemia and the accumulation of lead in the kidneys were prevented by the addition of dietary iron. They suggested that supplemental iron inhibits lead absorption into the body.[2]

Magnesium and Manganese

These two minerals get mixed up on the tongues of many people.

Magnesium helps the body absorb calcium, vitamins C, E, and B complex and is important to the health of the nervous system. Convulsive seizures and retarded weight gain have been observed in dogs fed a magnesium-deficient diet.

Magnesium appears also to help prevent lead toxicity. A recent study with lead-fed rats showed that the addition of magnesium to the diet increases the excretion of lead and actually draws accumulated lead out of bone and other tissue sites, thus reducing the toxic effect.[3]

Little is known about the requirements for manganese. It is involved in activation of various enzymes related to the proper utilization of vitamins B_1 and E. It is necessary for normal reproduction, bone and cartilage growth, collagen formation, fat metabolism, and pituitary gland function.

Potassium and Sodium

These minerals work in conjunction to maintain a normal fluid balance between the cells. It is necessary for them to be kept in proper balance in order for nerves to respond properly to stimulation and transmit impulses to the muscles and for smooth contraction of the muscles.

Sodium is usually taken into the body in the form of salt—sodium with chlorine. There is inadequate data available to permit determination of minimum requirements for these substances.

A sodium deficiency can lead to fatigue, listlessness, loss of equilibrium, exhaustion, inability to maintain water balance, decreased water intake, retarded growth, dryness of skin, and loss of hair.

Signs of potassium deficiency in an animal are restlessness, poor growth, muscular paralysis, a tendency to dehydration, and lesions of the heart and kidney.

Selenium

This micronutrient has been receiving much attention in recent years for the apparently effective role it plays against heart disease and cancer in both animals and humans. In areas where soil is the most deficient in selenium, medical researchers have found higher incidence of disease. Studies with test animals show that dietary selenium at levels above those recommended as required can increase the effectiveness of the immune system.

Selenium, like vitamins C and E, is an antioxidant. It counteracts the damaging oxidative process at the cellular level, working intimately with vitamin E.

Selenium is recognized as an essential nutrient for dogs, primarily as a result of studies conducted with other species.

Zinc

Zinc is a very useful addition to the supplementation program. Every day more and more is being learned about the activity of zinc and how vital it is in the production of enzymes, the maintenance of healthy hair coat and skin, and just how important it is to the healing process.

The ancient Egyptians, more than three thousand years ago, used salves containing zinc to promote the healing of wounds. Three millennia later, modern medicine is rediscovering zinc power.

Researchers have reported that wounded and burned rats fed diets containing extra amounts of zinc healed faster than rats getting a standard diet. In a clinical experiment at the human level, zinc-supplemented women recovered in half the usual time from a gynecological operation called a vulvectomy. A large majority of women experience complications and slow healing after this surgical procedure, but with zinc these difficulties are substantially reduced.

Zinc, like vitamin C and the B complex vitamins, is burned up by stress. Surgery and injuries are blatant forms of stress. I will often suggest to clients that they provide some extra zinc to their animals following surgery or an injury. Zinc, like C, figures in the production of collagen and is needed in abundant supply when the body is attempting to heal a wound and new cells are being produced at a quickened rate.

A situation exists today that makes supplementation of zinc a real necessity. Scientists have determined the soils in over thirty states to be deficient in zinc. Further depletion is occurring as a result of the use of phosphate and nitrogen fertilizers. This deficiency is reflected in the zinc content of crops and continues up the entire food chain.

Zinc, as I mentioned earlier, is effective along with vitamin C in combating unwanted accumulations of lead.

Recently I have upped the amount of zinc I recommend for older dogs because medical science has found that this mineral has antibacterial properties and may protect the prostate gland from infection. Prostate trouble is fairly common among aging dogs.

Part Three

THE PREVENTION PLAN

7

How to Use the Plan

This is the action part of the book. It contains the "how to do it" information that will enable you to start an effective prevention program for your dog.

In Chapters 8, 9, 10, and 11, I discuss how vitamins and minerals are beneficial in specific stages of canine life: pregnancy and lactation, puppyhood, adulthood, and old age. Simply refer to the stage of life that applies to your dog.

In Chapters 12, 13, and 14, I explain how to purchase vitamin and mineral supplements, how much to use, and how to administer the supplements. You will find charts with my recommended dosages for each stage of life.

If you follow the instructions, and they are essentially what I tell my own clients, then the whole process is quite uncomplicated. Once you have the supplements in hand, the actual administration takes only a few seconds daily.

The prevention plan is a simple and quick method of enhancing the minimum levels of nutrition that are present in your dog's commercial diet. It is an attempt to cover the gaps that may exist in the animal's nutrient intake, to address any special needs or dependencies on particular nutrients, to reduce allergic reactions, to strengthen the organs and the immune system, and in general to make the animal a better show dog, hunting dog, or a livelier companion for yourself and your family.

One question I am often asked is how long it takes for the supplements to work. If you are not trying to treat any particular condition but simply want to raise the level of your dog's health, it's a matter of about ten days or two weeks till you begin seeing improvement. Sometimes the results come even sooner with the disappearance of minor problems, like scratching, and the appearance of youthful vigor. The time factor depends on the individual dog and its individual biochemical status.

It is important to remember that vitamins and minerals work at the cellular level. Unlike powerful drugs that are designed to attack specific problems quickly, nutrients are nature's own compounds and work deep down and all over. Their pace is nature's pace. The whole body is being systematically repaired and reinforced at the foundation and that's why it takes time to see results on the surface.

I always tell my clients to be patient and not expect overnight results, although I have seen and heard of wonderful things happening very rapidly. Given time, your dog's problems will lessen or even disappear. Over the long haul, he may just not get sick anymore like he used to.

It is absolutely vital to stay with the program. Keep it up. Don't stop the supplements as soon as your animal perks up and problems disappear. Don't get the idea that the dog doesn't need the supplements anymore.

Over the years many a client has returned with a sick dog that I had previously put on a supplement program. The first question I ask is this:

"Are you still giving the vitamins and minerals as I recommended?"

The frequent answer: "No, I ran out," or, "I stopped as soon as Fido improved."

I tell them what I'm telling you right now. When you stop, the animal will go right back to the condition he was in prior to supplementation. He'll be the same old animal again, vulnerable to all the lead, toxins, germs, and stress that come his way. He'll go from optimal to satisfactory or less than satisfactory health, from increased to lessened resistance against disease, from A-OK to just OK or maybe not so OK.

Prevention is a lifetime consideration. Once an animal is optimal, you have to keep him that way. There is no reason a dog shouldn't be healthy throughout all stages of life, when providing it with the basis of good health is as simple as the prevention plan I have designed.

Let's start prevention first where life begins and discuss the pregnant and lactating bitch.

8

How Supplements Help
Pregnant and Lactating
Dogs

Pregnancy and lactation is a time of severe biochemical stress.
The female is providing for anywhere from two to a dozen puppies. It is necessary that she be nutritionally fit to cope with this
added burden.

The point is strongly made by Dr. Roger Williams: "It has
been amply demonstrated throughout the entire animal kingdom
that during the period of pregnancy, nutrition must be at a particularly high level. It has been found repeatedly that specific
diets supporting the adult life of rats, mice, dogs, cats, chickens,
turkeys, fish, foxes or monkeys will not be adequate to support
anything approaching the nutritional requirements for normal
reproduction."[1]

There is ample medical evidence—both on human and animal
levels—showing that deficiencies in any single nutrient can lead
to reproductive failures and fetus malformation. Vitamin A and
the eyeless piglets was a startling example of such a deficiency.
Zinc deficiency in rats has been shown to cause resorption of fe-
tuses and gross abnormalities in 90 percent of the young that
make it through birth. A manganese deficiency in rats, mice,
guinea pigs, chickens, and hogs causes inner ear defects and
equilibrium problems in the offspring.[2] Deficiencies of B_1, B_2,
pantothenic acid, B_6, biotin, folic acid, and B_{12} can cause fetal
loss. Conversely, no adverse effects have been reported from ex-

cessive dosage of any of the B complex vitamins.[3] The Bs are very essential for good pregnancies.

Roger Williams points out that if nutrition is good, most animals are vigorous, healthy, and prolific, and if their diet is excellent, they likely will produce healthy offspring. Nutrition can be upgraded in a number of ways, he says, such as by adding more and improved protein, improving the mineral balance, and "introducing a better assortment of vitamins in ample amounts."[4]

By introducing ample amounts of supplements, I have been attempting to achieve just the kind of nutritional enhancement that Williams is suggesting. The bitch's diet is being reinforced and so is her ability to produce vigorous, healthy, and alert young.

According to the NRC's *Nutrient Requirements of Dogs*, pregnant bitches will require slightly more food than normal, most of this increase coming during the last third of pregnancy. The requirements of a lactating dog may soar to three or more times over its normal intake.[5]

The extra food is consumed by the animal because of the extra amount of nutrition she needs. I personally don't think that the quantity of food is the vital factor. The animal requires more nutrients, not more bulk, but she has to take in the extra bulk to get the extra vitamins and minerals needed to pass on to the young. I have seen many of my clients' pregnant and lactating animals. If the animal is on supplements, I generally find that she will eat a little more than normal but not twice as much. The animal doesn't need all the extra bulk because she is getting the extra nutrients from the supplements.

You are well aware by now of my opinion of commercial dog food. The pet food industry maintains that all the dog needs is right there in the food. In my experience this is far from the truth, especially during pregnancy. When animals get dietary supplements, many of the problems of pregnancy are eliminated. When the animals are fed commercial food alone, the problems appear in force.

The pet food companies are forever stressing protein. It's like a broken record. All the while they serve up inferior protein. Protein is extremely important but it is also necessary to have enough of the key nutrients—such as the B complex factors—to metabolize and enhance the utilization of protein.

For the bitch trying to supply added nourishment to her young, the last thing she needs is to be fighting a second front of stress in the form of impurities and additives and poor protein. This is an important time to read labels and try to keep the food as free from preservatives and additives as possible. Do provide the supplements. These extra nutrients will help the bitch resist disease, prepare her for the real heavy stress of whelping and nursing, and promote the health and development of the puppies taking form inside her.

A bitch on good supplements is going to develop a stronger immune system to fight off disease and infection. If there were no other reason, this strengthening of the body's defenses would alone be reason to supplement. An optimally healthy pregnant bitch will have more effective antibodies to pass on through the placenta and milk to the puppies. This means more protection for them.

Smoother Whelping with Vitamin C

Back in the sixties when my son and daughter were growing up, we had three German shepherd bitches as pets. One year we decided to breed the best-looking of the three, a beautiful two-year-old named Rasha. She became pregnant and one night about two months later she started whelping.

One characteristic of large breeds is that they have long whelpings, and frequently one or two or even more pups die—or are born with defects—because they have been in the birth canal too long without oxygen. The problem usually stems from the bitch becoming exhausted after delivering several puppies. The uterus muscle that contracts to push out the newborn simply runs out of steam. The condition is called atony and is fairly common to the shepherds, Great Danes, Saint Bernards—the big dogs. But it can happen in small breeds as well.

It is imperative to do something to get the remaining puppies out quickly. You can use something like a posterior pituitary extract—an injection. This stimulates uterine contraction and is sometimes given to women to induce labor.

In the case of Rasha this is what I did. After going fifteen or sixteen hours, in which time she had delivered five puppies, she finally became exhausted and couldn't whelp anymore. After the injection however she was able to squeeze out the last two puppies.

A veterinarian is not going to sit up all night with somebody's bitch and help the animal whelp puppies. Nor is the average person going to get pituitary extract and syringe and inject his dog. What the typical dog owner will do is rush the animal into the veterinarian's office or to an emergency clinic if one is nearby. Usually a cesarean operation is then performed. The vet goes in and retrieves the remaining animals so there won't be any severe complications. The cost of such an operation is $200 and up, and I used to do them all the time before I began using supplements.

The experience with Rasha was strong enough so that we spayed our other German shepherds. It was only much later that I learned what vitamins could do to eliminate the drama and anxiety of puppybirth, but by then my children were older and not much interested in taking care of puppies.

The initial revelation that supplements enhanced the whelping process came during an experiment I conducted to see if vitamin C could prevent hip dysplasia in puppies. The first dog in the trial was a German shepherd bitch and we put her on sodium ascorbate powder, an excellent form of vitamin C, at the time she was bred.

The owner, a local breeder of shepherds, called excitedly after the bitch whelped to report that the whelping had taken place in half the normal time. Later, about two weeks after lactation, we found that the mammary glands were tucking right up into the dog's body. There were no lingering and sagging teats as often is the case with dogs. Impressed, the breeder said he wanted to keep trying the C on other dogs. A few months later he reported a remarkable whelping in which a champion German shepherd bitch delivered ten healthy puppies in ten hours. Previously, the breeder said, this dog had averaged twenty hours to deliver a litter.

As other breeders began trying the vitamin C, I received similar enthusiastic reports. Deliveries were smoother and quicker with healthier and more alert puppies. The eyesore of saggy teats was eliminated. The mother returned quickly to her prepregnancy form.

At this point a brief comparison to the human experience is in order. Dr. Fred Klenner, the North Carolina physician who pioneered vitamin C therapy in the United States, has repeatedly shown the benefits of large doses of this vitamin in pregnancy. In over one thousand deliveries he consistently reduced the time and pain of labor. The babies were so noticeably healthy that they were called "vitamin C babies" by the staff of the local hospital.[6]

Klenner and other doctors who followed his example have been using 10,000 milligrams of vitamin C daily. Compare this to the recommended daily allowance of 65 milligrams suggested by the National Research Council.

We know that dogs are poor producers of vitamin C. The stresses of pregnancy severely tax the liver enzyme system where ascorbic acid is produced. I feel that the bitch cannot make enough to overcome the stresses and meet the needs of the multiple lives inside her. Furthermore, she gets no help from the food she eats. The manufacturers are convinced the dog is making all the vitamin C it needs and so they don't add any in the food. The dog's own supply of vitamin C may be further strained by the need to detoxify some of the impurities contained in the diet.

Given this background it is not surprising to find similar benefits from supplementation when you compare the human female, who makes no vitamin C, to the canine female, who doesn't make enough.

— The quick recovery of the canine teats is related to the power of vitamin C to maintain the elasticity of the connective tissue. Klenner reported that the area around the womb—the perineum—of his patients always returned quickly to previous firmness. "Virginlike," he said. Furthermore, there were few or no stretch marks.

— My clients consistently report whelping time cut in half. Klenner talked in terms of three- and four-hour labors. Again, the elasticity of the perineum in woman and dog facilitates the enormous stretching necessary to make room for the emerging infant or pup. Also: Vitamin C has exceptional antifatigue power. The struggling females seem to have more strength and energy.

Klenner's "vitamin C babies" were all noted for their exceptional health. The same can be said for the "vitamin C puppies." Rarely is there a litter runt.

One of the causes of miscarriages in dogs is brucella canis. This very contagious microbe is related to the family of bacteria that commonly infects herds of cattle, goats, sheep, and swine. In the human, the brucella bacteria causes undulant fever.

Many dog breeders have experienced episodes of brucella infections with their bitches. The animal becomes pregnant but aborts halfway through the cycle. Tests often trace the problem to brucella.

I have been told by four different breeders that the addition of megadoses of vitamin C to an already existing program of vitamins and minerals resulted in the disappearance of brucella-related abortions. My assumption is that the vitamin C stimulates the immune system activity against the microbes. Although my opinion is based on limited data, I feel it is worthwhile to mention it. Breeders who are experiencing a brucella problem might like to try vitamin C. The regular preventive dose for a bitch will do.

Vitamin E for Pregnancy

Another wonderful pregnancy supplement is vitamin E. My interest in E was aroused by one of my assistants at the hospital. This young lady became pregnant and one day mentioned to me that she had read about vitamin E and how it was supposed to strengthen the muscles of the uterus. She was going to try it for her pregnancy, she announced. Her doctor had given her the OK. With the onset of labor, she was duly rushed to the hospital and barely arrived there when she gave birth. She had good strong uterine contractions and a good healthy baby.

Her experience inspired me to try vitamin E on pregnant dogs.

I was concerned about atony—the stalling of the tired uterine muscle at the time of whelping. This was still before my deep involvement with vitamin C.

I had seen many puppies die in the womb because they were ready to come out, ready to breathe, but the bitch was exhausted and unable to push out the last of the litter. The longer the pups are in the uterus, once whelping begins, the greater the chance of death or damage to the tiny brains, and of injury to the mother.

The results with vitamin E were generally quite good. Whelping was definitely made easier and it soon became routine for me to recommend 50 or 100 IUs at the time a dog became pregnant.

Years later, I found that when vitamin C and vitamin E are used together in liberal doses during pregnancy, the effect is exceptional. The problem of uterine exhaustion is eliminated.

In Ireland, Dr. N. H. Lambert reported good results many years ago using vitamin E to overcome the atony problem.

"In one kennel of Pekingese dogs," he reported in 1955, "practically every bitch for several years had suffered from uterine atony at parturition [time of birth]. This led to many forceps deliveries and caesarean sections. During the past eighteen months, vitamin E has been given daily to each bitch in this kennel from day of mating to parturition. Each bitch has whelped naturally and rapidly. There have been no retained placentas, and lactation has been abundant."

The result was very encouraging because of the general frequency of uterine atony, Lambert said.[7]

Vitamin E's technical name is tocopherol. The word comes from the Greek: *tokos,* for childbirth, *pherein,* for bringing forth, and *ol,* for oil. Thus it is the "oil of fertility." The name was applied after the original research showed vitamin E–deficient rats to have reproductive failures. Deficient dogs are similarly affected.

Many animals that are supposedly getting adequate amounts of vitamin E in their daily feed still have difficulty with conception. Sometimes it takes amounts over what is regarded as normal to enable an animal to conceive. There is a need for more because of stress or biological individuality. The needs, remember, differ from person to person, animal to animal.

In the Canadian study with race horses that I mentioned earlier, the researchers examined the impact of supplemental vitamin E on a group of thirty-four broodmares, including twenty-one that were either barren, maiden, or difficult to mate. Seven stallions in the experiment were also supplemented.

Tocopherol markedly increased female fertility, the report said. Fully 88 percent of the broodmares conceived when bred to the supplemented stallions. Their previous five-year breeding record was 66 percent of foals.

On their part, the stallions showed better breeding behavior, more libido, less nervousness, better sperm, and better condition after the breeding season.[8]

Dr. Wilfrid Shute, the vitamin E man, sums up these kinds of findings by saying that vitamin E simply seems to increase physiological effectiveness in every way—including ovum and sperm activity.

Shute, himself a prominent dog breeder, has left his mark on other breeders. Many have followed his suggestions and use vitamin E in their kennels.

At the Heying Teckel Kennel in Southern California, Fred Heying has been supplying his blue-ribbon dachshunds with extra vitamin E for years.

"We feel it helps the bitches because they always pop out big and healthy litters," he says. "We never have trouble with the whelping."

In my practice I had one dramatic case of "instant fertility" through vitamin E. It involved a five-year-old Yorkshire terrier that had been given away to a woman by a breeder because the animal couldn't become pregnant. The dog was a real aristocrat.

The woman brought the dog to me and I told her to put it on 50 IUs of vitamin E.

The next time the animal came into heat, she was bred, and she had three beautiful puppies. The breeder, who had tried in vain to breed the dog with several different males, was shocked when she heard the news.

I have found that vitamin E is helpful in cases where animals have a tendency to miscarriage. A three-year-old miniature poodle would abort every time she was bred. I put the animal on 50 IUs of vitamin E and she conceived and held the pups. I could only assume that either there was a deficiency of vitamin E or the reproductive system in the animal was simply made more effective with the vitamin.

Anne Rogers Clark, at her Surrey-Rimskittle Kennel in Maryland, has successfully used vitamin E at the strength of 100 IUs daily to prevent cleft palates and the tendency toward "swimmers" among English springers and English cockers. The incidence is greatly reduced with vitamin E, according to Mrs. Clark. "Grab puppies," or "swimmers," are the great big puppies who you think just eat too much and therefore can't get up on their feet. They lay around in the litter box, feet sprawled out and helpless.

Mrs. Clark's dogs are routinely getting a multiple vitamin and mineral product throughout their lives. As soon as a bitch comes into season the animal is given added vitamin E. This is continued through breeding and the entire pregnancy period.

Milk and Hair Coat Protected

A good supplement program must have plenty of the B complex vitamins. They are vital for the development of healthy little nervous systems. Some Bs are involved in stimulating the production of red blood cells and others in the production of good antibodies that the mother will pass on to the puppies. Pantothenic acid will help the mother cope with the stress of pregnancy.

Stress depletes zinc. Studies have shown that pregnant women tend to have low zinc levels. This mineral is far too important to be in deficit at this critical time. Zinc is related to proper collagen formation and body growth and utilization of nutrients. It is also essential in wound healing. Every puppy in the womb is connected through an individual placenta to the uterine wall. When a puppy is whelped, the placenta pulls away, leaving behind a raw area that is prone to infection. The sooner it heals the better. Zinc helps the process.

Many a breeder is familiar with a condition called eclampsia. It is similar to milk fever in cows. The nursing bitch develops the shakes, muscle spasms, an unsteadiness and stiffness in the legs, a high temperature, and convulsions. The animal can die. Milk production shuts off early in this condition and the bitch will reject the puppies. All breeds may be affected, but it is most common in small bitches with large litters. From my experience, one out of every twenty pregnancies involves a case of eclampsia.

We don't know for sure whether this condition is due to a calcium deficiency or not. The increased demand for calcium during pregnancy and lactation may be a prime factor. When this happens, the dog is brought in for a standard treatment of a calcium gluconate injection. In a matter of minutes, the shaking subsides. By next morning, the dog is fine and we send her back home to resume her nursing duties.

It is important for the pregnant and lactating bitch to be on a supplementation program that includes calcium. Not an excess, remember. The amount in a good multiple vitamin and mineral supplement will usually suffice. I have never seen a single case of eclampsia involving a dog on a supplementation program.

The program seems also to take care of congenital abnormalities. I used to frequently see tiny Chihuahuas, teacup poodles, and Pomeranian pups born with open craniums. The bone hasn't knitted together in one area of the cranium and the only thing covering the brain is the thin sheath of skin. These slits vary in size. On dead puppies, I have run my finger over some openings as narrow as a pencil point and others almost as wide as the diameter of a dime. The least amount of pressure causes seizure and death, which is usually what happens. Nothing can be done to treat this condition.

Many people consider this a genetic problem. Maybe, I say, but over the years I noticed that bitches on supplements don't produce these abnormalities. I feel the problem may be due to a deficiency of any one or more nutrients in the dog's food.

"She blew her hair coat!" That's bad news for any pet owner, but especially the owner of a show dog. A blown hair coat is one result of the excess stress of pregnancy and lactation. The bitch starts losing hair and her coat becomes scruffy and lackluster. This sorry state is unfortunately fairly common. It can take months for an animal to regain her previous rich hair coat.

Once I put a four-year-old German shepherd champion on the

supplement program. Previously, she had had two difficult whelpings, had lost pups and blown her hair coat each time. As a result of taking the vitamins, she delivered healthy puppies in half the time and didn't blow her hair coat. The owner showed her a couple of weeks after she had weaned the puppies. Supplemented dogs don't blow their hair coats!

One side benefit of the vitamin and mineral supplementation program is that it extends the breeding life of a bitch. Normally, when a dog reaches the age of five, I feel that her breeding life should be stopped because she is unable to cope with the stresses of puppy-bearing as well as when she was younger. This is especially true for the smaller breeds. In my practice however I have seen supplemented eight-year-olds coast through pregnancies and then produce good healthy pups. An older bitch that does become pregnant will greatly benefit from the supplementation program. There is an increased need for vitamin C because aged animals produce less C than they did in their younger days. An aging animal also needs more vitamin E.

One interesting case of vitamin E and a "December pregnancy" was reported by Lambert in Ireland. A small ten-year-old terrier bitch had aborted on two previous matings. For the following mating with the same sire, vitamin E was administered daily from the day of mating until delivery. The bitch gave birth to three live puppies and suckled them without difficulty.[9]

Cheaper to Supplement than Operate

As a rule, I don't try to push clients into a vitamin or mineral program. I have learned from experience that many people simply don't have enough awareness of nutrition to sustain a program over the long run. Pregnancy is one time though where I will march out all the ogres to help persuade an unmotivated client: increased stress, lowered resistance, risk of disease and deformities, complications of whelping and uterine exhaustion, the impurities in commercial food. I will appeal from the health standpoint or even the financial standpoint. Whatever works.

"You can pay a few dollars for some vitamins now or pay two

hundred fifty dollars or more for a cesarean operation later on," I say. "Take your choice."

I feel that dystocia, the medical term for delivery complications, happens often enough to justify this tack of persuasion. Before my work with vitamins, fully 95 percent of the cesareans I performed were on animals suffering from uterine exhaustion. Now, with dogs on supplements, I never see this problem. There may be the extra large puppy or a puppy in an abnormal position lodged inside the birth canal, and obviously vitamins won't help that predicament, but the program dramatically improves the odds for trouble-free deliveries.

TIPS FOR PREGNANCY

1. If you are planning to breed your dog or if you know she is pregnant, take her to your veterinarian for an examination. The vet will check the dog's general health, look for any possible complications, and test for parasites. If there is to be any treatment for worms or parasites, it should occur at the beginning of pregnancy, if at all, because the stress of chemical toxins in the treatment may be harmful to the animal's strained immune system.

2. If the bitch has not been on a vitamin and mineral program, *this is the time to start.* (See Chapter 13 for how much to give your dog.)

3. Commercial dog food is highly processed and full of additives and impurities. If you haven't done it before, try to seek out a product that has the fewest listed chemical preservatives. Some products have none at all.

4. During the second half of the two-month pregnancy, try to put a limit on the dog's activities. Don't go romping with her at the beach where she might get a chill. Don't play ball or Frisbee with her. Don't exhaust her. Limit the vigorous activities so she can gather her strength for the coming ordeal. Try to keep her away from other dogs. They may be carriers of disease or parasites.

5. Choose a warm, quiet place where you want the bitch to whelp and set up a whelping box or suitable container. You can feed her there to get her used to it. This will generally prevent an animal from going into a closet or some other off-limits place to do her birthing. Don't line the whelping box with cloth as puppies can get tangled up and suffocate. Newspaper will do.

6. If a bitch goes through two hours of heavy labor without producing a pup, this means there are problems. It is advisable to take the dog to a veterinarian as soon as possible. By heavy labor I mean contractions every five to ten minutes. If this continues much longer than two hours, the animal can become extremely weak. A large puppy or a puppy in a horizontal or posterior position may be causing the problem. It will require a veterinarian to make the diagnosis and choose the proper course of action. The longer the delay in taking the bitch to the veterinarian, the weaker the animal becomes. If a cesarean is performed, the anesthesia that is used can actually cause the death of an exhausted dog.

9

How Supplements
Help Puppies

"Stress," says Dr. Hans Selye, the foremost authority on it, "is inherent in the activity of life itself."

If the stresses are excessive or prolonged, the efficiency of the body's machinery deteriorates. Cells break down, reducing resistance to germs and increasing vulnerability to disease. If diet is adequate, the damage of stress can be repaired. If it is not adequate, the stage is set for illness.

Stress is a puppy's shadow. It's right there to greet him the moment he comes through the gates. Puppyhood is measured by trials of pain, diarrhea, injections, insects, worms, bacteria, and viruses. In a relatively short period of time, the animal goes from one strange setting to another, from one adjustment to the next.

For two months, the period of canine gestation, the puppy has taken form and wallowed in the comfort, warmth, and security of the womb. Then suddenly out he tumbles into a jostling world of squealing littermates. He has to start fending for himself, fighting and elbowing the other pups for nipple time.

A few days later, the pup gets his first dose of man-made misery: tail docking and the removal of dewclaws. Tails and "thumb" claws are snipped.

Man-made or nature-made, the road is paved with stress. That's why I recommend that a puppy be put on supplements as early as possible—from the day the animal is born or from the day it is acquired.

By supplementing his diet from the start you are helping him keep his guard up and repel the constant threats around him.

Extra vitamins are going to strengthen tiny nervous systems and improve the functioning of the organs. They will enhance growth rate, letting the dog reach the maximum size and intelligence for his breed. They will accelerate the healing process after puppyhood operations like tail docking and ear cropping. They will also protect against sudden infant death, an insidious, mysterious baby-killer that puzzles modern medicine.

Among humans, sudden infant death is the leading cause of mortality from age one week to one year. Babies, kittens, pups, calves, all species are seemingly vulnerable. The very young seem healthy one minute and are dead the next. In dogs, I have heard of many cases where half or even whole litters are inexplicably wiped out.

I recall one case of seven Doberman pinscher puppies. All appeared quite normal when they were brought in on the third day after birth to have the tails docked and the dewclaws removed. About a week later, I received a call from the owner who told me how each day there was another dead puppy in the litter. The weather was mild, so that was not a factor. I did a postmortem on two of the puppies and found nothing unusual. The woman didn't want to have blood tests performed, which might have yielded clues.

I gave the remaining two puppies an injection of vitamin C, hoping this would boost their immune systems enough to fight off the phantom killer. Both survived and are alive today.

The woman was a first-time client. She was not aware of my program. Her bitch had not been on vitamins and minerals at any time and neither had the puppies. Her attitude was that animals take care of themselves. I feel that had the pregnancy been reinforced with supplements, the whole litter probably would have survived.

In the medical world, there are many theories about sudden infant death. But there is very little agreement. In Australia, Dr. Archie Kalokerinos contends that sudden infant death is related to a vitamin C deficiency. He feels that a minor infection, or an immunization, can stress the immune system in a deficiency state beyond its capabilities and produce rapid death. Dr. Kalokerinos was a district physician among a rural aboriginal population in the sixties and was confronted with a sudden death problem that was decimating aboriginal babies. When conventional methods failed, he turned to vitamin C and found it an effective tool. He was able to practically eliminate the problem.[1]

Dr. Kalokerinos had determined that the aborigines were nutritionally impoverished. Most babies received inferior formulas and those that were nursed were getting poor quality mother's milk. The result was weakened immune systems and, all too often, sudden infant death.

With dogs, I feel that a taxing pregnancy followed by the susceptibility of the newborn can set the stage for sudden death. A pregnant bitch eating a suspect diet, receiving no vitamin C in her food, is severely stressed by the pregnancy.

Now, if the pregnant bitch is put on a good supplementation program, one that includes plenty of vitamin C, she will then develop good immunity to pass on to the pups. And once they are born, if the pups receive a daily ration of vitamin C themselves, the protection is essentially doubled. No more sudden death. That's what I have found.

Dehydration, caused by diarrhea, is another major problem with preweaned puppies. For some reason, probably a bacterial or viral infection, the puppy has the runs. It stops nursing. In this situation, everything is going out and nothing is going in. Because of its small size, it doesn't take long for the animal to lose an excess and fatal amount of fluids. In a few hours, the animal can die.

I recall a whole litter with bad diarrhea and the lady who owned the animals decided to take the matter into her own hands. She injected penicillin into their tiny thighs. All she did was cause nerve damage and a type of leg paralysis. The whole litter had to be put to sleep.

If we can strengthen the immune system of puppies, they will be able to resist the microbes that lead to sudden death and diarrhea and dehydration. There will be no reason to attempt something as idiotic or desperate as injecting penicillin into tiny puppies.

Puppies nurse for three or four weeks, a time of enormous growth. The little bodies demand good nutrition. The mother's milk is the pillar of the puppies' health—present and future.

After a few weeks of nursing, the pups begin to grow teeth. The suckling becomes a constant grind to the bitch. She in turn becomes physically and perhaps even psychologically sore because of the tiny teeth beating on her teats. She starts rejecting the puppies. The period of weaning begins.

The weaning puppy is usually introduced to cow's milk, baby cereal, or some kind of commercial puppy chow. For convenience, many people will use a commercial product immediately. If this is what you choose, do watch for preservatives and additives in the product and try to keep them to a minimum. Remember these are very sensitive little creatures. Supplementation during this period will protect the puppies from the sudden onset of impurities and chemical additives.

I personally prefer to see a puppy weaned for several weeks on human baby cereal combined with cow's milk. I have found the cereal and milk regimen better than a commercial kibbled product not only because of the additives but also because the kibbled product may be too coarse for an infantile intestinal tract. Make sure the milk is boiled and then cooled before you use it. The boiling deactivates certain factors in the milk that can cause diarrhea. Don't ever give a young puppy milk without first boiling it. This is a ranking cause of puppy diarrhea. A little honey can be used in the cereal in the beginning to promote feeding. I don't recommend sugar for the animal but honey can be used moderately at this time.

Cottage cheese can be mixed in with the cereal for added protein. When the puppies are around seven or eight weeks old, meat can gradually be introduced in the form of good ground hamburger, slightly browned.

The primary purpose of supplementing the diets of preweaned puppies is to bolster their immune systems, to protect them from microorganisms. I have found vitamin C alone is totally effective to do this job. Pediatric vitamin C drops, available at your nearest drug store, is all that is needed.

As the puppy is weaned from mother's milk, it can also be weaned from vitamin C drops and introduced to the full spectrum of vitamins and minerals. Tablets should be crunched up and sprinkled onto the food. Don't administer whole tablets to small puppies. They can become lodged in the throat and you'll have a problem. For more details on administration of supplements, refer to Chapter 14.

Buying Puppies—Some Words of Caution

At around six weeks of age, weaned puppies are separated from mother and littermates and shipped, sold, or given away.

When pups are shipped by air long distances from breeder to pet shop, they are tranquilized, caged, and stashed away with the baggage. In the best of times, a healthy adult dog will suffer from the experience of air travel. Some animals die. They are put into baggage compartments where the temperatures can range from zero when the plane is aloft to over a hundred degrees when the aircraft is standing in the summer heat. Additionally, in airtight compartments filled with baggage, there may be insufficient oxygen available.[2]

It is no wonder that the trauma of shipment often creates woeful arrivees that are suffering from diarrhea, coughing, vomiting, dehydration, and loss of appetite. I know of one pet shop that had been purchasing puppies from out of state breeders. Almost 50 percent of the puppies were dying en route and the majority of the survivors were sick. Finally, the owner stopped the practice of long-distance deliveries and confined his purchases to local or regional breeders. The health of his stock improved greatly. Puppies are just not strong enough to handle the tremendous stress of such an ordeal. My impression is that the animals coming from out of state are the ones with the most problems who will eventually die sooner or require a great deal of care.

Clients who administer a supplement program are not beset with the typical transportation problems. I have been told by a number of breeders that even when they ship puppies over long distances, the supplement-fed animals arrive in better shape with less wear and tear than if they were not supplemented.

Most pet shop owners maintain a hygienic setting for their puppies. Nevertheless I have seen many shops where the conditions are poor. Some places are not well ventilated. The pups are kept in cages without any sunlight. No sunlight means that vitamin D can't be activated and vitamin D, as we have seen, is important for healthy skin and bones. Under poor conditions, it doesn't take too long for body defenses to crumble, making the puppy an easy target for germs. And there will be plenty of those around if the environment isn't clean. Even in the best of situations the pet shop owner knows that disease can strike his puppies without warning. Kennel cough is a critical financial problem in many shops. Wherever you have any accumulation of dogs, in a kennel or pet shop or dog show, the kennel cough virus is a very real and common threat. Since dogs in a pet shop are kept closely confined, an outbreak of kennel cough will affect most or all of the dogs present and the resultant nasal discharge and hacking cough are not the kind of qualities that will attract buyers.

One typical case I had involved a Basenji pup about twelve weeks old. Basenjis are an ancient breed that hail from Africa and have a yodellike yelp instead of a bark. They are an extremely intelligent and individualistic breed. This particular animal was brought in scrawny and with no appetite. It was suffering from diarrhea and kennel cough. The owner wondered whether he should bring it back to the pet shop where he had paid a lot of money for the animal. But he had grown attached to the dog in the short time he'd had it and really wanted to keep it.

I told the owner that a good vitamin and mineral program would bring his dog around. He agreed to try.

In three weeks he returned with the dog to get inoculations. At first I thought he had exchanged the animal. But it was the same Basenji pup. It had gained weight, was alive and perky.

Many veterinarians are anti–pet shop. It is easy to put a pet shop down. I have tried to encourage some of the shop owners in the San Jose area to use supplements as a means of improving the health of their animals. Healthier-looking dogs translate into more sales. Recently, I attempted to make the point with an owner by taking on one of his animals, a cocker spaniel pup, that had pussy discharges from the eyes and a slight cough and was in generally poor condition. The shop owner had tried to cure the animal with antibiotics but without success. For four days, I kept the animal and administered a solid vitamin and mineral program. I gave it no medication. I brought it back without the discharge, without the cough. A healthier specimen. I think I made my point. The owner said he would start incorporating supplements into his daily rations.

The trouble with pet shops is that some owners want to put bare necessities into the animal and nothing more. For a minimum outlay, they could have puppies that radiated health. They would have more buyers. They would benefit in the long run.

When buying puppies from a pet store, here are three good tips to keep in mind:

1. Try to find out where the animal came from. Pups bred and sold in the same area tend to be healthier animals.

2. Do take a good long look at the puppy before you buy it. It should be more than cute. It should be healthy. Don't buy it if it doesn't appear to be in good condition.

3. Make any purchase contingent upon an examination by a veterinarian. Bring the animal to a vet. It will cost a few dollars but the price is well worth it. If the dog gets passing marks, then go ahead and conclude the deal. Horses are examined medically before purchase, and I see no reason that this practice shouldn't apply to dogs.

You have seen the doggie in the window. You have fallen in love. You have determined the animal is healthy. You have bought it and taken it home. For the pup a change of address means coping with a change in the bacterial flora. In the pet shop, or breeder's kennel, or somebody's kitchen corner, where the pup was born and weaned, there existed a particular population of bacteria. This bacterial environment is different from the environment in your house. For a little animal living very close to his bacterial surroundings, the change is abrupt. We humans are a whole lot bigger than a puppy but we can get bacterial culture shock too; for example, when we travel from North America or Europe to the tropics.

In the new environment, stress is everywhere. Stress is alien bacteria. Stress is new food and new impurities. Stress is a child playing with the puppy, lifting it up and dropping it.

Often in this adjustment period, young dogs will develop upper respiratory problems, bronchitises, or diarrhea, simply as a consequence of change.

Every veterinarian sees his share of newly acquired puppies brought in—and ailing. If the case is serious enough, I will keep the animal and treat it. But very often I will advise the owner to start using a good multiple vitamin and mineral product along with some extra vitamin C. In a few days, I'll get a call from the happy owner that the puppy is improved.

My comment on these kinds of situations: Why let them happen at all? Put the animals on a program from the start. Protect those little bodies and tiny nervous systems that are under constant attack.

Immunization: Injected Stress

Immunization is the next big trauma a puppy faces. Around nine weeks of age, pups are usually taken to the vet for vaccination against distemper, hepatitis, leptospirosis (a disease carried by rats), and para-influenza. Later, pups return for a rabies shot.

What occurs with immunization is that the organism causing the disease is injected into the dog's body in a modified, toned-down form. In essence, the animal is receiving a mild dose of the disease. A normal, healthy body responds by producing antibodies, which then circulate throughout the bloodstream. Should the dog come into contact at a later date with the same disease-causing organism, the antibodies are present in the system and mobilize to fight off the invader. This is the same way that smallpox and polio vaccinations work with humans.

The shock of immunization is rather severe for a three- or four-pound German shepherd, let alone a three- or four-ounce Chihuahua pup. The typical canine immunization shot carries a multiple warhead—several organisms at one time.

Sometimes body cells and tissues will actually become overwhelmed and die in reaction to an immunization. As they die, the cells give off histamines—poisons—which are absorbed into the bloodstream. Some animals become very ill from this tide of histamines. We often then see some of the symptoms of the disease that the puppy has been vaccinated against.

If an animal is unhealthy or stressed at the time of immunization, it will not produce the antibodies. A presumed measure of protection is thus nonexistent.

I once had a case of a six-month-old Australian shepherd that was brought in suffering from demodectic mange, a common parasitic problem. The dog also had classic distemper symptoms. In questioning the owner, I learned that the animal had had the mange condition at the time it had been immunized for distemper a few months earlier. What happened? The dog, trying to fight off the mange, had been in a stressed, weakened state when inoculated. It never produced the antibodies against distemper. The mange had gone untreated and remained a constant drain on the animal's constitution. Along came a distemper virus and challenged the animal. There were no defenses and no antibodies. The virus won and the dog lost.

I have seen this pattern over and over again. A woman told me about her dog that had been sick at the time of immunization. Three months later it came down with distemper and died. The dog should not have been vaccinated at the time it was ill. Although it recovered from the illness it was not protected from distemper. No antibodies had been produced. When challenged by distemper, it had no immunity.

The brochures that accompany the vaccines specify that the animal should be in good health when vaccinated. This is a vital detail. No matter how minor a condition seems, do not vaccinate until it has cleared up and the dog is fully healthy again. Treat the condition first. Vaccinate later.

From my experience, I feel that when young animals are given supplements of vitamin C and other vitamins and minerals, the antibody production and immune response in general are definitely enhanced. Vitamin C is a potent antivirus, antibacteria, and antihistamine agent, and it spearheads the resistance against invading organisms. I don't believe that a puppy under constant stress is capable of producing enough of this vitamin.

The puppy will also benefit from extra B complex vitamins. Pantothenic acid, along with vitamin C, is important to the proper functioning of the adrenal glands. The adrenals manufacture cortisone, an essential chemical in stimulating the lymph glands, which in turn manufacture antibodies. B_6 is also needed for good antibodies. Researchers have found that animals

deficient in pantothenic acid and B$_6$ experience a sharp decline
in antibody production, and even when they are vaccinated their
immunity is not boosted.[3] Still other scientists have shown that
diets lacking in B$_2$, B$_3$, folic acid, and biotin also result in an impaired immune response to vaccinations.[4] As a puppy struggles
with stress, it is these water-soluble vitamins that are used up
rapidly by the body. The B complex in the food is not enough.
The young dog needs supplementation.

Puppies are prone to infections in the respiratory tract. A common occurrence is for bronchitis to develop into a pneumonia
condition or a pleurisy, an infection of the lungs or lung membrane. A puppy can get a bad cold, what we call an acute nasal
catarrh. Vitamin A, in good supply, protects the mucous membrane lining of the respiratory tract. If this vitamin is in short
supply, millions of cells in the lining die and serve as fodder and
stepping stones for increased bacterial activity. Vitamin A is also
a necessary factor in the production of antibodies and white
blood cells.

We can't forget vitamin E. Pituitary hormones are necessary in
this whole antistress process. These hormones are dispatched in
the blood to the adrenal glands. They act as messengers, telling
the adrenals that the body is under stress and to hurry up and
produce some cortisone. There is more vitamin E concentrated
in the pituitary gland than in any other part of the body, and it
is believed to protect, through its antioxidation ability, both the
pituitary and adrenal hormones. Similarly, it rides shotgun for
the vitamin A circulating in the body.

It is pretty clear then that your puppy needs the whole team
of nutrients. You can't take a chance on any deficiency at this
critical stage of life.

Making War on Worms

One of the more pathetic sights a veterinarian encounters is
the young puppy brought in with a potbelly sticking out of
an otherwise cadaverous body. The poor creature is stunted,
shaking with convulsions, has a dry and dull hair coat, and
suffers from persistent diarrhea. The cause is roundworms, long,

spaghettilike parasites, a common source of early puppy distress. The worms can be picked up in two ways. First, an infested mother can pass them on to her pups before their birth. The larvae migrate through the blood and eventually reach the intestines, where they grow into adults. If a pup has the worms he will usually start to show the effects at around five or six weeks of age. You may notice worms the puppy throws up or passes out in his bowel movement.

The second manner of infestation is when a young dog ingests dirt or water that contain worm eggs. Again, the eggs will wind up in the small intestine and grow in size, absorbing a good deal of the food that would otherwise be used by the dog.

In the intestines these parasites give off toxins that are absorbed through the intestinal membranes into the bloodstream. These poisons can reach the brain and cause seizures. I have seen numerous young puppies brought in with the typical potbelly and seizures. The pups have never been wormed nor were the mothers checked for worms when they became pregnant. Upon pregnancy, a bitch should always be examined for worms. This can prevent problems later on. I have seen too many young dogs so riddled with parasites that there was no way they could survive. The parasitic stress saps their defense mechanisms, leaving the dogs wide open to bacterial and viral infections. The dog is weak and running on a deficit of vitamins and minerals. Much of his food isn't being absorbed. He is in a state of systemic chaos. There may be degeneration and malfunction of organs and parts.

To this battered state is added the deworming chemical, essentially a poison. It is supposed to kill off the parasites but it may kill off a weakened puppy as well. This is a situation of damned if you do and damned if you don't.

I vividly remember the frantic phone call one Sunday morning from a sobbing woman. Her puppy was dying.

"It's just lying there," she said.

I asked her for details.

"The puppy had worms," she said. "I went to the supermarket and bought a preparation and used it according to the directions. Now the dog is dying."

There was nothing I could do for the animal. It was too far

gone. On autopsy, I found a swollen liver. Apparently the liver was unable to cope with the chemical dewormer. The product had killed the worms that were infesting the small intestine. The damaged liver was unable to detoxify the chemical, however, and it circulated through the system and caused the death of the animal.

How does nutrition come into play? Insufficient protein and a low iron intake have been long recognized as factors that severely reduce a dog's resistance to worms. If the animal is well nourished, the body has a greater defense capacity. Solid nourishment and a vitamin and mineral program cannot keep the worms out. But once they are inside and doing thei. dirt work, an optimal diet will ease the stress of the ordeal, strengthen resistance and minimize the effects of the toxins of both the parasites and the deworming compounds.

Raymond and Margaret Hickel, who raise champion Cardigan Welsh corgis in San Fernando, have a simple antiworm program they claim is highly effective. From four weeks of age on, all their dogs get a daily garlic and parsley tablet. The Hickels described their program to me.

We have never had to worm dogs for roundworms since we started using garlic some thirteen years ago. Periodically we take stool samples from the dogs for a routine lab check and every time the report is negative.

For the very young pups we recommend crunching up the tablets. Later on the dogs will take the tablets whole and crunch them up in their mouths. The dogs seem to love the taste and lap them right up. The parsley neutralizes the garlic odor.

We don't have a problem with fleas either and think that maybe the garlic may have something to do with that too.

Garlic is one of the oldies but goodies of folk medicine. Dr. Paavo Airola, in his book, *The Miracle of Garlic*, reports that garlic is an ancient remedy for worms and was used by the ancient Chinese, Greeks, Romans, Hindus, and Babylonians Fresh garlic cloves, as well as the modern tablets, are all seemingly effective. A Czechoslovak study found that extracts of garlic are effective in treating animals infested with ticks—the carriers of encephalitis. Garlic is also said to have powerful antibiotic, antifungal, wound-healing and even tumor-inhibiting abilities.[5]

I would certainly suggest garlic as a fine natural preventive. It may spare a puppy, and an older dog as well, a great deal of grief.

The Ear Crop Drama

The ear crop. Another milestone on the calendar of puppy stress. Breeds like Boxers, Dobermans, Great Danes, Schnauzers, and Pit Bulls are brought in to the veterinarian at around ten to twelve weeks of age for the prescribed surgery. These dogs by nature have floppy hound ears and traditional standards of canine fashion call for surgical reshaping.

Ear cropping originated in Europe. Years ago when dogs chased wild boar on organized hunts, sportsmen became aware of a particular canine vulnerability. The driven boars would often lash out and bite the floppy ears of their pursuers, which bled profusely. Hunters decided to trim their dogs' ears to deny the boar a convenient target and to protect the highly valued dogs. Over the years, in nonhunting settings, the ears were trimmed for appearance' sake and this became the norm.

At the vet's office, the dog is anesthetized. The cartilage and skin of the ear are cut into the set pattern for the breed. Once this is done the only remaining problem—and what a problem!—is for the ears to stand erect.

I use a special set of wire racks I had designed. The ears are placed into the racks and taped in such a way so as to leave the cut edges exposed to the air. This aids in the healing process. The racks also provide an upward direction and support for the ears and promote the ability of the animal to hold the ears upright.

One week after surgery I have the dog return. I check the stitches, clean the ears and racks. The healing process is continuing. The ears, still sore, are reracked. A week later, the client and dog return. The ears are healed. They don't hurt the animal anymore.

Until I began using vitamins and minerals in my practice, it was extremely rare for a dog's ears to stand soon after the racking. It took weeks and even months. Now, I would say that practically every puppy that is on a supplement program has a set of fine erect ears two weeks after surgery when the racks are removed. There is no need for further treatment. Occasionally I will even see ears standing as soon as the dog comes out of the anesthesia.

I am convinced that supplementation is the reason why the ears are standing so quickly. Before the supplements I used to experience the typical frustration of all veterinarians in doing ear crops. I would estimate that for every success I had there were maybe ten failures. To this day, ear cropping results are generally so poor that some states have even banned the surgery. Because ears frequently won't stand, many veterinarians avoid the frustration and potential client dissatisfaction by simply not offering the service. They just cannot guarantee the success of the operation. So what then is the purpose of cosmetic surgery that doesn't work? I know from talking to colleagues that there are many times when veterinarians resort to special plastic implants in order to produce erect ears.

Let me explain my theory of why ear-crop surgery is so unsuccessful. The puppy is undergoing rapid growth. Bones, ligaments, muscles, all the parts are expanding madly. The animal is teething. These growth processes utilize enormous amounts of vitamins and minerals. The vitamin C supply is being severely taxed to build collagen—the cement of body tissue. Huge amounts of vitamin C are being used in the development of the teeth alone.

The nutrient value of the food the puppy eats is questionable. There may be an actual situation of undernourishment at this critical time. There is, of course, no vitamin C in the food.

In the middle of all this natural and intense growth cycle, along comes the client and presents the puppy for the cosmetic ear crop. Another dimension of stress is added, along with another order for collagen. Remember that the ear is basically cartilage covered with skin. If the dog has weak cartilage, the ear won't stand erect. The cartilage depends on collagen and plenty of vitamins and minerals, especially vitamin C.

What you are doing is asking a body undergoing extreme physiological changes and stress to find the extra resources needed for the unnatural function of keeping ears aloft. Where is the funding to come from? If you consider the resources required just to deal with the natural growth and challenges of puppyhood, the added burden of the ear crop takes on whimsical proportions. If you are going to increase the demand on the young dog's body, then you must increase the nutrients accordingly. This is why a puppy on a good supplement program, with plenty of vitamin C, heals faster from an ear crop and has the wherewithal to point his ears to the sky.

Strong Collagen for Good Growth

I can't emphasize enough the importance of adequate vitamin C and all the other vitamins and minerals that support the production of collagen. It is so critical to a growing puppy.

Puppyhood is a period of extreme and concentrated growth. We humans take a leisurely seventeen or eighteen years to do our growing. Within a year, smaller breeds of dogs are full-sized. In two or three years, big dogs have reached maturity. All this pell-mell growing is a constant form of stress to the young dog. The natural output of vitamin C is burned up rapidly.

My prevention program calls for considerably higher doses of vitamin C and other nutrients for the larger dogs than the smaller ones. Generally they will receive more than twice the amount given to smaller animals. The larger dog is undergoing much more stress and much more physical growth. It is imperative that he have plenty of the nutrient factors that relate to collagen and stress and he certainly isn't going to get all he needs in commercial dog food.

Hip dysplasia is the most notorious of the puppyhood bone and ligament problems, and I will talk in considerable detail about it later in the book. Meanwhile I want to discuss some other less celebrated but nevertheless serious skeletal problems that afflict large-breed animals.

With the larger breeds you constantly have a touch-and-go situation, with a skeletal system that needs to grow fast enough and strong enough to keep pace with the rapidly increasing bulk of muscle and fat. The skeletal system often can't keep up.

A classic example is a phenomenon we often see with Doberman puppies where the wrists buckle out and it looks like the animal has rickets. It is a very pathetic sight and can happen from one day to the next.

The problem is ligament laxity. The dog is not producing enough collagen, which gives strength to the ligaments, tendons, and bones. The wrist ligaments of the rapidly growing puppy stretch thin and can no longer hold the weight or the joint together, so the wrist bulges out in a constantly flexed position.

I remember a few years ago treating three Dobermans out of the same litter with this very problem. I administered 3,000 milligrams of vitamin C (sodium ascorbate) intravenously and dispensed vitamin C powder with the instructions to give a quarter teaspoon (1,000 milligrams) in the food daily. In three days the wrist condition had returned to normal.[6] The vitamin C built up the collagen rapidly. I have now treated this problem with vitamin C a number of times and find that the wrists straighten out in an average of three to four days. The maximum has been ten days.

Hypertrophic Osteodystrophy

Hypertrophic osteodystrophy. Also known as panosteitis. Big names that mean trouble for big puppies. The coverings of the long leg bones become inflamed, swollen, and painful. The front feet may splay and the hind legs become cow-hocked. The puppy will limp or not want to walk at all. There is often diarrhea, high fever, and pneumonia involved. Most animals will overcome the condition in time. Many, however, have died of complications or been put to sleep because of the pain and pathetic sight that is produced. Usually dogs between the ages of three to eight months are affected.

Hypertrophic osteodystrophy—HOD for short—was diagnosed as far back as the thirties. It was said to have something to do with low blood levels of vitamin C and it resembled a human condition known as infantile scurvy. But in the face of the al-

ready established concept that dogs produce all the vitamin C
they need, the C connection was not vigorously pursued. The
French veterinarian who first described the condition in 1938
used only 50 to 100 milligrams of vitamin C and/or the juice of
one or two lemons. His results were ambiguous. Some animals
quickly healed. Others didn't.[7]

In 1957, a team of Boston veterinarians diagnosed seven dogs
with HOD and also found low vitamin C levels in their blood.
They suggested the reason was a temporary disturbance of the
vitamin C assembly line—the liver enzyme system. A dose of 100
to 200 milligrams per day of vitamin C was administered to the
dogs with "no obvious clinical improvement." Spontaneous improvement appeared to take place when the dogs stopped growing, the veterinarians reported.[8]

In 1962, Dr. J. R. Holmes of the University of Bristol in England described the same condition in two boxers and one collie
cross. He too found the low ascorbic acid levels and said the
problem was "suspected skeletal scurvy," due to an inability in
some animals to produce adequate vitamin C. After antibiotics
and anti-inflammatory drugs failed, Holmes used 500 milligrams
of vitamin C daily—the largest amount used to this point in treating HOD. One boxer responded and within four days was walking, although the hind legs remained weak for two months. The
collie cross was reported walking normally, eating well, and free
from pain in twelve days. The other boxer, whose condition was
apparently more advanced than in the other two dogs, died two
months into the treatment. Autopsy revealed many of the symptoms of scurvy, including internal hemorrhaging and degeneration of muscle tissue.[9]

In 1979, two Finnish veterinarians, Maria Vaananen and
L. Wikman, documented two cases of HOD. The first was a five-
month-old German shepherd. Antibiotics, aspirin, an anti-inflammatory drug, and a change of diet were all tried without success.
Subsequently, 500 milligrams of vitamin C were given intravenously. Keep in mind that intravenous administration is always
more effective than oral. There was slight improvement but then
a relapse. The dose apparently wasn't high enough. The veterinarians decided to drop all medication. Boldly, they increased
the vitamin C to 3,000 milligrams. The dog's condition showed

rapid improvement and after two weeks the animal was ready to be discharged.

The second case involved a Great Dane. Since medication had proven ineffective, no other treatment except 3,000 milligrams daily of vitamin C was administered. Two days later, the dog was able to stand and began to walk a little. After four days, an accompanying fever was gone, the appetite had returned, and the dog was able to walk quite steadily. In twelve days, the Great Dane was discharged.

Like the veterinarians before them, Vaananen and Wikman had observed signs indicative of scurvy: fever, pulmonary infection, diarrhea, swollen and painful joints, and, through X rays, porous and hemorrhaging bone tissue. There were immune system and collagen disturbances—both areas in which vitamin C has a major role.

The Finns suggested that "the mere growth, in large fast-growing breeds, requires such an enormous amount of collagen that the ability of the liver to produce a sufficient amount of vitamin C is exceeded." They concluded that it was "advisable to supply vitamin C to dogs of the giant breeds during their most intensive period of growth at the age of four to eight months."[10]

I was glad to see the Finnish evaluation because it confirmed what I have been advocating for years: the need for large doses of vitamin C. I have long felt that most of the bone problems of dogs—the giant breeds in particular but not exclusively—are due to the inability of the liver to produce enough vitamin C to keep up with the speeding growth and development. Much of the vitamin is derailed for nongrowth activities, such as detoxification of impurities and toxins and the other stresses I have mentioned. There just isn't enough available to sustain good growth.

Years ago in my practice I used to see cases of HOD. I don't see it anymore when dogs are supplemented with adequate amounts of vitamin C. What I consider adequate is a few thousand milligrams orally of vitamin C given daily to those big growing puppies. Refer to the puppyhood dosage chart in Chapter 13 for my specific recommendations. I have listed doses for the different sizes of dogs. If the doses seem high to you, keep one very important thing in mind: I have found them effective in preventing puppy afflictions like HOD and hip dysplasia. The chronology of the treatment I have just described clearly indicates the justification of high doses. Had the earlier investigators used megadoses, their results would have been better. These animals are so stressed that it is going to take large doses to prevent or repair collagen breakdown and build a blood level of ascorbic acid to counteract the other symptoms that are involved, such as diarrhea, infections, and fever.

The history of this disease alone, with the documented proof of its relationship to scurvy going back to 1938, makes it very hard for me to understand why many veterinarians still cling to the concept that dogs produce all the vitamin C they need. What does it take to make them believe?

Supplemented Pups Eat Less

The NRC says the growing puppy will eat twice as much food as the maintenance level of adult dogs. In my practice I don't see this gluttonizing, just as I don't see it in lactating bitches. When a puppy gets vitamin supplements, the ravening appetite is greatly diminished. Once the hunger has been satisfied and the adequate vitamins and minerals taken, the puppy has no need to gorge itself. Instinctively it will reduce intake if it is on good supplements. Excessive appetite in an animal is a sign of needed nutrition. It eats more of the commercial dog food, not because it is so enamored of the food, but because it needs more to get more nutrition.

TIPS FOR PUPPYHOOD

1. If purchasing an animal from a pet shop, finalize the deal only after having a veterinarian examine and OK the dog. This will minimize the possibility of you buying a sick dog.

2. Supplement as early as possible—from the day the pups are born or the day of purchase.

3. Maintain the lactating bitch on vitamins and minerals. She has a specially increased need for more nutrients. Her own good health and the good health of the puppies are on the line.

4. Don't permit the immunization of a sick puppy. A sick puppy may not develop immunity and can become even more weakened from the effects of the vaccinations.

5. Don't allow wee puppies to be handled by outsiders. All the fondling should wait until at least five weeks. People carry organisms that can infect a vulnerable puppy. Furthermore, bacteria vary from person to person. The puppies have a hard enough time as it is adjusting to local bacteria. Don't add to the burden. The pups may be cuddly, but they are very vulnerable.

6. Don't subject puppies to the out-of-doors until they have had immunization. If you have bought a new puppy, keep it at home, don't take it to the store or on a walk with you, until it has had its shots. Outside your front door are legions of what we call "street viruses" just waiting to attack a young, vulnerable puppy. Keep in mind as well that excessively hot or cold weather, or any sudden temperature changes, can stress a small puppy and lower its resistance to disease.

7. Good housekeeping is important. Young puppies defecate nonstop. Keep the area as clean as possible of fecal matter to minimize the activity of germs.

8. Keep the animal out of drafts. Most puppies are quartered on the floor in a basket. In wintertime especially, cold drafts can sweep in under closed doors or opened doors and lead to upper respiratory problems. I suggest placing the puppy box or basket in a room where there are no doors leading to the outside.

9. Make sure the puppy has a nice warm area. Many people ask me at what age a puppy can be kept outside. From my experience, not before three months. The immunizations first, remember. A barn or a garage is suitable. Be aware of abrupt temperature changes because a young puppy will have difficulty acclimating.

10

How Supplements
Help Mature Dogs

I am always pleased when clients tell me how their pets have hurdled through puppyhood without any of the usual troubles. The dogs have been on a supplement program for one or two years and are strong, alert, and energetic young animals.

If all goes well and they aren't banged up in an accident or a dog fight or fall victim to a parasitic infestation, then I don't see them very often. Perhaps once a year for an immunization or a checkup and that's it.

Typical is a local woman who breeds tracking bloodhounds who comes in with a dog only when an immunization or a health certificate is needed. She keeps her animals on a solid program and reports that they have increased endurance as a result.

Let's say your dog is grown up. He has survived the wars of puppyhood although he may be wearing some of his wounds. He is apparently healthy or not so healthy or downright ailing. The idea now is to jack him up to optimal health.

The first thing to do is to purchase supplements and start your dog on the program. In Chapters 12, 13, and 14 I tell you what to buy and how to gradually build up the vitamin level in your dog's food to an optimal amount.

How much you can improve the health of your animal depends on his past. If he has been sickly, the supplements are going to boost the immune system and he will have much more resistance to disease.

If your dog has been eating inferior dog food for years and as a result has a damaged liver and kidneys, I can't promise you new organs with the supplements. What they will do is to stop the deterioration where it is. Let's hope the condition is not already so advanced as to cause ill effects in the animal.

If your dog has arthritis, the supplements won't turn him around so that he won't have arthritis anymore. They will ease the pain, though, and enhance mobility.

As the animal ages, the tissues begin to deteriorate and the dog's susceptibility to disease increases. The supplements can slow down the degenerative processes and prolong the youthfulness of the body.

In my practice I have seen animals turned around. I have seen scores of lifeless creatures that would just lie around and lift their legs, sniff a little, and occasionally bark. Maximum activity would be tail wagging. We'd put them on a vitamin and mineral program and they would come alive. They seemed to find things to do. They become alert and interested and more playful.

Winterize with Supplements

The young dog has matured and is now put out-of-doors. Along comes the first winter. While the master is snuggled comfortably inside his house with the thermostat on high, many an animal is out shivering in the cold. The experience can be very stressful.

Invariably, a few days after the onset of cold weather, owners of young dogs begin a veritable parade into veterinary hospitals. The dog is limping. One day it's the left front leg. The next day the left rear leg. Usually only one side is involved.

What apparently is happening is that the side the dog is sleeping on comes into contact with a cold surface and a muscular ache develops. It is similar to the kind of problem we humans have when we open a window and expose ourselves overnight to cold air. We wake up with a pain and call it neuralgia.

The first winter is likely to be more jolting to an animal than subsequent ones. After being out-of-doors two or three winters a dog seems to acclimate. Studies have shown that warm-blooded animals acclimated to cold have a greater resistance and an enhanced capacity to produce body heat than animals not pre-exposed to cold.[1]

Still, winter is winter and it can get cold enough to lay low the hardiest of dogs. The winter of 1978–79, for instance, brought record low temperatures and snow to much of the United States. A veterinarian in Chicago reported treating upper respiratory conditions in large numbers of dogs that had been running around loose in the bitter cold and snow. She observed many runny noses and eyes and deep coughs. If the owners didn't seek immediate treatment, these symptoms worsened into pneumonia.

Some dogs that live in cold climates or continually lie on cold surfaces will eventually develop some kind of arthritic condition. Joints become inflamed. There is pain and immobility.

Supplementation is a good way to insulate your dog against the cold. In scientific experiments, extra vitamin C and pantothenic acid have been shown to be highly protective for both humans and animals exposed to cold. In my practice I have found that the supplementation program helps the young dog overcome the stress of his first winter and increases his tolerance of lower temperatures.

Doris Wear, who raises whippets and fox terriers at her Stoney Meadows Kennel in Cecilton, Maryland, told me that despite the severity of the 1978–79 winter she had fewer problems than normal. She attributes this to the daily addition of 250 milligrams of vitamin C to her dogs' diets that she started during the preceding year.

"When the weather gets horrid," she said, "and the dogs go out in the cold, the whippets will come down with diarrhea and the terriers get sore throats and cough. The minute I see loose stool or hear any coughing, I will hit those dogs with 500 milligrams two or three times a day. This has really helped stop problems."

Vitamin C was the most recent addition to a diversified supplementation program at Stoney Meadows that included bone meal, wheat germ, and brewers' yeast, and for brood bitches and older dogs, kelp and a multiple vitamin and mineral. The C made a noticeable difference, even with an otherwise solid program. It proves once again that dogs benefit from extra vitamin C.

Out on the California coast we don't experience the kind of winter beating that most of the country gets. But we do have sudden changes in temperature. For instance, here in the San Jose area, the mercury will hit 70 degrees during the day and then plunge 30 degrees within a half-hour of sunset. At the beginning of the season, a lot of dogs are affected by this sharp drop and come down with respiratory ailments.

Whether it is cold all of the time or part of the time, a good vitamin and mineral program is going to keep your dog out of harm's way.

Coping with Heat

While winter presents special problems to the dog, so does summer. Many animals, especially the long-haired breeds, have trouble with the heat. Bear in mind they are wearing an overcoat on days you are wearing shorts. Dogs don't have sweat glands as humans do. It is very difficult for them to give off heat. They have to depend on the pads, the muzzle, and the tongue to give off this excess heat. Who hasn't seen a panting dog with his tongue hanging out and dripping a puddle on a hot summer day? This is the animal's way of coping with the heat.

One of my clients is a breeder of Akitas, the largest of the Japanese breeds. This dog originated in the northern regions and has a thick hair coat.

One particularly hot summer my client was showing his animals. He called one day to say that one of the dogs was just wilting. It would pant endlessly and couldn't seem to take the routine that was mandatory for the show. I recommended he give the dog salt tablets—the average human dosage. The next time I saw him he said it had worked. The dog was able to go through all his disciplines without a problem.

These heavy breeds lose a great deal of salt from an intense exchange of heat through the pads, muzzle, and tongue. It is a good idea to replace the depleted salt when a dog is in obvious difficulty during very hot weather. Typical signs of distress are the heavy panting, listlessness, fatigue, dizziness, or a loss of equilibrium. Salt tablets can be purchased at any drug store.

The salt tablets may not be necessary however if the animal is on a good supplementation program, especially one that contains vitamin C. Studies conducted with miners and industrial workers operating in conditions of extreme heat showed that supplemental vitamin C enhanced their tolerance to high temperatures and protected them from heat prostration.[2] Other studies have shown that high temperature is a serious stress that accelerates the bodily destruction of vitamin C and simultaneously increases the need for it to maintain biochemical balance. Animals that already produce their own supplies of ascorbic acid have been shown to benefit from supplementation. A Russian scientist supplemented the diets of rats with 15 milligrams per kilogram of body weight and improved their resistance to heat.[3] In America, chickens and laying hens subjected to extreme heat were given 100 to 200 milligrams of vitamin C per kilogram of food with a resultant improvement in growth, egg production, and eggshell strength.[4]

Boarded Dogs

When you go away on vacation or for some other reason have to leave your dog in a kennel, you are going to leave behind one unhappy dog. The animal is going to be very disenchanted about removal from routine and familiar surroundings. He is now caged and would like to escape if he knew how. He is getting a different diet than what he is used to. All this will be very stressful to him.

Stress, as we have seen, depletes the water-soluble vitamins—B complex and C. When these are in low supply in the body, the stage is set for disease.

I will discuss kennel cough, a common affliction of boarded dogs, later in the book. Let me say here that kennels are parade grounds for all kinds of dangerous organisms. Even if kennel owners maintain a high level of hygiene, there is still an ample number of germs lurking about the premises. An animal on supplements is better protected to withstand the threat of kennel disease.

Neutered and Overweight

There are two primary reasons for an overweight dog. One is lack of activity. A backyard or apartment dog is going to have a tendency to put on weight unless he gets in some regular exercise.

The other cause is alteration. The male has been castrated, the testes removed. The female has been spayed, the ovaries removed. The removal of these reproductive glands directly affects fat metabolism. This is because the hormonal secretions—testosterone of the testes, estrogen of the ovaries—are involved in the body's utilization of fat. Without them there is a greater fat deposition in the tissues. Six months after the operation you begin to see your dog growing fat.

Some veterinarians feel they can control the weight of these desexed animals by controlling the quantity of food; cutting down their daily rations. But it is important to remember that when you cut down on the amount of food you are also cutting down on the amount of vitamins and minerals and other nutrients.

As a result of decreased nutrient intake these animals may be more susceptible to disease. I have seen several cases of animals that have been put on "reducing diets" and while they lost weight they also developed skin, liver, and kidney problems.

Personally, I don't advocate this cutting back of the food. If the dog is a little buxom or overweight, better this than health problems. I suggest to pet owners that they simply allow the animal to eat what it needs because most animals will not gorge themselves. The neutered animal will not eat any more than the non-neutered animal.

If you are following a veterinarian's advice and are cutting back, then I would suggest this as a particularly good time to initiate a supplementation program. The supplements will replace what has been lost by the reduced rations.

A neutered dog that has some room to roam or is being exercised regularly is less likely to put on weight than a confined neutered dog.

In my practice, I try to convince clients who want to have their animals neutered that we can perform instead a partial spay or a vasectomy. The added expense is minimal. In the partial spay, the uterus and cervix are removed but the ovaries are left. The female will go into heat, will have the desire for intercourse, and will be able to have it, but she will not be able to reproduce. Moreover, she will not spot blood and not have the problem later on with weight gain.

The male will similarly continue to behave normally, but will not be able to impregnate a female.

By choosing these options you are keeping the animals as near natural as possible. You are not desexing them. It is another way to go for individuals who are concerned about the health and welfare of their animals and who don't want to be bothered by puppies or accusations from neighbors that "your dog did it."

By leaving the gonads intact in this manner, you also avoid another problem: urinary incontinence. This is an inability to control the urine flow. When the animal reaches five or six you begin to see puddles of urine on the floor where the dog has been lying. Bladder control is affected by the full neutering operations. The urine trickles out. This can be remedied with hormones but that means extra time and money spent in veterinarian visits and administration of hormones. I feel the partial neuter offers a good alternative.

TIPS FOR ADULTHOOD

1. **Supplement your animal's diet.**

2. **When the weather is cold or rainy, bring your dog inside where it is warm and dry.** This will minimize the risk of muscular aches and the potential for arthritis later on.

3. **In very hot climates, the animal should be provided with an abundance of fresh water.** Don't confine a dog in a hot sunny area without shade. Under no circumstances lock your pet in a car on a hot day. Even if the windows are opened a crack, the inside may become like an oven. The stress is extreme and many dogs die in hot summer months as a result of their owners' carelessness.

4. Be careful with dogs around horses. I have had to treat many dogs that were kicked or stepped on.

5. If a dog is going to be traveling with you, find out first how the animal takes to the car. Go for a trial spin and observe the reaction. Some animals, like humans, suffer from motion sickness. If the animal is to be tranquilized, try the tranquilizer a week or so before the trip. There are some drugs that will make a dog violent, drowsy, or nauseous, or will make it start salivating excessively. Be forewarned. If you are air-shipping an animal in a nonpressurized freight compartment, don't tranquilize. Breathing will be difficult in any case at high altitudes and a tranquilizer will only make the process more difficult. Beware if the dog has a known heart problem. Make inquiries with the airline company about pet shipping conditions.

11

How Supplements
Help Aging Dogs

In the aging process, the internal organs lose efficiency. The liver
won't function at its previous capacity. It has been filtering a
lifetime of impurities. The pancreas isn't producing adequate
amounts of enzymes that are vital to the digestion of food. The
kidneys are probably in bad shape. About 80 percent of dogs
eight years or over have chronic interstitial nephritis, a degenerative kidney condition caused in large part by the excess protein and impurities in commercial diets. So the kidneys don't
filter as they used to. The bladder isn't the same either. Many an
older dog will urinate where he lies or sleeps. Dog hearts are
fading as well. The chronic valvular disease that has developed
often leads to death.

If they could talk, from the big dog down to the low-slung
dachshund, they would be complaining of aching backs. There
are many spinal problems with old dogs.

Your dog may eat, sleep, and laze around the backyard or living room sofa and that pretty much is the limit to his activity.
He is no longer stimulated by flies, cats, or bones as he was when
younger. He's reaching the end of the line.

By now your dog has been around so long he is a fixture in the
family. Taking him for a walk has become ritual. The animal has
grown up with the kids or been a favorite hunting dog or a great
performing show dog or maybe just a good, constant companion
for a long, long time. There is a close bond between you and
your dog. It hurts to see him slowing down and ailing.

The supplementation program can put the brake on your dog's physical deterioration. It won't turn him into a six-month-old puppy again. It won't repair all the internal damage that has piled up over the years. But it will put some new juice into the old hound and rejuvenate him to some or even a considerable degree. Resistance to disease and infection is increased. Failing organs, suffering from deficiencies of this or that nutrient, are recharged. They cope and function better. I have seen this happen many times. Clients have called or written to tell me about wondrous recoveries and "born-again" dogs. I have seen some animals who were so ill they were about to be euthanized. Yet when put on a vitamin and mineral program they lived one, two, or three years more and in seemingly less pain.

Clyde, a ten-year-old collie cross, is owned by Charlie Milazzo, one of my clients. Clyde couldn't control his bladder or bowels any longer and was constantly surrounded by flies. He wouldn't eat, was listless, and had a rough hair coat. He was declining rapidly.

Mr. Milazzo wanted the dog put to sleep. Tears welled in his eyes as he told me how close the dog was to him, how much the loss of his long-time companion would mean.

I asked him if he was willing to try vitamins and minerals. I couldn't offer any guarantees, but Mr. Milazzo said he was game as long as there was any kind of a chance. I gave him a powdered vitamin and mineral preparation and told him to give the animal a teaspoonful in its food once a day and force feed the dog if necessary to get him started.

A couple of weeks later, Mr. Milazzo returned and wanted to know if vitamins and minerals had the same effect with humans. What effect, I wanted to know.

Well, Clyde was up and alive, able to control his urine and bowels. The dog was running, jumping, and barking.

As I write this book, the dog is still doing fine. It has been over a year since Mr. Milazzo came in with the intention of putting Clyde to sleep. The Milazzos were so impressed that they started taking supplements themselves.

The supplements, as I said earlier, are intended to affect the whole body—the whole cellular environment—rather than specific symptoms. If the foundation is strengthened, all the parts benefit.

As the whole body becomes healthier, individual symptoms diminish.

Here's a typical example. Aging dachshunds are prone to spinal disc problems. They also seem to suffer from a lot of skin ailments. One day a seven-year-old dachshund was brought in by its owner. The animal was paralyzed in the hind quarters with a bad disc condition. The skin was a mess. The dog had dry, scaly skin and quite a few bald spots. I put the animal on a substantial vitamin and mineral program with abundant A, C, and E.

A month later, when I saw the dog again, his back had improved. There was more use of the hind quarters. The condition was progressively improving, the owner told me. The skin looked more pliable and softer, and hair was starting to grow back in places.

Working at the cellular level, the vitamins and minerals were strengthening the collagen of the vertebral ligaments and enhancing circulation and nourishment in the skin. The dog was more active. Obviously inner organs were getting nutrients that the commercial dog food was not supplying. From nose to tail, the dog was benefiting. That's the way vitamins and minerals work.

Take the case of an aging hunting dog, seven or eight years old. He's having trouble keeping up with the pack. The back is weakening. The hind quarters are starting to sway. The master no longer takes him on the hunting trips he has been making since the age of six months. The dog hears the engine start on the pickup truck and hears the excited barking of the younger dogs. But there are no more trips for him. There is humiliation along with physical deterioration. The dog feels unwanted, worthless, left out.

An engineer who keeps a pack of Labrador retrievers once brought in such a suffering animal. I was using only vitamin C at the time and had the man start giving the dog 2,000 milligrams daily with the food. In a few weeks the dog showed tremendous improvement. His back problem seemingly vanished. He had new zip and could keep up with the rest of the dogs. The last I heard the animal was ten and still running with the pack. The engineer, after this experience, put all his dogs on a vitamin C program.

There is no question that an adequate supply of nutrients is related to the health and longevity of dogs. If your dog had been on a preventive program he would likely be entering old age without many of the typical problems: cataracts, deafness, arthritis, and heart and back problems.

I have observed a happy absence of arthritis among dogs regularly maintained on vitamins and minerals. Years ago, before I was involved with supplements, it was pretty common for me to see seven- or eight-year-olds limping into the office in pain from arthritis. Nowadays I generally see arthritis only in new dogs or dogs belonging to clients who don't follow the program.

Medical investigators have spotted a number of nutrient deficiencies in human arthritis sufferers. Studies have pinpointed A, B_2, B_3, pantothenic acid, B_6, vitamin C, magnesium, calcium, phosphorus, and other minerals.[1]

Furthermore, the very aspirin that is often recommended to ease the pain of arthritis—both in humans and animals—causes further deficiencies of nutrients. Aspirin has been determined to accelerate the urinary loss of calcium, potassium, vitamin C, and all the B vitamins.[2]

It is vital to adequately nourish the cells that are involved in the fluid, bone, joint, and muscle activity if arthritis is to be prevented. Supplementation is insurance against arthritis.

C and E—The Age Fighters

All the nutrients on the team are needed to promote rejuvenation. Vitamins C and E, however, seem to stand out. To see changes in an old dog it is vital to supply these two versatile vitamins in abundance, but in the process do not neglect the other members of the team.

I have increased the amount of vitamin E for older dogs as compared to adult dogs. This is because E is regarded as the best cellular antioxidant. An antioxidant, we have seen, is a substance that blocks oxidation (or damage) of fatty substances in individual cells, a process associated with aging.

Vitamin C is also an effective antioxidant. However, I have cut down the amount I want you to give your aging dog. This is because vitamin C has a tendency to put a dog on a natural high. I don't want the older animal suddenly becoming hyper and doing things beyond his capabilities. This may kill him. If the older dog is very active then he can remain on the adult level. See Chapter 13 for the precise dosages.

Let's examine how vitamin E affects aging.

Down at the microscopic level of the cells, life is a battlefield. Enemies abound: viruses, bacteria, toxic chemical molecules. If nutrition is good, the cells are strong. If nutrition is poor, the cells are weak. Cells are continually challenged. Strong ones can fight off the invaders. Weaker ones cannot meet the challenge. The toll of dead and wounded cells mounts with the years.

Scientists have known for some time that one of the primary factors in this aging battle is the oxidation process. Oxygen is vital for life, and yet when oxygen molecules react with vital fatty membranes and components that are present in each cell, these parts are said to undergo "peroxidation" and become damaged. The function of enzymes and proteins and other minuscule mechanisms inside the living and working cell are impaired. Eventually the cell can stop functioning altogether. The process multiplies. More and more cells are knocked out. Tissues deteriorate, become hardened and lifeless. Systems go awry. Death follows.

Scientists have measured the accelerating pace of this degenerative process. They have observed it in the tissue of the heart, blood vessels, brain, muscle, liver, adrenal glands, and reproductive organs.

The scientists have also seen how vitamin E, a fat-soluble substance, mixes right into the fatty cellular parts and protects them from peroxidation. What happens is that the vitamin E actually sacrifices itself to the oxygen molecule to form a harmless compound.

A number of animal studies have demonstrated this life-protecting ability of vitamin E. Dr. L. H. Chen of the University of Kentucky has shown the effect of vitamin E on the age-related increase of oxidative damage to liver cells.

Vitamin E was added to the diet of laboratory mice of all ages and it indeed reduced peroxidation of the cells. But Chen noted that the amount of vitamin E that was adequate to protect the liver in young and adult mice was not enough to protect the liver from peroxidation in very old mice. This was because the rate of peroxidation increased with age. A higher level of supplementation was thus necessary to provide protection against the ravages of accelerated old-age peroxidation.

Chen suggested that "there is an increased requirement of vitamin E as aging progresses in order to protect tissue from peroxidation. It is possible that in animals of older ages, vitamin E or another antioxidant is required in relatively larger quantity in order to slow down the oxidative deterioration of tissues and thus prolong the life span."[3]

Chen said this might easily apply to aging humans. I definitely feel it applies to aging dogs.

The nutrient requirements as formulated by the NRC do not take into consideration whether an animal is adult or aged. The recommendation is the same for both. What is in my mind a questionable standard for the adult may be a downright deficiency level for the aged animal.

Back in the early sixties in the beginning of my clinical practice, I began to notice that dogs were playful and frisky for the first three years of life. Afterward, there appeared to be a steady drop in vitality. When the dogs reached five or six they seemed to be older than their years. They acted ten or eleven. This was the general impression I had. I felt something was wrong. Something had to be wrong. It didn't seem normal to me.

I began looking around for ways to rejuvenate these "old-young" dogs. I read about the work done by the Shute brothers in Canada with mice and vitamin E and particularly at how they were able to seemingly reverse the aging process. I thought I would try this with dogs and see what happened. I did try it and I observed a tremendous change. Shute, as a dog breeder, noticed the same thing with his animals. So did other breeders to whom he recommended vitamin E. So did Dr. Lambert, the Irish veterinarian who put old hunting dogs back into the field with vitamin E.

By the NRC scheme of things, a 22-pound dog should be getting about 11 IUs of vitamin E in an average daily ration of a half-pound of food. On this dosage, older dogs have back problems, skin problems, heart problems, all kinds of problems. When we supplement that dog with 100 or 200 IUs of vitamin E, the same problems diminish or disappear.

Here are two reasons why these good things happen:

1. Vitamin E, above basic levels, increases transportation of nutrients to the far reaches of the circulation system. In effect, it is like using a semitrailer truck to deliver the goods instead of a small pickup truck. The result of this improved transportation is better circulation and a heart that doesn't have to work so hard to pump blood and all the nutrient constituents in blood to the extremities.

2. The efficiency of the immune system declines with age. Studies with mice have shown that old animals have only a quarter or even less the immune response of younger animals. In one experiment, the addition of vitamin E to the diet of mice was found to bolster the declining immune system.[4]

Vitamin C, like vitamin E, is an antioxidant. It has the ability to trap and deactivate tiny molecular fragments caused by peroxidation. These fragments, called free radicals, disrupt and damage cellular structures and set off chain reactions of destruction. Vitamin C and vitamin E work together as an antioxidant team to stop the sabotage of peroxidation. In this interaction, C increases the effectiveness of vitamin E.

Since C is produced naturally in a dog's liver you might think it would rush to the rescue in any case of vitamin E deficiency. Unfortunately there's a hitch. The very liver enzyme system where ascorbic acid is manufactured is highly susceptible to the same abominable peroxidation process.

Dr. I. B. Chatterjee of India is one of the world's leading authorities on ascorbic acid synthesis, and I asked him whether peroxidation taking place in the liver would impair a dog's ability to make C. Probably so, he replied. He has found that animals of other species produce less C as they age. An old goat, for instance, has about one-fourth to one-third the production of a young goat.[5]

Chatterjee has shown in experiments that a vitamin E deficiency sharply decreases the vitamin C output in animals. This deficiency, we have seen, probably exists in all aging animals unless they are supplemented. Chatterjee also found a similar drop in C production when laboratory animals were deficient in vitamins A, B₁, and B₂.[6]

Whatever the biochemical dynamics, it is a good bet that your old dog is producing less C now than in the past. Research conducted forty years ago did indeed show that older dogs generally have lower vitamin C blood levels than younger dogs.[7] The consequences are known and are not pleasant. Lower blood levels of vitamin C in dogs have been positively linked over the years to all sorts of trouble: skeletal scurvy, skin problems, tumors, inflammations, a weakened immune system.

Chronic subclinical scurvy is the insufficiency of vitamin C that affects many dogs most of their lives. This subtle state of scurvy is highly apparent during puppyhood when dogs are unable to manufacture enough ascorbic acid to meet the fierce demands of their rapidly growing bodies. In the later years, it is seen once again when the already limited output is further crippled by nutrient deficiencies and by the damaging effect of peroxidation on the liver.

Collagen, remember, depends on vitamin C. Collagen is the cement of the body that keeps cells and tissue components in place, much as concrete keeps the bricks of a wall in place. Strong collagen is vital in the early part of life and must be maintained in later life as well. If the supply of vitamin C diminishes then the cement starts to come apart. The tissues deteriorate just as a wall crumbles. The tissues become less resistant to disease and less able to carry out their specialized functions.

Aging has been associated with deteriorating collagen and a vitamin C deficiency in both humans and animals. The strength of collagen, for example, is a key factor in the ability of body tissue to resist the invasiveness of proliferating tumor cells. Weak collagen means weak resistance.[8] This helps to explain the increasing risk of tumors among aging dogs.

In summary, deficiencies of vitamin E and vitamin C are intimately connected to disease and the aging process. Clearly, supplementation is in the best interest of your old dog.

Frequently people ask me if vitamins and minerals can help very old and decrepit dogs, animals that are barely alive. This is a hard question to answer. I have seen some feeble old dogs come alive with the program, but I have also seen others for whom the program was too late. Obviously the sooner you can put your dog on supplements the better.

By now I have managed to restore enough hopeless cases that word has gotten around about the veterinarian in San Jose who saves dogs with vitamins. As a result I will see many a cast-off from other veterinarians, dogs brought in to me as a last resort after more "orthodox" treatments have failed.

If an individual brings in an animal near death and I feel it has any kind of a chance to live with less pain, then I will try vitamin therapy. The owner has to recognize though that it is a chance and it may not work. I make no claims for life extension. I only say that the chance to live longer is increased. The ultimate decision in cases like this lies with the pet owner.

If the dog is receiving medication, vitamins and minerals will not interfere with the action of the drugs. Instead they will actually correct deficiencies that are created by many drugs. So adding the supplements can generally help an ill dog.

My suggestion would be to consult with your veterinarian in a case like this. There is nothing to lose and perhaps something to gain: added time with your cherished old pet.

TIPS FOR OLDER DOGS

1. Supplement! A must!

2. Make sure an older dog has plenty of water at all times. Aging kidneys are generally not functioning well and an animal needs more water to assist in elimination.

3. Older dogs have a tendency to collect dental tartar. This can promote oral bacteria growth, infection, and loss of teeth. Yearly dental attention is advisable. Your veterinarian can perform the necessary oral cleanup.

12

What Supplements to Buy

I hope I have convinced you that your dog needs extra vitamins and minerals. The next step is for you to go out and buy them.

But what to buy? There are a bewildering array of supplements on the market, as any visit to a health food store will tell you at first glance.

If you read my instructions carefully they will spare you a good deal of confusion.

For an animal other than a preweaned puppy, you will be making two stops. The first is at your veterinarian or favorite pet shop. There, you purchase a good multiple vitamin and mineral product for pets. It must have minerals as well as vitamins. Don't just get a multivitamin and forget the minerals, as a lot of people do in buying supplements for themselves. Your veterinarian or pet store owner may be able to help you select a good product that has been specially designed for animals. There are a number of excellent products to choose from.

These items are marketed either in tablet or powder form. I prefer the powder because it is easier to administer. You can readily add and mix it right into the dog's food. There are good tablet products as well, and they can be crunched up and sprinkled onto the food. Some of them are flavored with meat, and the dog will likely gobble these up right out of the palm of your hand. It really doesn't matter which form you choose.

If you select powder, stay away from the bulk products. These are items that list on the label a minimum vitamin guarantee per pound of powder. They don't tell you how much a teaspoon or tablespoon will give you, and this is the kind of daily dose you are concerned with. There is no convenient breakdown. A label will say 110,000 IUs of vitamin A per pound and leave the mathematics up to you. It doesn't mean a thing to somebody who wants to give his animal 3,000 IUs.

The product you buy should tell you what the dosage is per tablet or per spoonful.

After you purchase your multiple vitamin and mineral supplement at the veterinarian or pet store, you continue on to stop number 2—a health food store. There, I want you to buy two things: vitamin E capsules and vitamin C powder.

First, vitamin E. If you have a small dog you can buy the vitamin in the 100 IU capsule size. If you have a larger dog, you can buy the 200 or 400 IU size. The size is clearly written on the labels in large print. Refer to the appropriate prevention plan chart on the following pages for the dosage that suits your dog.

There are two kinds of vitamin E: natural and synthetic. Many people argue that a natural product is superior to a synthetic one because it always contains some unknown factors that a man-made product won't have. I would agree with that thinking, but in my practice I have had as good results with the synthetic as with the natural. The clincher might be price. A bottle of a hundred capsules of natural 400 IUs will cost around three times the price of a similar bottle of synthetic capsules. Health food stores often have the synthetics on sale.

Price is one way you can tell the difference between the two. Another is by their scientific names written in the smaller print on the label. The natural vitamin is called d-alpha tocopherol. The synthetic has an extra letter "l." It is called dl-alpha tocopherol.

Both supplements work. It depends solely on whether you want to pay more or less.

Vitamin C is of paramount importance to me, as you well realize by now. None of the popular multivitamin and mineral products made for pets will have as much vitamin C as I recommend. Most of them won't have any at all.

In my practice, I advise clients to use the slightly alkaline form of vitamin C: sodium ascorbate. This is because ascorbic acid, the more common type of vitamin C, is on the acidic side and might cause some initial minor heartburn or gastrointestinal upset. Ascorbic acid has a 3.0 pH as compared to 7.4 for the sodium ascorbate.

You may not find sodium ascorbate in the powder form. Some health food stores don't stock it. They may only have sodium ascorbate in tablets. If that is the case, then purchase the tablets and order the powder for the next time. The powder is half the price of tablets and easier to administer.

If the store has no sodium ascorbate but only straight ascorbic acid vitamin C, then go ahead and purchase the ascorbic acid, but ask the clerk to order some sodium ascorbate for you. I will tell you shortly how to administer the different kinds of vitamin C. Whichever form you use, the procedure is very simple.

Tablets of vitamin C of the ascorbic acid kind come in a wide variety of sizes and accompanying features. I have seen them in 100 milligram, 200 milligram, 250 milligram, 300 milligram, 500 milligram, 1,000 milligram (1 gram), and 1,500 milligram sizes. Purchase the size that is most appropriate for your dog according to the charts.

Some vitamin C products say "with rose hips." This is not an important distinction. It merely means that a very small and insignificant amount of rose hips, a natural source of vitamin C, is contained in the product. Still other vitamin C tablets will say "with bioflavonoids." The bioflavonoids are the pulpy part of citrus fruit, right under the outer skin, and are actually a separate vitamin: vitamin P. They aid in the absorption of vitamin C and contribute to the health of the small blood vessels—the capillaries. These products tend to cost more, and while they do add another dimension, I have not found them to be necessary in my program. If you buy a vitamin C product with rose hips, you are wasting your money. If you buy one with bioflavonoids, you are getting something worthwhile for the price. But a vitamin C product that contains ascorbic acid and nothing else is totally adequate and this is what I recommend when sodium ascorbate is not available.

There are no varieties of sodium ascorbate as there are of ascorbic acid. It's found simply as sodium ascorbate. Tablets usually come in the 1,000 milligram (1 gram) size.

If possible, buy the powder. It's cheaper. You may find a bottle that says vitamin C crystals. Powder and crystals are one and the same. The bottle will state how much vitamin C is contained in a teaspoonful. Normally, there are 4,000 milligrams (4 grams) to a full teaspoon. If you are administering 1,000 milligrams, then you use ¼ of a teaspoon. If 500 milligrams, then ⅛ of a teaspoon, etc.

Whatever form of vitamin C you use, make sure you store the bottle in a dark and cool place and keep the lid tightly closed. Vitamin C can lose potency rapidly from heat, light, moisture, and air. I always keep my supply inside a cabinet.

If you have preweaned puppies, you need make only one stop: your favorite pharmacy. There, pick up some vitamin C pediatric drops for human babies. From my experience, vitamin C is a critical factor at this stage of life since it will stimulate the immune system and greatly reduce the risk of sudden death and viral and bacterial infections. When the puppies reach the weaning stage they can then be introduced to the full range of vitamins and minerals. In the meantime, they will be receiving their nutrient supply from their mother's milk.

In summing up, these are the stops and the purchases you need to make:

1. A veterinarian or a pet shop for the multiple vitamin and mineral product.

2. A health food store for the extra vitamin C and vitamin E.

3. For the preweaned puppy, a pharmacy for the pediatric drops.

The lazy man's method: If you don't want to make two stops, you can do a one-stop shop at either a supermarket or health food store. Purchase a regular human-type multiple vitamin and mineral product, but look for one that's in line as much as possible with my recommended dosages. Purchase the separate vitamin E capsules and vitamin C. My choice for a one-stop shop would be a health food store, because it will have a larger variety of products and may even have multis for pets.

13

How Much to Use

The following charts represent my idea of safe, effective, and manageable daily vitamin and mineral dosages. These levels have successfully prevented or minimized disease in many hundreds of dogs, from the noblest of blue bloods to the shaggiest of mongrels.

Essentially, with the major exception of vitamins C and E, my recommendations follow along the general formula lines of popular pet multivitamin and mineral products. As I said in the previous chapter, I want you to purchase a good veterinary multivitamin and mineral product. You'll find one in your veterinarian's office or in a pet shop or in a health food store. Read the dosage instructions on the label and administer to your pet accordingly.

Ingredients will, of course, vary from product to product. Some will have things that others don't have. But don't be confused and don't be concerned. The only differences I am concerned with for this prevention plan are the vitamin C and E levels. The veterinary multivitamin and mineral products do not have enough vitamin C and vitamin E. Most don't have any vitamin C at all. This is why I am asking you to purchase extra C and E.

The nutrient levels in multiple vitamin and mineral supplements for pets are largely based on the nutrient requirements for food as determined by the National Research Council. In other words, the dog will receive supplementally in powder or tablet what he should be getting in his food. The NRC requirements for food are basically minimum nutrient guidelines for adequate health and maintenance which I believe fall short of providing optimal protection against the many stresses encountered in a dog's lifetime. As I have said before, there also remains the question of whether the dog's commercial food even contains these minimum levels.

The multiple vitamin and mineral is, in effect, guaranteeing the NRC quantities. It is something you personally have control over. You may not know what the dog is actually getting in his food, but you know what he is getting in the supplement. When you add the extra C and E, which enhance utilization and transportation of the other nutrients as well as doing so many other important jobs in the body, you are giving your dog the best possible chance for optimal health.

The blueprint calls for three separate items:

1. A multivitamin and mineral. Follow the dosage instructions on the label of the product.

2. Extra vitamin C. Follow the dosage that I recommend in the appropriate chart for your animal.

3. Extra vitamin E. Follow my recommendation in the appropriate chart.

This scheme applies for all animals except preweaned puppies, who will be taking drops.

For individuals who want to use human multivitamin and mineral products, try to find a tablet as close as possible to the dosages I suggest. This may prove to be difficult. To simplify matters, use a low potency human multi for a small dog and a medium potency multi for a large dog. But you will still have to use additional vitamin C and E. For instance, if you buy a multi that contains 30 IUs of vitamin E and I recommend 100 IUs for your dog, there is a shortfall of 70 IUs. However, vitamin E doesn't come in a 70 IU size. You will have to buy capsules in 100 IU potency, which is the smallest commercial size. Now the dog will be 30 IUs over the recommendation. Don't worry. The extra vitamin E is very unlikely to cause any problems. Vitamin E is extremely nontoxic. If anything, the animal will benefit. If the product contains, for example, 300 milligrams of vitamin C and I recommend 1,000 milligrams, then administer vitamin C in either tablet or powder form in the amount that brings it close to the recommended figure.

Each individual cycle of life dosage chart will be divided into four columns denoting the size of the dog. Small dogs are those weighing up to 20 pounds as adults. Medium breeds are those from 20 to 50 pounds. The large are from 50 to 100 pounds. And the giant breeds are the big guys over 100 pounds.

Dosages throughout are expressed in micrograms (mcg.) and milligrams (mg.) and International Units (IUs). One thousand micrograms equal one milligram and one thousand milligrams equal one gram.

Dosage Charts

1. PREWEANED PUPPIES

Supplementation consists of vitamin C pediatric drops. Dosages are figured in milligrams according to the size of the animal and its age. The dosage of the drops is increased after the first five days and then again after the second five days. Maintain the last dosage until weaning, when the puppy will gradually be switched onto a tablet or powder form of supplementation.

VITAMIN C

SMALL BREEDS			MEDIUM BREEDS		
1–5 days	/5–10 days	/to weaning	1–5 days	/5–10 days	/to weaning
20	35	65	35	65	100

LARGE, GIANT BREEDS		
1–5 days	/5–10 days	/to weaning
65	100	135

2. WEANED PUPPIES

Follow the instructions on the label of the multiple vitamin and mineral product you buy. Dosages are determined according to weight of animal. For example, if the label of your product says to provide one tablet for every ten pounds of body weight and your puppy weighs only five pounds, then simply break the tablet in half. When the animal reaches ten pounds, give him the whole tablet.

The multi will contain some vitamin E. This is sufficient for the young puppy. My recommendation is to hold off on purchasing vitamin E capsules until the puppy is about six months old, and then to begin gradually bringing the animal up to its normal adult dose.

Vitamin C dosage should be based on the following schedule:

SMALLER BREEDS

	SMALL	MEDIUM
First six months.	250 mg.	500 mg.
Six months to one year, gradually increasing to adult level.	250 to 500 mg.	500 to 1,500 mg.

LARGER BREEDS

	LARGE	GIANT
First four months, gradually increasing.	500 to 1,000 mg.	750 to 2,000 mg.
Four months to eighteen months, gradually increasing to adult level.	1,000 to 3,000 mg.	2,000 to 6,000 mg.

Note: The doses shown here are for normal conditions. If puppies are placed in high stress conditions such as obedience training, or any type of training program, or become working dogs, then I suggest that their daily vitamin C dosage be gradually increased so as to eventually bring them up to the level of the active and working adult dog.

For example, a normal large dog will receive 1,000 milligrams daily by four months of age. This will be gradually raised to 3,000 milligrams by eighteen months. However, if the dog enters a training program or begins actively working, the doses should be raised accordingly to bring the animal up to 6,000 milligrams by eighteen months.

3. ADULT DOGS

Dosages of vitamin C are given according to the activity of the dog. An active or working dog receives the higher dose.

	SMALL	MEDIUM	LARGE	GIANT
Vitamin C	500 to 1,500 mg.	1,500 to 3,000 mg.	3,000 to 6,000 mg.	6,000 to 7,500 mg.
Vitamin A	1,500 IU	3,000 IU	5,000 IU	7,500 IU
B_1	0.5 mg.	1 mg.	2 mg.	4 mg.
B_2	0.5 mg.	1 mg.	2 mg.	4 mg.
B_3	15 mg.	30 mg.	50 mg.	75 mg.
Pantothenic Acid	3 mg.	6 mg.	10 mg.	15 mg.
B_6	0.75 mg.	1.5 mg.	3 mg.	5 mg.
Folic Acid	33 mcg.	66 mcg.	112 mcg.	170 mcg.
B_{12}	6 mcg.	15 mcg.	30 mcg.	45 mcg.
Biotin	12 mcg.	24 mcg.	42 mcg.	60 mcg.
Vitamin D	100 IU	200 IU	400 IU	400 IU
Vitamin E	100 IU	200 IU	200 IU	400 IU
Calcium	15 mg.	30 mg.	50 mg.	75 mg.
Phosphorus	11.5 mg.	23 mg.	40 mg.	57 mg.
Iron	9 mg.	18 mg.	30 mg.	40 mg.
Sodium	175 mg.	350 mg.	500 mg.	1,000 mg.
Potassium	50 mg.	100 mg.	150 mg.	200 mg.
Manganese	0.75 mg.	1.5 mg.	2.6 mg.	3.75 mg.
Zinc	10 mg.	10 mg.	30 mg.	30 mg.
Magnesium	10 mg.	20 mg.	50 mg.	75 mg.
Copper	1 mg.	2 mg.	3.5 mg.	5 mg.
Iodine	0.2 mg.	0.4 mg.	0.7 mg.	1 mg.
Selenium	12 mcg.	25 mcg.	50 mcg.	50 mcg.

Remember: You will be purchasing a multiple vitamin and mineral product for pets, along with separate vitamin C and vitamin E supplements. With the exception of C and E, the dosages shown here represent what is generally found in commercial multivitamin and mineral formulas. Dosages of individual nutrients will vary from product to product, but don't be confused by this. For your animal, follow the dosage instructions on the label of the multi product. Then add the extra vitamin C and E according to my recommendations here.

4. PREGNANT AND LACTATING DOGS

Your female will start displaying some signs that tell you she is pregnant. Watch for unusual weight gain, a swelling abdomen and rib cage, a filling out of the breasts, and increased appetite.

When you notice any of these telltale signs, switch her onto the pregnancy program. If your female has been bred, then start the program as soon as possible.

There are only two differences between this and the regular adult prevention dosages.

1. Vitamin C. The pregnant and lactating bitch receives the high adult dose that would normally be given to a working dog.

2. Vitamin E. The larger breed bitches receive 50 percent more vitamin E than normal to help guard against atony—uterine exhaustion.

Maintain the multivitamin and mineral supplement level according to the instructions on the container label.

	SMALL	MEDIUM	LARGE	GIANT
Vitamin C	1,500 mg.	3,000 mg.	6,000 mg.	7,500 mg.
Vitamin E	100 IU	200 IU	400 IU	600 IU

5. AGED DOGS

Vitamin C doses have been cut down 50 percent from the adult levels. Again, doses are allotted according to the activity of the dog, with higher levels given to the more active animals. Very active dogs can remain on the adult dose.

For older dogs, I have doubled the amount of vitamin E over the adult level.

Maintain the multivitamin and mineral supplement level according to the instructions on the container label.

	SMALL	MEDIUM	LARGE	GIANT
Vitamin C	250 to	750 to	1,500 to	3,000 to
	750 mg.	1,500 mg.	3,000 mg.	4,000 mg.
Vitamin E	200 IU	400 IU	400 IU	800 IU

14

How to Administer
Supplements

Vitamin and mineral supplements are really concentrated forms of food. They should be given to the animal at mealtime. This way the supplements will be metabolized at the same time and with the same digestive juices that the dog is producing to handle his food.

Doling out the supplements is easy. Some of the veterinary multis are meat-flavored and the dog will eat them from your hand or out of the bowl with the rest of the food.

Powdered supplements can be sprinkled onto the food and mixed in with it.

The vitamin E is a simple matter of pricking the end of a capsule with a pin or sharp object and squeezing the contents onto the food. I know of some dogs who will readily eat the capsule.

I don't advise people to start popping pills down a dog's throat. Many animals will resent this and might bite at the hand that is trying to help. I haven't heard of any clients losing fingers but a few have told me their dogs have snapped. I have heard of some dogs turning tail when they see the tablets coming. If the dog won't take the tablet out of your hand or out of the food bowl then crunch it up and sprinkle the pieces onto the food. Mix the pieces in with the food.

Some animals may resent vitamins and minerals being added to their food. The main reason is the particularly strong aroma of the B complex vitamins. The dog may not like it. To make sure the supplements are accepted, I use the "sneak attack" method.

You start with a minute amount, well below the recommended quantities. That way the animal isn't likely to detect anything different. Every two or three days, you increase the dose. It may take a week or ten days for a finicky dog to be brought up to his appropriate dosage, but I have found this method succeeds in fooling even the most sensitive of dogs.

Vitamin C Bowel Tolerance

Now for vitamin C. The slightly alkaline form of vitamin C—sodium ascorbate—will usually be more gentle on the dog's tummy than the more acidic type, straight ascorbic acid.

Large doses of vitamin C, if given at once, can cause temporary diarrhea in the beginning when an animal is not used to it. This is the only commonly encountered side effect of this extremely nontoxic vitamin.

Diarrhea can be avoided by slowly bringing the animal up to the recommended dose rather than starting him off with the full load. If you do encounter diarrhea or soft stool while you are increasing the doses, then just cut back the next day to the previous lower level you used, and stay with it. That will be your dog's optimal dose. Another method to avoid the diarrhea is to administer the C in divided doses over the day. One in the morning and another at suppertime.

Dr. Robert Cathcart of Palo Alto, California, is a general practitioner and a long-time user of megadoses of vitamin C. Based on his experience, he coined the term "bowel tolerance concept" in regard to vitamin C.

Cathcart found that if an individual is ill or under extreme stress, that individual can take much more vitamin C than under normal circumstances without having diarrhea. More is actually needed by the body in these conditions and thus more is tolerated. This is because large amounts are being used up by the body to fight the toxins of disease and to maintain biochemical balance.

The principle holds true for animals. I have seen dogs with hip dysplasia take five times as much vitamin C as another animal the same size. Normally, that much would bring on diarrhea.

While I have been talking about the sodium ascorbate form of vitamin C you may have been wondering about the sodium part. Isn't that bad for the heart?

Dr. Fred Klenner has used massive doses of sodium ascorbate for years and found that even his cardiac patients benefited from it. No problems, he told me. To this date I have not observed any harmful effects in dogs. I have only seen them benefit. It is worthwhile to mention that the sodium content of sodium ascorbate is only 10 percent. Thus if you are administering 1,000 milligrams of sodium ascorbate to your dog, one tenth of that, or 100 milligrams, is sodium. The rest is vitamin C—ascorbic acid. The added sodium salt buffers the acid, making it slightly alkaline.

Compared to the amount of sodium (salt) the dog is getting in his food regularly, the supplemental sodium is a drop in the bucket. An adult 20-pound dog, for instance, eating a typical daily diet of about 200 grams of food (less than a half pound), would be ingesting anywhere from 900 to 3,500 milligrams of sodium. The same dog taking my suggested dose of 1,500 milligrams of vitamin C in the form of sodium ascorbate would be getting only an additional 150 milligrams.

Still, because of the general medical taboo against sodium for heart patients, I am reluctant to recommend sodium ascorbate to you if your dog has a known heart problem. If you prefer, vitamin C in the form of ascorbic acid can be used. The benefits are just as good.

In my prevention plan charts, I have listed ranges of vitamin C and suggested that the higher ranges be given to very active dogs. These figures are based on what I have found to work well for a large number of animals.

If you want to find an accurate level for your individual dog, you can apply the bowel tolerance concept. Increase the vitamin C gradually until the animal develops a soft stool. When this point is reached, back off to the next lower level, to where the dog didn't have the soft stool. This would represent the maximum level for the particular dog at a particular time. The level probably will shift from time to time depending on stress and activity. You may not want to bother with this kind of fine tuning exercise. If you simply follow the general recommendations you will be covering your dog's needs nicely. If you do encounter soft stool at any time just drop down the level of vitamin C.

Puppy Drops

For the preweaned puppies, you will be buying and using vitamin C drops made for human babies. They come in small bottles with droppers that enable you to squirt the liquid directly into the puppies' mouths. The label will tell you the milligram potency in a dropperful and you can compare that with the preweaned chart to figure how much to administer.

The pups can be given drops two or three hours after birth. Lift the animal gently, cradling it in the palm of one hand, and with the other hand slide the dropper inside the mouth and squirt in the recommended amount of liquid.

If the little pup is walking, that makes it easier. All you have to do is hold his head back gently with one hand and insert the dropper with the other.

All this takes a matter of a few seconds for each pup. Insert the dropper, squeeze off a round of drops, and move to the next one. You can do a litter of ten pups in a couple of minutes.

Just as you slowly wean puppies off mother's milk, you can wean them off the drops as well. I would suggest a transition where you apply the drops to the food and then gradually introduce the powdered or crunched-up tablets.

Never give tablets to a preweaned puppy, and be extra careful with a newly weaned puppy. You don't want a tablet getting stuck in a tiny animal's throat. I have heard of very young and small animals choking to death on deworming capsules. Don't give tablets to toy breeds. Crunch up the tablets and sprinkle into the food.

Part Four

SHUTTING THE DOOR ON DISEASE: PREVENTING AND MINIMIZING COMMON DOG DISORDERS WITH VITAMINS AND MINERALS

15

See Your Vet First

Unless you went to veterinary school as I did, I don't think it is wise for you to play doctor with your dog when the animal becomes sick. Take the dog into a veterinary hospital for a proper diagnosis. Once you have the diagnosis you will find that the treatment the vet prescribes for the dog can be enhanced with supplements. Many drugs that are given to animals and humans for specific problems actually interfere with biochemical balances and create new problems. I have always found vitamins and minerals supportive of medication. The better the cells are nourished, the better the body can respond to medication and the quicker the recovery. If you are considering supplementation in addition to standard treatment, it is a good idea to consult with your veterinarian. Perhaps you will be lucky enough to have a veterinarian who is attuned to vitamin and mineral therapeutics and can give you positive guidance. If not, there should be such an individual in each community, and it may be beneficial to seek that person out.

The idea of the prevention plan is to use supplements to prevent and minimize disease and infections, and to develop a strong immune system. The goal of the plan is the creation of optimal health.

In Part Four, I will examine some of the common canine conditions I handle in my practice. These are problems of concern to most dog owners. I will discuss how vitamins and minerals are applied specifically to these ailments.

16

Allergies

Symptoms: **Common reactions are skin disorders, vomiting, and diarrhea. Other reactions range from flatulence and behavioral changes to convulsive seizures and a weakened immune system that can lead to disease. Sneezing and runny noses are more associated with human than canine allergies, although they do turn up now and then in allergic animals.**

Years ago I had a case of a boxer who was brought in with a swollen face. I injected it with a steroid to bring the swelling down and kept the animal overnight. The next day the dog looked normal again and I had the owner pick it up.

Two days later the dog was back again with the same swollen face. I repeated the treatment and the condition cleared up again.

I suspected the dog was coming into contact with some substance that was causing an allergic reaction. I personally returned the dog to my client's house during my lunch hour and had him turn the animal loose to see where it went and what it was putting its face into.

The client lived in an industrial area. On the other side of his backyard was an open area behind a fiber-glass factory. The dog sniffed around the yard for a few minutes and then headed for the open area. We followed. There was a pile of discarded fiber glass next to the building and here the dog started digging, clawing up the hairy material as if he were looking for a bone. By the time we got there, the animal's face was already swollen. Most creatures are sensitive to fiber glass but don't readily come in contact with it. This dog did and had a dramatic allergic reaction.

I mention this case in order to demonstrate that a dog, just like his master, can be allergic to absolutely anything he eats, drinks, touches, or inhales. Substances that evoke an allergic reaction are called allergens. They can be the pollens of ragweed and grasses, mold spores from mildewed material and fungus, house dust, a flea bite, food, drugs, carpeting, fiber glass. Anything. Both dog and his master can be allergic to any natural substance and likewise to any of the unnatural compounds of modern chemistry found in pesticides, herbicides, preservatives, food coloring, and the pollutants in the air. One of the hazards of the scientific age is a chemical blitz of our environment and both the bodies of humans and pets have been unable to adapt fast enough to the stressful inundation. Since dogs eat predominantly highly processed, highly cooked commercial food, there exists a probability that this type of diet has upset natural metabolic processes and caused some irregularities in digestive, enzyme, and hormonal function.

Both dogs and cats evolved on diets of raw food, including raw meat. Dr. Francis M. Pottenger, Jr., a California doctor, conducted a ten-year study with cats and found, among other things, a relationship between cooked meat and a lowered threshold of allergic resistance. Compared to cats fed raw meat, the animals given cooked meat developed skin lesions and allergies that became "progressively worse from one generation to the next."[1]

Authorities on allergies tell us that a healthy individual or animal can be exposed to pollens and molds and environmental chemicals without seeming to suffer. The body's manner of adaptation is complex and incompletely understood. In a body that has an inherited tendency toward allergy or has been insufficiently nourished, however, the stress of an ever-present allergen in the environment will cause a breakdown sooner or later at the biochemical level. Problems can then crop up anywhere in or on the body. The allergens cause cellular destruction and when cells die they give off a toxin called histamine. You know the term antihistamine. This is a medication taken to counter the effects of an allergic reaction. The histamines are cast into the bloodstream where they circulate and perform all kinds of biochemical mischief. Often they find their way to the skin and as a result the dog will begin scratching or will develop hives, rashes, or swelling. This initial problem can then be complicated by continual rubbing, licking, chewing, and scratching. The skin is damaged and infection can take hold.

What vitamins and minerals can do for all this potential trouble is to strengthen the body's resistance to allergens. Both vitamin C and pantothenic acid, for instance, are essential in the production of the adrenal hormone, cortisone. This substance is secreted into the bloodstream and acts as an anti-inflammatory and antihistamine agent.

Ascorbic acid is the natural antihistamine, produced in the liver and used by mammals for millions of years. The liver is supposed to increase ascorbic acid production when the animal is under stress, but this response is sluggish in most canines and felines under physiologic stress. Perhaps once, when the dog was on its own and eating *au naturel*, vitamin C production was more efficient. Domestication, the cooked diet, and the proliferation of chemicals have possibly impaired the canine's natural vitamin C–producing ability. By supplementing, we are fortifying this disability.

A one-year-old terrier female was admitted into my hospital with a history of sneezing and excess tearing from the eyes. These symptoms appeared only when the dog was in the client's backyard. Since it was springtime, it was felt that pollen or some similar allergen was causing the condition. I injected the animal with a steroid and gave the owner steroid tablets to be administered twice daily to the animal. One week passed and the condition had not improved. I then prescribed a stronger steroid tablet for the dog, to be taken for five days. At the end of this time there was still no improvement and the dog was becoming lethargic from the drug.

The owner was initially opposed to vitamin therapy but now agreed to try it. The dog was brought back and five grams of sodium ascorbate were administered intravenously and vitamin C powder was dispensed, to be given to the animal at the dose of one to two grams daily in the food. The following day, the client telephoned stating that the patient was free of all symptoms.

A little Lhasa apso suffering from the same kind of a problem was brought in. At first I thought it might have a foxtail burr lodged in the nose and this was causing the sneezing. This is a fairly common predicament and one of the hazards of sniffing. Upon examination, I found the nasal passages clear of any foreign object, although I did find considerable inflammation and mucous secretion.

I questioned the client and learned that there was a great deal of foliage in the backyard, including a broad-leafed acacia tree. This tree gives off a large amount of pollen in the spring. I guessed that this might be causing the problem.

I gave the animal a steroid to reduce the swelling and in a few hours the nasal passages had normalized and the sneezing stopped. Steroids have both anti-inflammatory and antihistamine action. But I didn't want to keep the animal on steroids for the whole spring, so I recommended the prevention plan. We were soon able to boost the animal's resistance so that it was not bothered by the backyard pollen. By now it has been habituating the same backyard for three years without a recurrence of sneezing.

Although vitamin C is generally effective by itself, I prefer using it along with the other vitamins and minerals. The whole team. I want pantothenic acid involved. I want vitamin E involved since it too has been shown of late to be effective against allergies. In tests with both laboratory animals and humans, Japanese dermatologist Dr. Mitsuo Kamimura has demonstrated that vitamin E supplementation reduces or eliminates swelling caused by injected or topically-applied allergens.[2]

Occasionally an animal that is being immunized will have an allergic reaction to some substance in the preparation. I have vaccinated dogs for rabies and, about fifteen minutes after pulling out the needle, found the animals swelling up. Usually around the lips and eyes. They would show signs of obvious discomfort. Sometimes the hepatitis vaccine will cause a corneal opacity—what we call "blue-eye"—and this will last about ten days before clearing up.

These types of startling reactions are uncommon. Perhaps one dog out of a hundred will show them. In my practice I have never seen a supplement-fed dog react negatively to an immunization. This doesn't prove anything, of course. The supplemented dogs may not have been among the reacting animals even if they were not taking vitamins and minerals. I do remember a couple of cases in which previously reactive dogs sailed through immunizations after they were started on a prevention program. I believe the supplements do protect to some degree an otherwise allergic animal.

In my experience the reactions of allergic dogs on a good program are greatly minimized. In many cases, the allergy symptoms disappear.

There are cases where the allergens are so unceasing and so potent and the dog so weak that even the supplements cannot make a large impact. Nevertheless, the least thing they will do is minimize the suffering to some degree and over a period of time build up the animal's resistance. The steroids that are usually prescribed are going to make the animal drowsy and lethargic if used for long. Steroids are known to interfere with the body's chemistry. One way is by causing depletion of potassium, and any depletion of this mineral can lead to listlessness and weakness.

While allergic disease often responds quite readily to steroid therapy, the symptoms usually return just as readily soon after the therapy is discontinued.

Food Allergies

One common problem encountered by veterinarians is food allergy, and while it may be common it isn't simple to find exactly what's causing the trouble. The best approach to a suspected food allergy situation is to change the diet and put the dog on a vitamin and mineral program. The importance of changing the diet is this: if day after day the dog is eating substances that are allergenic, then the vitamins and minerals can only do so much. The stress can be greater than the protection.

Dr. Alfred J. Plechner, a West Los Angeles veterinarian, is a leading investigator into the problem of food allergies in pets. High on his list of common major offending foods is beef. In his practice he has found that about 40 percent of Old English sheepdogs suffer from a hypersensitivity to beef antigens and they react whether the beef is pure or in the form of kibble, meal, biscuits, bones, rawhide, or chewsticks. The least allergenic of meat products fed to dogs and cats, according to Plechner, is lamb. Problems increase progressively with chicken and chicken by-products, fish, pork, horsemeat, and then beef.

Plechner says he has seen a significant number of dogs and cats that just cannot eat meat.

Other main allergenic offenders are wheat, wheat germ, wheat germ oil, corn, corn oil, peas, beans, nuts, eggs, milk and milk products, shellfish, fish, processed fish, fish oils, chocolate, fresh fruit, tomatoes, grapes, pineapples, mushrooms, yeast, foods containing yeast, spices, and additives used in food preparations.[3]

Plechner says he has even found some animals allergic to B complex vitamins. I have not run across this problem in my practice. I feel the incidence may be fairly rare. Some humans are allergic to yeast and since B complex vitamins are usually prepared from yeast, this could be the source of an allergic reaction in dogs. An alternative to yeast-based Bs is rice. There are some vitamin products that use rice as the source of their B complex factors. If you find your dog is allergic to yeast then I would suggest trying rice. You can find these products at health food stores.

The message in Plechner's list is that really anything can cause an allergic response. He has found, for instance, that many animals will react to dry food products. Not only is the beef in the meat meal causing a problem, even though the protein may be of inferior quality, but so are the other allergenic ingredients in the package, such as dairy products, wheat, and corn.

To accommodate hypersensitive animals, Plechner developed a meat substitute that avoids most of the common allergens. It is made from soymeal, brown rice, carrots, celery, garlic salt, and water.

Veterinarians have known that dogs suffer the same susceptibility to allergies as humans ever since 1922, when facial swelling in certain dogs was induced by the feeding of foods to which they were sensitive. Veterinarians believe that the vast majority of allergies related to food cause either diarrhea, vomiting, or dermatitis (skin problems).

Plechner has traced cases of chronic bronchitis, hepatitis, kidney ailments, and spontaneous convulsions to food allergies. His attitude is that a dog owner has to shop not for the best food but for the food that will cause the fewest problems.

Dr. K. W. Chamberlain, a veterinarian in Plainview, New York, who specializes in allergic problems, estimates that 30 percent of the allergy patients in his practice have some degree of food hypersensitivity. The substances he has found most offensive are horse and pig products, milk, eggs, food dyes, and preservatives.

By carefully monitoring what a dog eats and what his reactions are, an owner can sometimes draw a bead on what may be upsetting the animal. Says Chamberlain, "A history of conditions such as diarrhea with or without vomiting, skin rash, and pruritus [scratching] caused by changing foods can be a helpful lead to food allergy. The occurrence of signs within a certain amount of time (thirty to sixty minutes) after eating is another clue. On the other hand, if the condition is a perennial one, but it is intermittent, and the patient is fed varied diets, then an attempt should be made to correlate the reactions with the feeding of certain foods."[4]

The matter of allergies is complex and not thoroughly understood. Multiple reactions can be caused by one or more allergens and they can change with time. Testing for allergies can be a long and expensive proposition and not many veterinarians specialize in this work. If your animal develops diarrhea, vomiting, or a chronic skin problem, consult with a veterinarian. If an allergic condition is involved, the vet will be able to treat the symptoms and if he is not set up for allergic testing he may be able to refer you to someone who is.

In the meantime, there are two things you can do on your own. One is to start your animal on a solid program of vitamins and minerals. Two is to consider the dog's diet. Be highly suspicious of food that is eaten every day. An allergic reaction may be lessened or eliminated merely by switching diets or elements in the diet. Avoid products that contain chemical additives.

17

Cold-weather Muscle Pain (Limping)

Symptoms: **A sudden onset of limping during wet or cold weather.**

This is a problem frequently encountered at the onset of a young dog's first exposure to winter or cold, wet weather. The animal is fine when he goes to sleep and the next morning you see him limping.

The condition is basically a muscular soreness and inflammation caused by lying on a cold surface. Local nerves will be affected, giving rise to a neuralgialike condition and pain. One or more limbs can be affected. Pain and limping can occur one day on the right side and the next day on the left. The dog has simply decided to sleep on the side that doesn't pain him. The susceptibility to the cold then causes the neuralgia and limp on that side.

First and foremost: Anytime your dog starts to limp bring him to the veterinarian immediately. X rays will be taken. The possibility exists of more serious conditions such as hip dysplasia, osteoarthritis, or HOD, and X rays can best diagnose these.

In my practice, if a limping animal is presented during a spell of cold weather and X rays rule out any of the aforementioned problems, I will treat the dog for neuralgia. I will keep him for a day and administer sodium ascorbate (vitamin C) intravenously at ¼ gram per pound of body weight morning and evening—up to a maximum of 25 grams. When the dog is discharged, the owner is given a supply of powdered sodium ascorbate with directions to add a preventive dose daily to the animal's food.

Vitamin C is a great protector against the cold. A number of Canadian studies have demonstrated this fact.

At a time like this I will usually take the opportunity to pitch a good all-around vitamin and mineral program to a client. Pantothenic acid is another good cold weather insulator, and factors like calcium, magnesium, and the other B complex vitamins will help fortify the nervous system.

Even with supplements this limping may return. The severity of the cold is a factor. So is the age of the dog. As it matures it is less susceptible. In general, the animals seem to tolerate the cold a lot better with supplements and the duration of the limping, if it returns, is greatly minimized.

It is imperative to give an animal sufficiently warm housing. The garage is fine but if a dog is sleeping on the cold cement in the garage he may still come up limping. Get the animal up off a cold surface. Use a thick rug or a pallet of some kind. Put the dog house in the garage.

Thus, a combination of good housing and a vitamin and mineral program will serve as effective protection against the cold. Administer supplements according to my suggestions in Part Three. Remember that a young dog has to become acclimatized to the cold. A small effort on your part can help the process.

18

Convulsive Seizures

Symptoms: Minimal attacks usually last less than a minute. They typically begin with the dog appearing frightened and making what appear to be vigorous attempts to escape. For this reason, the condition used to be referred to as canine hysteria or fright disease. The dog then stiffens, becomes immobile, and champs rapidly with the mouth, as if trying to remove a morsel of food with its tongue from the throat. There is often a foaming saliva. These minimal attacks may generalize into a maximum, or grand mal, seizure where the animal undergoes violent spasms. The champing develops into jaw and neck muscle spasms with violent shaking of the head. There follows rigidity of major muscles over the body. The attack subsides with a relaxation of the jaw, a running motion of the legs and often with urination and/or defecation. Afterward, for several minutes, the animals have a glazed look and appear dazed.

Spontaneous convulsions affect dogs far more than any other domesticated animal. Despite investigations into possible causes, the disorder remains pretty much a mystery to veterinary scientists. Different researchers have linked the problem to genetics, emotional reaction, food allergies, and hormonal and biochemical influences.[1]

Seizures strike any breed at any age. Veterinary textbooks say that this problem is seen more frequently in dogs over two years of age, but I have seen it occur in puppies, and so violent that it kills them.

It has long been known that a deficiency of vitamin B_6 or any interference with its function can cause seizures in any mammalian species, including man and dog.[2]

In my experience, animals that are on a good vitamin and mineral program don't seem to suffer seizures. I know that may sound unscientific, but nevertheless this is my observation. Whenever an animal is brought into my office suffering from seizures, I ask the owner if the dog has been on supplements of any kind, and invariably the answer is no.

My treatment calls for a variation in the prevention plan dosage and, if the seizures are severe, the added use of a central nervous system depressant like Dilantin or Mylepsin.

First the vitamins. B_6 seems to be a common feature in many seizure situations. I will increase the B_6 to about 50 milligrams daily for an average-sized dog and 100 for the larger breeds.

I also increase the B_3 level. Fifty milligrams for an average dog and 100 for a larger animal. Niacinamide, one of the common forms of B_3, seems to be very helpful in combating this problem. I was turned on to this several years ago by a woman who called me while I was appearing on a San Francisco radio talk show. The woman had a little poodle that was having convulsive seizures. She started to give the animal 25 milligrams of niacinamide and in a week or so the attacks stopped. The woman had previously been using only a nervous system depressant. While helping, it also made her dog dopey so she stopped using it. The seizures returned. After reading about B_3, she went out and bought a bottle of tablets and started feeding them to her dog. The dog responded and there were no more attacks, the woman said.

When dogs are brought in suffering from grand mals, the more severe seizures, I will use the central nervous depressant. The drug has no curative powers but will act to sharply reduce the degree of the seizures. It will also make the dog listless. In some cases, the drug's effectiveness on an animal will cease over time.

I keep the dog on the combination of depressant and vitamins for thirty days, by which time I feel we have built up the nervous system. Then we slowly wean the animal off the depressant during the following thirty days, leaving him eventually under the influence exclusively of the vitamins and minerals. In most cases, this approach is successful.

Typical was the story of an 85-pound Doberman that had a history of violent seizures. The owners were considering putting the animal down. I first put the dog on Dilantin to keep the seizures under control. But I didn't want the dog maintained on the medication indefinitely. This doesn't solve the problem. I placed the dog on a supplementation program and slowly weaned him off the drug. Now the dog is living a seizure-free life without drugs.

If your dog suffers from seizures, the first course of action is to consult a veterinarian. Likely, the vet will prescribe a nervous system depressant. You can then help the healing process by supplementing the dog. But do inform the veterinarian of your interest. He will probably not mind. You will find, as I have, that with the supplements you can eventually stop the drug or reduce the dosage significantly. The benefit in doing so is worth emphasizing. Instead of a tranquilized dog functioning at 50 percent, you can have a 100 percent animal again.

Parasitic-caused Seizures

Seizures can also be the result of a worm infestation. Internal parasites will release toxins that have an adverse effect on the nervous system. Roundworms are frequently involved.

I will routinely run a fecal examination on a dog suffering from seizures. If a suspicious quantity of eggs is discovered, then I will deworm the animal. First I will inject the dog with a half gram per pound of sodium ascorbate. The vitamin C is a natural detoxifier and will also boost the animal's resistance to the chemical deworming agent that is used. The worming procedure is toxic and I want the animal protected as much as possible.

By keeping your animal on a preventive dose of vitamin C and other essential nutrients, you can provide that high level of protection in case of a worm problem. The vitamins and minerals cannot prevent the infestation, but they will buffer the animal against the toxins of both the worms and the deworming chemical itself.

It's a good practice to maintain the dog on a preventive dose of vitamin C for at least two weeks after a deworming. This is insurance against reaction to any residual toxin. The best practice, of course, is to maintain the dog on a permanent program of vitamins and minerals.

The possibility exists that chemical additives and high lead in the dog food and environment may contribute to an epileptic condition. Both factors can affect the nervous system in a harmful manner. Thus it is a good point to try and purchase diets for your animal that are as free of additives as possible.

19

Eye Problems

Cataracts

Symptoms: **The tissue of the lens of the eyes changes from normal transparency to an abnormal opacity, resulting in gradual loss of vision. Cataracts are regarded as a symptom of old age and are common in dogs.**

There have been a number of reasons put forward as to why people and animals develop cataracts. Some of the reasons suggested are nutritional deficiencies, diabetes, and low thyroid activity, and some say the condition is a normal symptom of the aging process.

I have not personally had the experience of treating cataract cases with vitamin therapy. In a number of human studies, vitamin C has been determined to improve vision in elderly people suffering from cataracts. The slowing down of ascorbic acid production in the aging dog and a possible connection to cataracts has not been investigated to my knowledge.

Dr. L. O. Brooksby, a Hawaiian veterinarian, has reported excellent results using a combination of vitamin E and selenium therapy in about three hundred cataract cases and related eye conditions. His procedure consists of intramuscular injections once a week for five weeks, followed by capsules twice a week for six weeks.

Typically, Brooksby says, a response is noticed by the third injection and sometimes even after the first.

"The owner reports that the dog appears to be more aware of its surroundings," Brooksby reports. "Animals that previously collided into furniture are reportedly able to move more freely without bumping into objects."

One of the most joyous recoveries was made by a ten-year-old Shih Tzu with bad cataracts. The animal had been bumping into household objects and had even fallen into the swimming pool when left alone outside. After the third injection, the dog was actually catching Frisbees in the air.

Brooksby used veterinary vitamin E–selenium products in his therapy.[1]

Dr. Wilfrid Shute told me of an interesting case with one of his old Doberman pinscher champions that had stopped siring and gone blind with cataracts at the age of seven:

> I put the animal on 300 IUs of vitamin E because I wanted to restore his fertility, and did I ever.
>
> The dog had missed several bitches for about two years. After starting him on the E, the first bitch got pregnant and had four pups, the second bitch had eight and the next one twelve. I used to joke about not daring to breed him again.
>
> The vitamin E also regained that dog his sight. In three months the cataracts cleared up.

In his own private practice in Canada, Shute said, several of his cardiac patients who were taking vitamin E reported that the vitamin had eliminated their cataracts.

Dr. Geoff Broderick, a nutrition-minded veterinarian on Long Island, New York, had a case of canine cataracts that he successfully treated with vitamin A. He used 20,000 IUs a day and in two-and-a-half months the condition had greatly improved.

There are many different types and causes involved with cataracts. My opinion is that a good diet and supplementation program will contribute to preventing them and may, as the above cases show, eliminate them should they occur.

Conjunctivitis

Symptoms: **The linings of the eyelids become very red and inflamed with an accompanying mucous discharge. When infected, the area becomes pussy.**

The conjunctiva is the mucous membrane lining of the eyeball and the inner surface of the eyelid. It is also the source of most canine eye problems, which can range from a slight reddening of the conjunctival tissue to a severe infection full of mucus and pus.

I believe that chronic conjunctivitis is a symptom of a weak immune system, an external expression of an internal problem. The eye is exposed to a steady stream of bacteria in the air and the animal's resistance is too weak to prevent infection. Very often a dog with this kind of constant eye problem is also experiencing disorder elsewhere—in the skin, in the intestinal tract, in the liver, or the lungs. The dog is simply unable to fight off bacterial predators and lives a life of routine subnormal health.

Many long-haired dogs have a constant battle with eye irritation as a result of hair getting into their eyes. Hair is a first-class trash collector. It picks up anything blowing in the wind and germs from any surface the dog rubs against. Hair-borne bacteria and other organisms easily find their way into the eye and cause irritation, inflammation, and infection.

I regularly treat dogs with chronic ocular discharge caused by hair in the eyes. We either remove the hair or do it up nicely out of harm's way in a ponytail.

Some owners are reluctant to permit removal of the hair. They subscribe to a durable myth that says if you cut the hair away the dog can become blind. According to the myth, the hair is needed to filter the sunrays.

Years ago I had a case of a Lhasa apso with severe conjunctivitis caused by hair continually getting into the dog's eyes. The lady who owned the dog was a staunch believer in the myth, and it took some doing to persuade her to let me cut away some hair.

Afterward I applied some local antibiotics and dispensed some medication to the woman. The condition seemed to clear up. But once the medication was used up, the conjunctivitis returned. I understood at this point that the dog had a very poor immune system. My next move was to strengthen the inner defenses. I encouraged the owner to put the dog on a good supplement program. After this was done the eyes cleared up. The woman kept the hair away from the eyes and maintained the dog on supplements and had no further problems.

Vitamin and mineral supplementation will perk up the immune system. My standard treatment has been to use antibiotics for local and immediate relief and the supplements for strengthening the immune system.

Orbital Gland Disease

Symptoms: **A gland in the inside corner of the eye becomes enlarged and protrudes.**

The orbital gland, also known as Harder's gland, is situated in the lower inside corner of the third eyelid. It is a rather common occurrence for this gland to become somehow irritated or infected and then puff up. Frequently it appears in one eye first and then later in the other. The gland will swell up out of the corner of the eye and protrude. The unsightly appearance is alarming to the owner.

Surgery is the only effective treatment because the enlargement, once it occurs, is permanent.

I see this condition fairly often but I have never seen a single case involving a dog that has been routinely taking vitamins and minerals.

20

Heart Problems

All nutrients are essential for the good health of the heart. The heart differs in no way from other tissues in the body. Single or multiple deficiencies of the various essential nutrients—vitamins, minerals, amino acids, fatty acids—can have a profound effect on the heart and its performance.

I believe that by providing a balanced array of extra vitamins and minerals to the dogs in my practice I have been able to build healthier cardiovascular systems. There are no statistics I can pull out to prove my point. I can only say this: I just don't see as many heart patients in my practice these days as I used to in the beginning.

The prevention plan I have designed serves as a therapeutic basis for canine heart patients. When a client brings in an animal with a degenerative heart condition I will suggest the supplements as a routine course of action.

Among the individual supplements, vitamin E stands out as the great heart protector. The work of the Shute brothers—Evan and Wilfrid—in Canada over a forty year period demonstrated the effectiveness of vitamin E supplementation in rejuvenating ailing hearts and circulatory systems and protecting healthy ones.

Vitamin E usage among breeders and handlers is fairly widespread today, due largely to the influence of Dr. Wilfrid Shute. As a breeder, show judge, and former president of the Doberman Pinscher Club of America, Shute was able to personally introduce vitamin E to many people in the dog world.

Shute's influence reached the attention of Dr. N. H. Lambert in Dublin. Although Lambert's landmark work goes back thirty years, it is as valid today as it was then. At the Third International Congress on Vitamin E, in Venice, Italy, in 1955, Lambert described some of his experiences with vitamin E supplementation in more than 1,200 dog and cat cardiac cases.[1]

Cardiac disease is relatively common in the dog, particularly in older animals, and Lambert found that vitamin E–treated dogs . . .

appear to regain a feeling of well-being, exercise tolerance is increased, and many owners remark on the fact that their dogs regain their youthful behavior. The coat and skin improve immensely, which is probably explained by . . . [vitamin E] promoting the health of the sebaceous glands.

It has been observed that in most cases a slight beneficial effect is noticeable even within forty-eight hours after starting vitamin E therapy. Originally small doses of alpha tocopherol [vitamin E] were used and these seemed to help many cases. But further experience with high dosage levels, as suggested by the studies of the Shutes, has shown that larger doses (100 to 150 IUs daily) are much more effective. Many of the therapeutic failures, clinical and otherwise, mentioned in the literature, may be ascribed to inadequate dosage.

Lambert went on to say that the marked improvement in the general condition of treated animals was due not only to enhanced circulation but also to the ability of vitamin E to restore normality to various tissues and organs such as the liver, testes, and stomach.

From the start, Lambert's experience with vitamin E and canine cardiac disease was dramatic. The first case, in 1945, involved a nine-year-old griffon bitch. The animal was dying from heart disease and also suffered from an inflammatory uterus condition. Prior treatment had been unsuccessful. Placed on vitamin E, she made a spectacular recovery, Lambert said, and "became quite rejuvenated in her ways and lived for another six years." She eventually died from senile decay, having taken vitamin E every day during those years.

Heart disease is a common occurrence in the sporting breeds, Lambert noted. Dogs are inactive from one day's work to the next, perhaps for weeks or months, and few are given any preliminary training prior to the opening of the shooting season. As a result, heart strain is common. These breeds, of course, also contract the same diseases as other breeds and develop the same symptoms. But, as Lambert pointed out, the consequences are often much more severe because enforced exercise too early in their convalescence hinders the recovery process. Vitamin E was found to be very beneficial in a large number of these dogs, many of whom were restored to full usefulness.

One four-year-old Irish setter, while working in the field, would get attacks resembling cramp or angina. The animal would suddenly stop and stand, hind quarters raised and the fore quarters lowered, and apparently in pain. The attacks lasted about five minutes and recurred several times during a shoot. A cardiovascular problem was suspected and the dog was placed on 150 IUs of vitamin E daily. No further attacks occurred after the first day of therapy.

A tricolor cocker, seven years old, had been tiring very easily while out on the hunt. In addition, the owner reported that the dog appeared to be practically deaf. Examination revealed a valvular murmur and the early stages of congestive heart failure. Vitamin E at 150 IUs was prescribed. The dog made a gradual recovery and eventually returned to the field, its exercise tolerance increased and its hearing returned almost to normal.

Lambert reported good results with racing greyhounds. A circulatory condition called "greyhound cramp," in which the animal stops short in the middle of a race, was cleared up with vitamin E. Others dogs that tired easily or were running badly were supplemented with E. The results were excellent. Also-rans became winners, he said.

Lambert emphasized the necessity to keep dogs on a good, high maintenance dosage of vitamin E. If this is not done, he said, sudden relapses tend to occur and these can be fatal.

"We believe that alpha tocopherol therapy is not a cure, any more than digitalis or insulin is a cure," he said. "It is supportive and restorative treatment and must be kept up."

Lambert documented the importance of continuing supplementation. In one instance, a nine-year-old Irish setter had been diagnosed for cardiac degeneration and congestion of pulmonary circulation. Once a fine gun dog, the animal now had a persistent cough that grew worse on the slightest exercise. Vitamin E was prescribed and the cough improved considerably. The owner stopped the treatment and the cough returned in force. Upon resumption of vitamin E, the cough ceased in a few days. The dog was maintained on vitamin E and was able to return to the field once again.

I had a similar experience in my practice, though not with a big hunting dog. Just the opposite, it was a little seven-year-old Chihuahua. The dog had a degenerative heart condition which I diagnosed as valvular insufficiency. The animal was spiritless and coughing—a persistent, dry, hacking cough is symptomatic of the condition. I suggested a daily regimen of 100 IUs of vitamin E. In short order, the animal began to improve. It became spunky and the coughing subsided considerably. From time to time, however, the owner would allow the vitamin E to run out, and whenever she did, the dog would start showing signs of the ailing heart in three or four days. When she resumed the vitamin E, the dog improved.

Valvular insufficiency, also known as chronic valvular endocarditis, is relatively common in dogs. In my practice, most of the canine heart disease involves this problem. What happens is that over a period of time there is a thickening of the tissue around the valves. The valves are unable to perform adequately and the heart has to work harder to pump enough blood. This can lead to heart failure and death.

The thickening of the valves can occur as a result of stress. By now you know the cycle. The animal undergoes some form of stress. The resistance is lowered. Microorganisms carried by the blood attack and inflame the endocardium, the thin membrane that lines the internal surface of the heart. Heartworms can also be involved. Nature's way of repairing this irritation is a thickening of the tissue and even formation of scar tissue. Result: The valves do not open and close properly.

Among the virtues of vitamin E is the prevention of excessive scar tissue production and even, according to the Shute brothers, the ability to melt away unwanted scar tissue. Vitamin E then is the key to a healthy heart.

The doses I recommend for prevention also serve as therapeutic doses. For the adult, 100 IUs for the small dogs, 200 IUs for the medium and large animals, and 400 IUs for the giant breeds. For older dogs, I double these doses. See Chapter 12 for my suggestions on purchasing vitamin E.

Along with vitamin E, I always like to see an animal taking the full range of vitamin and mineral supplements.

As far as vitamin C is concerned, I am reluctant to suggest sodium ascorbate even though dogs with heart problems in my practice have taken it without any problems. The medical establishment believes a curtailment of sodium in these cases is desirable. My suggestion then, for ailing hearts, is to use the ascorbic acid form of vitamin C, dividing up the doses two or more times a day to prevent the possibility of any digestive disturbance.

21

Hip Dysplasia

Symptoms: **An affliction of puppyhood marked by the rather sudden appearance of limping, often several hours after vigorous activity. Lameness in the rear legs, and usually one leg is favored. The dog may be in pain and may whimper as it walks. It may drag itself up from the lying position. Appetite and activity often decline. Five to six months of age is the critical period, although general incidence ranges from three months to two years. Common to larger breeds but can strike smaller breeds as well.**

Increasing numbers of breeders and veterinarians are effectively warding off this dreaded puppy crippler with a very simple potion: vitamin C. By following my suggestions in Part Three for supplementation of pregnant bitches and growing puppies you can also put a stop to hip dysplasia among your animals.

How this is possible is explained by the relationship of vitamin C and collagen and stress.

Collagen, you will remember, is the intercellular cement that binds tissue, that makes tendons and ligaments strong and strengthens all other structures in the body. Good quality collagen is dependent on an ample source of vitamin C.

Stress is the scourge of both man and dog. Stress undermines resistance to disease and germs in part by depleting the body's stores of water-soluble vitamins, namely vitamin C and the B complex group. Work stressed dogsled teams have displayed signs of scurvy, the disease that results from a vitamin C deficiency. Sickness diminished only when the dogs were given food containing vitamin C.

Consider now the puppy, a tiny and vulnerable animal undergoing constant assault from stress: environmental and emotional stress when the puppy is separated from mother and littermates and placed in new surroundings; toxicologic stress from deworming; immunologic stress from vaccinations; physical and mental stress from conformation and obedience training; stress from cosmetic surgery such as dewclaw removal, docking of tails, and cropping of ears; stress from teething; and stress from growing. Pups of the larger breeds grow especially fast and this puts an added load of stress on their developing bodies.

The chart on page 51 shows the low rank that dogs have among the animal kingdom's producers of vitamin C. For the size of the German shepherd, Great Dane, Saint Bernard, and other large dogs, canine liver production of vitamin C is paltry.

This poor production, along with the nonstop stress, results in chronic subclinical scurvy. The animal may not lapse into terminal scurvy but he will often become ill with some of the symptoms. Hypertrophic osteodystrophy (HOD), which I mentioned earlier, is one example. And so is hip dysplasia. Both conditions are related to deficient vitamin C and poor collagen.

The big-breed pup has an extraordinary need for large amounts of vitamin C. The vitamin is needed in laying down the collagen. He needs strong ligaments and tendons to hold bones and a heavy muscle mass in place. He gets no vitamin C in his food. If his liver doesn't produce enough, the animal is at risk, and from the worldwide incidence of hip dysplasia, it seems obvious that the liver of the domesticated dog is not up to the task.

The problem is located in the area of the hip socket where the head of the long thighbone (the femur) is shaped like a round ball and fits neatly and snugly into the concave hip socket (the acetabulum). The joint is held in place by a short, elastic, round ligament, supported by adjoining muscles. The fitting ensures rigidity and the synovial fluid between ball and socket provides lubrication for mobility. On the inner side of each rear leg is a tendonlike muscle, called the pectineus, that connects the lower end of the thighbone to the pelvis above. When the young dog is undergoing constant stress and not producing enough vitamin C, the quality of the collagen is below par. The pectineus muscle doesn't develop as it should to keep pace with the skeletal growth. The ligaments are not tough enough to hold the bulk of muscle and bone in place.

On the surface, all appears normal. The dog is a picture of health. The next minute he is a cripple. It can happen that fast.

The dog is jumping, running, chasing a Frisbee or a tennis ball, doing what young dogs do. There is tremendous pressure—the weight of the entire body—on the muscles, bones, tendons, and ligaments of the rear legs each time the dog pushes off or springs. The pectineus muscle has become taut as the bones grow larger. Tension is transferred to the head of the femur in the form of an outward lateral pressure. One vigorous leap and the ball is tugged away from the natural cradle of the socket. A small gap of varying degree is created in both right and left hip joints. You now have what is medically known as congenital coxofemoral subluxation and commonly called hip dysplasia.

Rapidly, from a few minutes to a few hours, the synovial fluid leaks out of the joints, causing inflammation in the adjacent tissue. There is now little or no lubrication in the joints. The rotation of the ball in the socket becomes grating and uneven. An inflammation occurs there too because of the lack of oil and irregular movements of the parts. Soon the animal is limping.

With time, scar tissue and ossification build up in the gap. This is nature's way of filling the vacancy. An osteoarthritic condition develops and contributes, I believe, a good deal of the pain. Sometimes the pain is so bad a dog will roach up his back in an attempt to alleviate the pressure on the joints.

Continued activity of the animal means continued irregular wearing of the affected joints. Thus there is more inflammation, more scar tissue and ossification. The effect is to push out the head of the femur even more, a process that doesn't stop until either the animal has stopped growing or the gap has partially or totally filled.

It is important to bring a young dog to the animal hospital at the first sign of limping. Many people will wait weeks before acting, hoping the limp is only a temporary thing. The delay only allows the arthritic condition to progress.

Hip dysplasia can be diagnosed only through X ray. The de-

gree of severity, that is the extent of joint separation, is defined
through a numbering system from zero to five. Zero means good,
flawless hips. Five means the worst has happened. I have one set
of pictures on my office wall of the worst case of grade-five hips I
ever saw. Both joints had separated so far that the entire bowl of
the acetabulum had filled solid with bony tissue.

The damage, once done, is permanent. Many animals are put
to sleep. Many vets will tell the owner there is nothing that can
be done except to put the animal on aspirin or corticosteroid
drugs. This will keep the pain and inflammation down. After a
time, however, the drugs lose their effect. Such prolonged treatment in fact may be inviting more trouble. Aspirin is known to
destroy huge quantities of vitamin C. Steroid therapy can cause
a potassium deficiency, water retention, and high blood pressure over the long haul.[1] It can also interfere with collagen production. I have seen dogs become lethargic and develop poor
hair coats after prolonged use of steroids. The effect of either of
these approaches is to invite a deterioration of the immune system and collagen quality. It has been found in humans that vitamin C supplementation can prevent or reverse the disturbances
created by extended usage of steroid drugs.

In my practice I will put the dysplastic dog on a good dose of
vitamin C and all the other vitamins and minerals. Vitamin C
has analgesic powers. It makes the animal more comfortable.
High doses of vitamin C have been determined to ease the pain
and swelling of human sufferers of osteoarthritis. The other nutrients will support the animal in many ways. One of them is to
prevent the arthritic condition from advancing due to any possible vitamin or mineral deficiency.

Many veterinarians today will suggest to a dog owner at this
stage that the animal undergo a pectinectomy, a surgical procedure I pioneered in 1968. The operation entails snipping the pectineus muscle, which is as taut as a piano wire. This procedure
eliminates the outward tension on the head of the femur. It also
eliminates some of the pain and the limp, depending on how far
the osteoarthritis has developed. There is no technique, however,
to restore the ball and socket to its predysplastic state, because
inflammation has occurred and calcified scar tissue and even
bone tissue have begun filling up in the socket.

Vitamin C *vs.* the Genetic Theory of Hip Dysplasia

The reigning myth—which unfortunately still clouds much of veterinary thinking to this day—is that hip dysplasia is an inherited condition. A limping, dysplastic dog, so the reasoning goes, begets other limping, dysplastic dogs. The protocol calls for drastic action: Destroy the dysplastic puppies or have them neutered, so there is no possibility to pass on dysplastic genes. I know of breeders who, even before the X ray was dry, would ask the vet to put the dog down. So severe has been the stigma, they were afraid to let it be known that their bitch or their sire had produced dysplastic puppies. If you were a breeder and word got out that your bitch was giving dysplastic puppies, you couldn't sell the offspring. You quickly and quietly brought afflicted dogs to the vet and had them put away. When hip dysplasia was involved, people talked in whispers.

Behind this proprietary stealth is a residue of heartache. Many breeders would provide a guarantee when they sold a puppy. If the dog turned up lame and was found to be dysplastic, they would give you another dog. But it doesn't take long to develop an attachment to a puppy, and I have seen many a grown-up sitting and crying over a young dog that was put to sleep. The story of hip dysplasia is written in tears.

An East Coast veterinarian connected to the Seeing Eye Dog program says that animals with zero-, one-, and two-degree hip dysplasia can be approved for training. Dogs with three-degree hips are not to be trained. They are neutered "to keep them from reproducing" and are handed over to individuals for pets. The four- and five-degree dogs "have to be put to sleep," according to this veterinarian. Furthermore, he recommends that only zero-rated dogs be allowed to breed and reproduce.[2]

Over the years I would hear of something like one hundred dysplastic puppies being put to sleep every year in the San Jose area alone. There probably were many more I wasn't aware of. Projected over the nation, there must be thousands of Saint Bernards, German shepherds, Great Danes, Great Pyrenees, and other large dogs that are destroyed each year because of the genetic concept.

Personally, I refuse to euthanize any animal I feel can be helped, and most of these animals can be helped.

The first medical observer of canine hip dysplasia was Dr. Gerry Schnelle, a radiologist at the Angell Memorial Animal Hospital in Boston. He published a paper in 1945 theorizing that this condition was genetically based and suggested sterilization of all pups in a dysplastic litter.[3] A recessive gene was responsible, he believed, and it should be simple to breed away from this gene so you wouldn't have the problem any more.

The veterinary and dog world jumped on the genetic bandwagon and everybody began trying to breed out the recessive genes. But it was apparently still there, as prevalent as ever, no matter what anybody did.

One Swedish doctor X-rayed army dogs and concluded that dysplastic animals produce 10 percent more dysplastic puppies than nondysplastic animals. More recently, some of the authorities who championed the genetic argument for years are slowly doing an about-face and talking about hip dysplasia being a biochemical problem. Out of this transformation came one of the most unusual statements I ever heard. A university specialist, a die-hard supporter of the genetic theory, now felt the problem as he saw it was 42 percent genetic! A 1978 report from Australia talked in terms of 25 percent.

In the sixties, the Orthopedic Foundation for Animals (OFA) came into existence, an organization established to gather data on dysplastic dogs and to issue certificates to nondysplastic animals. It was hoped this would facilitate selective breeding and help eliminate the problem. An individual had his animal X-rayed at the pet hospital. Then he submitted the film and a $10 fee to OFA. The X ray was reviewed and if the animal was found to have flawless hips, the owner was issued an OFA certificate. In an era of general acceptance of the genetic theory, possession of such a certificate greatly enhanced the marketability of a stud and breeding bitch and their offspring.

I was never able to find a genetic pattern. I saw males and females certified by OFA produce dysplastic pups and dysplastic parents produce normal offspring. My own experience was telling me that the genetic theory was wrong.

In 1968, an interesting paper was published examining hip dysplasia from the cellular level. The article focused on the involvement of the pectineus muscle and its effect on the ball and socket of the hip. The researchers felt that the pectineus muscle suffers from a state of atrophy in potentially dysplastic puppies.[4]

The vitamin C–collagen connection may be responsible, I suspected. I then set out to test my hunch.

It wasn't difficult to find breeders willing to cooperate in an experiment. Enough of them came into my office angry and frustrated over their hip dysplasia problem, which OFA certification was not helping at all.

My idea was to fortify the bitch and the newborn puppies with vitamin C. I hoped in this manner to prevent hip dysplasia by building stronger collagen. The first animal in the experiment was a two-year-old German shepherd with grade-three hips. She should have been neutered, according to the Seeing Eye Dog standards. The bitch was bred and immediately placed on 2,000 milligrams daily of sodium ascorbate. No difficulties were reported. The pregnancy proceeded uneventfully and the dog whelped much faster than usual. This, as I mentioned earlier, is one of the benefits of vitamin C during pregnancy. The dog produced eight normal pups, who in turn were placed on 50 to 100 milligrams daily of liquid vitamin C during early puppyhood. When the puppies were weaned, the liquid was replaced with powdered vitamin C providing 500 milligrams daily. This dose was maintained until the animals were four months of age. At that time the dosage was increased to 1,000 milligrams daily, then graduated to 2,000 milligrams over the next couple of months and kept at that level throughout the growth period.

Since those early days I have adjusted upward the amount of vitamin C I recommend for growing puppies, especially for young animals put under stress conditions such as training programs or work. See the chart for weaned puppies in Chapter 13 for precise dosages.

The original shepherd bitch was bred three different times, and out of thirty puppies, there was not a single case of hip dysplasia.

During a five-year period, I similarly monitored two other bitches. At the end there were a total of eight different litters where both mother and puppies were supplemented with vitamin C. In each case, one or both of the parents was dysplastic or had previously produced dysplastic puppies. Through all eight litters, not one puppy showed any dysplasia as determined by X ray.[5]

One of the litters I worked with belonged to a breeder friend who raised tracking German shepherds, dogs trained for mountain rescue work. The woman had one particularly handsome and fertile female who unfortunately had grade-three hip dysplasia. She bred the bitch twice to two different OFA-certified males and both times half of the litter developed hip dysplasia. She didn't want to breed the dog any more because she said she didn't want to bring any more cripples into the world. I badgered her into trying the vitamin C experiment and breeding the animal again.

We went to a third OFA-certified male because neither of the previous two were available. The bitch was bred and eleven puppies were whelped. The woman sold the offspring after they were weaned and provided the new owners with a supply of vitamin C for each animal. A stipulation of the sale was that the new owner had to supplement the puppies with vitamin C and bring them in for X rays when the animals were between eighteen months and two years of age. The time passed. The X rays were taken. To my delight, I found eleven pair of perfect hips. I took the pictures over to a veterinarian at a Seeing Eye Dog center and showed them to him. He looked first at the X rays of the bitch and said that at the center they would either have neutered the animal or put her to sleep. He looked at the X rays of the OFA-certified father and praised the hips. Then he began looking at the X rays of the puppies, and as he got to the end he was amazed. It was hard for him to believe that these eleven dogs came out of the dysplastic bitch who previously had produced dysplastic litters.

In 1976, I published an article in a leading veterinary magazine about vitamin C and hip dysplasia and, like most new ideas that tend to explode popular theories, my hypothesis came in for much criticism. But eventually I began receiving very positive feedback, particularly from breeders. Some of them told me that the program with vitamin C was so successful that when they sell their puppies, they incorporate into their sales agreements a clause stating that the pups are guaranteed dysplastic-free only if they are kept on the prescribed regimen of vitamin C.

In bygone years, breeders were reluctant to admit they had a hip dysplasia problem. It could affect their business. Now, people were admitting for all to hear: Yes, I had hip dysplasia in my kennels but I don't have it anymore. A Great Dane breeder in Australia wrote a letter to a veterinary journal proclaiming he had controlled his hip dysplasia problem by feeding vitamin C daily. A breeder of Saint Bernards in Seattle reports similarly he has totally eliminated hip dysplasia. I hear from other veterinarians who have tried the vitamin C approach that they too are overcoming the problem. What I am observing with my own clients and hearing from others convinces me that hip dysplasia is preventable with vitamin C. For me, the problem is solved.

The idea is to prevent hip dysplasia if you can rather than to look for ways to help a limping dog in pain that already has the condition.

Remember that pet food manufacturers believe that dogs produce sufficient vitamin C and so they don't fortify their food with vitamin C. Remember that a dog may not produce enough vitamin C to cope with stress and excess lead levels in his diet. This is particularly true of the fast-growing, large breed puppies. You need to bolster their ability to produce good collagen that is needed for strong ligaments and tendons. You need to supplement.

Carefully follow the prevention plan. If your bitch is being bred, start her on the vitamins and minerals immediately. If you have purchased a young puppy, start the animal on supplements without delay.

If it is too late and your animal is limping, he should still be taking plenty of vitamin C for its pain-killing and other beneficial powers. The regular preventive dosages, as I have outlined in the charts in Part Three, will be helpful to your dog.

Hip dysplasia is a problem that has anguished dog owners and breeders for years. The day has come that it no longer has to affect you and your dog.

22

Kidney and Bladder Problems

Chronic Interstitial Nephritis

Symptoms: Older dogs are commonly affected. The animal always seems thirsty and constantly drinks large volumes of water. As a result, urination is more frequent than usual. Urine is pale, sometimes colorless. In advanced stage of the disease, a dog will frequently vomit, lose appetite, and emit a foul, urinelike odor from the mouth.

Chronic interstitial nephritis is a common degenerative disease of older dogs. Fifty percent of all dogs are believed to have some degree of kidney malfunction. For dogs eight years and older, something like 80 percent may be affected.

This condition involves a gradual breakdown of kidney function over the years, caused by the constant and excess burden of impurities and poor-quality protein these key organs of elimination have to handle. The chemicals and inferior protein in most commercial dog food products are prime contributors to this degeneration. Remember too that the kidneys have to cope with toxic lead and other heavy metals and all the chemical toxins that reach the bloodstream via flea collars, sprays, deworming compounds, pesticides, and other environmental sources.

Chronic interstitial nephritis means an inflammation exists in the nephrons, the tiny tubes of elimination in the kidneys. There are about a million of these filtering tubes. They screen the passing blood for beneficial substances, collecting them in special ducts for recirculation, and excrete the undesirable material, the toxins and nitrogen waste products from protein breakdown.

This is what healthy kidneys will do. Nature never designed canine kidneys to handle the persecution that now comes their way. The result of endless impurities is overwork, irritation, damage, and deterioration after several years of life. Scar tissue replaces damaged kidney tissue and cannot perform the same job of filtering. Eventually, excess waste products are retained by the body. These poisons often collect in skin tissue and often cause poor coats and scratching. If unattended, the internal buildup of toxins can lead to vomiting, loss of appetite, and uremic poisoning and death.

One cheap product has been consistently involved in kidney disease, so much so, in fact, that here in the Santa Clara Valley the veterinarians call the disease by the name of the product.

One particular terrier I remember had spent a lifetime eating this food and died of a complete kidney shutoff and uremic poisoning. In a healthy animal, you should see kidneys the size of nice big walnuts. When I opened the dog for autopsy, I found two shriveled-up kidneys, half that size, and hard with scar tissue. I kept them in formaldehyde for many years to show clients just exactly what can happen to animals fed an inferior diet.

When the symptoms become pronounced it is often too late for the veterinarian to do anything. The kidneys are beyond repair.

I recall one case of an eight-year-old mongrel male. The dog had lived all those years on one of the most popular—and inferior—dry food products. The animal came in with a history of loss of appetite, loss of weight, and vomiting. It was inclined to drink large amounts of water and excrete typically colorless urine. The hair coat was rough.

I administered medication to stop the vomiting and because there was some degree of dehydration I put the dog on a solution of minerals to restore body fluid balance. A blood test showed high levels of urea and nitrogen, indicative of failing kidneys.

The animal didn't respond. Once an animal reaches this state it is generally too late. We had to put the dog to sleep.

Another case I had displayed all the same symptoms except the vomiting. This seven-year-old female responded, however. There was apparently more healthy kidney surviving in her than in the previous case. The owners were advised to make some dietary changes, namely to change to sources of good protein instead of bad, and to put the dog on a vitamin and mineral program. The dog came out of it pretty well. The owners were conscientious and followed the program faithfully. The dog lived on for several years.

Hill Packing Company's Prescription Diet K/D is a special-formula canned dog food designed for the dog with kidney disease. It is one of an excellent line of commercial products developed by a widely respected veterinary nutritionist, Dr. Mark L. Morris, that caters to the dietary needs of infirm small animals. Many pet shops and veterinarians stock this line. I usually suggest either using this product, which is simple to feed but somewhat expensive, or providing the animal a varied diet of good quality protein along with cooked grains and raw or cooked vegetables. By good protein I mean things like eggs, cottage cheese, yogurt, and fish. However, in order not to tax the crippled kidneys, the protein should be fed in moderation.

With dietary adjustment, I also recommend a preventive program of vitamins and minerals. The supplements, high in C, A, and E, will strengthen the surviving healthy tissue in the kidneys, help detoxify some of the accumulated toxins, and may even repair some of the structural damage.

I generally do not see chronic interstitial nephritis among the dogs that stay on a prevention program.

Stones

Symptoms: **Difficulty and straining to urinate. Only small amounts of urine are produced, accompanied with blood and sometimes pus.**

This is a fairly common condition in older dogs of both sexes. What has happened is that the urine has become overly alkaline, causing urinary salts, which ordinarily remain in solution, to crystallize into tiny clusters or stones. Bacteria, epithelial shreds, or foreign matter in the region can act as a rallying point for these stone formations.

Stones can occur in the kidney and urethra as well as the bladder, but I see much more of the bladder type than the others. The bladder is a reservoir and in the "lull" between inflow from the kidneys and outflow through the urethra, there seems to be a more conducive setting for stone formation.

If your dog shows signs of difficulty in urinating, take him immediately to the veterinarian. A veterinarian can X-ray for stones. If stones are present, surgery is necessary.

The possibility of actually dissolving stones through megadoses of vitamin C may promise a less jolting form of treatment than surgery for an older or fragile dog that might not stand up well to an operation. I have heard of two successful cases and I think they are worth mentioning here.

A woman wrote to me about her ten-year-old female terrier. It had been X-rayed and found to have bladder stones. Because the dog didn't appear to be in great distress and because of its age, the woman decided not to operate. Instead she put the dog on a program of vitamin C, 500 milligrams a day. After six months the dog had to undergo surgery for a uterine condition. While the veterinarian had the dog open he examined the bladder and found the stones were completely dissolved.

The second case was reported to me by Dr. Geoff Broderick, the Long Island veterinarian who successfully treated cataracts with vitamin A. He used 8 grams of ascorbic acid daily on a small-breed dog to dissolve a large bladder stone. The treatment took four months. In order to prevent any bowel upset, which might be expected because of the large amount of vitamin C, the vitamin was administered in divided doses over the day and the dog had no problem.

I intend to pursue this promising avenue of therapy. I would not suggest you try it on your own. If your animal is having difficulty urinating, bring it to the vet.

The administration of vitamin C seems to change the pH (alkaline-acid balance) in the urinary tract to the point where stones are dissolved or just do not form at all. In my clinical experience, I have found that animals on a good supplement regimen ample in vitamin C do not develop stones. Some medical sources claim that vitamin C causes kidney stones. I have never found this to be the case. Just the opposite, in fact. When I operate on a case of stones I encourage the dog owner to place the animal on a vitamin program. Most people don't want to go through the ordeal again with their animals, so they usually adhere to the program. I have never had a recurrence of stones in an operated animal that was receiving vitamin C. Actually, I like to recommend the entire program with other vitamins and minerals. Vitamin A, for instance, protects the health of epithelial tissue lining the bladder and may prevent a sloughing off of tissue particles that contributes to the formation of stones.

Stones very often irritate and inflame the lining of the bladder, causing hemorrhage. This produces a bloody and sometimes pussy urine. Inflammation of the bladder may also be due to a bacterial infection without stones. In either case, the condition is known as cystitis.

When stones are involved, the inflammation becomes pronounced enough to cause swelling and thickening of the mucous membrane lining of the bladder. This thickening makes the animal feel there is a need to void and it constantly is pushing to force the urine out.

This is a matter for the veterinarian to diagnose and treat. Normally, antibiotics will be given to destroy the bacterial infection. A good vitamin and mineral program will boost the immune system and generally prevent this kind of infection from taking hold. Thus both the stones and the cystitis can be prevented.

23

Skin and Hair Coat

The late Dr. Clive McCay of Cornell, in his important book, *Nutrition of the Dog*, stated that skin disease bacteria are continually present on the dog. If the animal is healthy, he noted, there is a strong natural immunity developed against skin disease.[1]

My comment to his comment is this: There must be a great number of unhealthy animals afoot because there is a great deal of skin disease. In my practice, I treat skin problems more than any other ailment. Other veterinarians I have talked to over the years say the same thing.

The hair coat is an extension of the skin and the two can be regarded as a single entity. Anything affecting the skin usually will affect the hair coat. Whether you talk of one or the other, it is important to bear in mind that a dog's surface appearance is a window of his inner health—or lack of it. Some experts contend that fully 90 percent of canine skin disorders stem from internal physiological disturbances.[2] Chronic low-grade ailments or major troubles that are brewing inside an animal's body often express their presence on the skin, the largest organ in the body.

Diagnoses of parasitic skin conditions can be made relatively easily and accurately. But it is the nonparasitic problems that turn dermatology into real detective work. Unfortunately, these are the great majority of skin problems. There are countless internal factors that can be involved and so many unseen and unknown physical reactions at play.

When talking about skin and hair coat, I feel you have to return to basics and good nutrition. A good diet is vital to the health of an animal and if he is healthy inside he is generally going to be healthy outside.

But can you confidently say your animal is getting good food? What about the impurities in dog food? What about the chemicals that color, preserve, stabilize, and flavor? Some of them have indeed been linked to skin disorders in experiments.

What about the kidneys that are required to filter a lifetime of impurities and in many cases a lifetime of excess protein? Any veterinarian who has been in practice for a month knows that most of the older dogs he sees are suffering from some degree of kidney degeneration. Overworked or malfunctioning kidneys don't filter out impurities effectively, nor do they properly handle the waste products of protein metabolism. The impurities and wastes recirculate throughout the bloodstream and provoke problems such as itchy or dry, scaly skin.

The first thing I do when I see an animal with a skin problem is to try and put it on a satisfactory food preparation, products that I have found to have either few or no impurities or chemical additives. At the same time I suggest that the animal be given a vitamin and mineral program in the expectation that this will fill some nutritional gaps and neutralize toxic substances that may be contributing to the trouble.

About 70 percent of the time these two factors work by themselves. If the problem doesn't clear up, then I turn to drugs or some other conventional modality along with the supplements and diet change. This generally takes care of the most stubborn cases.

A veterinarian will see a large variety of nonspecific skin conditions that fail to respond to usual methods of treatment. Often it is not until a nutritional approach is tried that the problem is solved. But since veterinary medicine is not a nutrition-minded profession, a good sum of money will often be spent in vain by the client before vitamins or diet are tried as a last resort.

One such case was reported to Dr. Wilfrid Shute. In the late sixties, a terrier breeder in Canada wrote to him with this story:

We sold a young puppy about two-and-one-half years ago and at six months of age the dog developed a skin condition with ulcers and such loss of coat that half of its body was actually bald. The people who owned the dog took it to at least half a dozen vets, who prescribed various treatments,

*with no results. They had spent over $800 during the two
year period and finally were advised to put the dog to sleep.*
*We were quite willing to replace the dog when we
suggested that they try Vitamin E. They gave 200 IUs daily
for two-and-a-half months and when I saw the dog again I
couldn't believe my eyes. The coat was long and the dog
was in beautiful condition with no trace of ulcers or rash.*[3]

In Ireland, Dr. N. H. Lambert reported fine results with
chronic skin ulcers in small animals by using vitamin E both
orally and directly on the skin. He cites one dramatic case of a
four-year-old bull terrier with chronic ulceration of the lower lip.
Many remedies had been tried over fourteen months to no avail.
Treatment with vitamin E healed the ulcers in fourteen days.[4]

Lambert used the same oral and topical approach to clear up
two cases of the "dry nose syndrome." One of the animals was a
nine-year-old poodle bitch being treated for a cardiac disorder.
For almost all of her life, the dog suffered from a warm, dry, and
crusted nose. Daily topical applications were necessary. If this
wasn't done, cracking and profuse bleeding occurred. While
treating the cardiac condition with vitamin E, the owner observed an improvement in the nose. The vitamin was then also
rubbed into the nose daily. "The result is that this bitch now has
a normal moist nose," said Lambert. "This is quite significant as
this condition of the nose is quite common in dogs and no effective treatment was previously known to us."[5]

In my practice I have had good success using vitamin C or vitamin A to clear up numerous conditions and restore healthy
skin. Years ago I had no good way to treat pyoderma, pussy
eruptions on the skin of young puppies, usually caused by bacteria. I would scrub the dogs with a disinfectant and apply steroid
creams and antibiotics. Improvement, if any, was slow. Sometimes the puppies would have to be destroyed. With the coming
of vitamin C into my life, I found the weapon to use against
pyoderma. I remember one litter of eight German shepherd puppies about eight weeks old. All of the animals had pyoderma on
their faces and paws. I administered an antibiotic along with one
to two grams of sodium ascorbate incorporated into the food.

Within one week the encrusted areas showed vast improvement and in twelve days the condition was gone.[6]

In a 1942 study, a team of veterinary researchers tested the vitamin C levels in the blood of 104 dogs. Within the group there were 13 dogs with nonparasitic skin inflammations and all were found to have below normal levels of vitamin C. The researchers treated the dogs with the vitamin and reported successful results.[7]

Whether it is vitamin C or vitamin E or vitamin A, the point I'm making here is that nutritional deficiency is a common culprit in skin problems. If there is a short supply in the body of any one or more of the nutrients the deficiency may reveal itself as a skin disorder.

Once I handled the case of a big Newfoundland that had a terrible skin condition. The dog, about eight, had a sparse hair coat and had been scratching for months. By nature the animal was black in color, but when I first saw him he was almost gray. The skin exuded a smelly discharge. Prior treatment had not proved effective. Steroid medication to stop the itching and inflammation was working only as long as the animal remained on the drug. Whenever the drug was used up and not refilled, the scratching and smelling started up again. The owner, a lady who had just moved into the area from the East, had heard about the vitamin veterinarian and thought I was worth a try.

After an examination of the dog, I suggested she start a supplementation program in the expectation that it would make up nutritional deficits and fortify the dog against stress. I told her also to change the dry dog food product she was using.

In two weeks the woman called to say that the dog was already showing improvement. A year later I saw the animal again and it had a luxurious black hair coat, the kind that Newfoundlands are supposed to have.

Most people aren't going to have the time or money to get involved in endless medical investigation of their dog's eternal scratching or hot spots or raggedy hair coat. This kind of veterinarian detective work is costly. Since nutrition is often the problem, putting the animal on a good vitamin and mineral program is a simple, economic, time-saving, safe, and usually effective therapy. Even if the condition has been complicated by infection or parasites and veterinary attention is required, adding supplements to treatment is a useful step that you can do yourself.

Generally, any dog that is kept on a prevention program is not going to have skin problems. He is going to display a good healthy exterior.

Many people like to add fat or oil to dog food in an attempt to stimulate a glowing hair coat. Some people swear by this. I don't. I have seen that saturated fatty acids from animal fats have a tendency to stimulate intestinal motility and sometimes cause diarrhea. If oils such as corn oil, linseed oil, safflower oil, or cod liver oil are used, they are known to increase the need for vitamin E.

Dogs on supplements don't need the extra fat or oil. The vitamins and minerals take good care of coat, skin health, and external appearance.

Demodectic Mange

Symptoms: **This parasitic condition usually starts on the head, around one of the eyes, and spreads. There is loss of hair, slight swelling in the area, and redness.**

This condition is often called the "red mange" and normally affects puppies or dogs under two years of age. The villain is a mite by the name of *Demodex folliculorum,* so called because of his affection for hair follicles. The mites are permanent boarders, living deep among the follicles, where they thrive and propagate.

Adult dogs seem to have more resistance to demodectic mange than young dogs, and they often carry the mite without exhibiting symptoms.

What typically happens is that when a mite-carrying bitch gives birth, the parasites located on her genitalia attach themselves to the puppies passing out of the birth canal. Since the pups come out face first, this is where the mites take hold and establish themselves.

The mites seem to remain passive and unnoticed as long as the puppy is not stressed. Stress, of course, is a companion to puppy-hood and before long the mites make their presence known. Patches of hair disappear from around the eyes and muzzle. The barren areas are red and slightly swollen.

When a dog shows symptoms of demodectic mange it must be brought immediately to an animal hospital. A diagnosis is vital. You don't want to wait. The mange can spread so swiftly that an animal soon sinks beyond the realm of help. I have seen cases where the entire bodies of puppies were affected. The veterinarian has to treat the infestation with a powerful insecticide to kill off the mites. The larger the surface that is treated, the more chemical is absorbed through the skin. The insecticide can cause seizures. Don't wait for the condition to spread. The dog may have to be put to sleep if the mange is body-wide.

Vitamins and minerals can help in three ways. First, they will reduce the impact of stress on the dog's body. You have read how nutrients like vitamin C and pantothenic acid have tremendous antistress action. A puppy on a prevention program will have increased resistance to stress and therefore increased resistance to mites.

Ample vitamins and minerals can also help detoxify absorbed chemical toxins from the insecticide once the animal has been treated.

The supplements help in yet a third way by stimulating the return of healthy hair. In the past when I treated dogs with the mange mite it would take a good six to eight weeks to see the hair growing back. With supplements, I now find hair growth in half that time.

Moist Eczemas (Hot Spots)

Symptoms: **Chemical, allergic, or parasitic irritation causes the dog to lick, bite, or scratch areas of the skin. Eventually the dog breaks through the skin, exposing underlying tissue.**

It starts with an anonymous insect bite. Or an anonymous allergic reaction. Or a chemical irritant that has lodged in the skin tissue. Then the molehill becomes a mountain. To deal with the irritation, the dog starts picking at the area with his teeth or claws, causing it to become devoid of hair. If nothing is done, the area grows and the dog breaks through the skin, causing an open wound. Sometimes the animal can dig deep into the underlying tissue. An untreated open wound is a target for infection. Flies may deposit eggs and soon there are maggots crawling around the wound.

Obviously you must not let the problem advance to this degree, because then it becomes a matter for immediate medical attention.

These hot spots will show up much more readily on a short-haired dog. It is the long-haired dogs that are more problematic. The wound remains hidden under a thick covering of fur.

A client once brought his collie in for a routine examination. He mentioned the animal was continually biting at the hind end. I moved away the hair and found an open wound teeming with maggots. I removed the maggots, applied medication, and there was no further problem.

Vitamins and minerals will strengthen the dog's internal defenses and enable him to resist bites, allergens, and toxins. Brewers' yeast is an effective antiflea weapon. Garlic is effective against mosquito bites. Supplements will speed up the healing once the dog has created an open wound.

You can deal with a hot spot problem if you catch it early enough. Many of my clients have reported favorable results with the following method:

1. Maintain the dog on a regular preventive program.
2. Mix a teaspoon of sodium ascorbate in a glass of water. Dip some sterile gauze or first-aid dressing into the solution. Dab the material onto the wound. The sodium ascorbate has healing qualities and tends to soothe and shrink the wound. Do this once a day. If sodium ascorbate is not available, you can use regular tea. This also has astringent power. Dab the tea onto the wound.
3. Take a vitamin E capsule, cut off a tip, and squeeze the contents onto the wound. Massage gently with your finger. Do this once a day also, preferably in the evening before the dog settles down to sleep. The E promotes quick healing of the skin.

This multiple treatment should heal the area in a few days.

Parasitic Dermatitis

Symptoms: **Biting, scratching, and damaging of skin caused by insects, with resultant inflammation and sometimes infection.**

During the warmer months, insects play havoc with a dog's skin. Fleas and ticks are the chief culprits. The dog will acquire a flea, the flea bites the dog, the dog bites back or scratches at the flea and damages his skin.

I have found that by adding 25 milligrams of powdered brewers' yeast per 10 pounds of body weight to the daily ration of dog food, you can eliminate this problem in about thirty days. I have heard it work even faster. In a few days, in some cases. Generally I find it takes a few weeks.

Brewers' yeast is rich in the B complex vitamins. When the dog eats it he develops an unusual aroma in his skin, apparently stemming from the B_1 fraction of the B complex. You yourself won't be aware of the odor, but the fleas and ticks are aware of it and don't like it. They leave and go hunting elsewhere.

Brewers' yeast can be bought in any health food store.

I suggest to many of my clients that they start feeding brewers' yeast to their pets in the spring and continue right on through the hot weather. That way you prevent the fleas from bothering your dog altogether. It's not a bad idea to routinely add brewers' yeast the whole year around. The extra B complex and good protein content of this foodstuff will serve the animal well.

By now you may be asking where does the flea collar fit into all this.

It doesn't. Not in my scheme of things.

I don't recommend flea collars. They contain an insecticide that can be absorbed into the animal's bloodstream and cause trouble. If there is sensitivity or systemic weakness or if the animal is ill or stressed, an increased risk of reaction exists. "Flea collar dermatitis," an angry-looking band of skin around the neck of dogs and cats, has been a common consequence of collar wearing. I have seen cases of animals becoming ill from the collar. They are listless and don't want to eat. When you remove the collar, they seem to perk up.

If a client is insistent that his animal wear a collar, I will make that individual aware of the increased importance of the supplementation program. The extra vitamins will team up to protect the pet from any chemical toxins.

Other than a miniature buckle and loop, the flea collar is not different from the insecticide strip you hang in your house, patio, or garage.

There have been many reported cases of skin irritation in hypersensitive people handling the collar or fondling an animal wearing one. On the packages are warnings that children should not handle the devices. Humans who come into contact with the pest strips are advised to wash the chemical off.

The skin of dogs is much more sensitive than the skin of humans and yet we put these devices on the necks of puppies!

Besides the possible harmful effect a flea collar can have, I feel they are absolutely worthless for what they are advertised to do. Fleas don't spend their lifetimes on the animal. They feed on the animal but live in carpets, furniture, animal bedding, sand, and grass. Fleas have to remain on the animal long enough to come into contact with the chemical of the flea collar. If the house or yard are infested, the animal is under ever-increasing attack from new generations of fleas. The flea collar may kill a couple of insects a day but others, by the numbers, will be thriving in the carpet or in the yard.

To effectively eliminate an infestation, you are going to have to use the flea bomb. If the source is in the yard and you spray there, remove the dog for a couple of days so he isn't exposed to the chemicals. Bring him first to the vet and have him defleaed. Then leave him with a neighbor.

If you suspect an infestation in the house there is one sure way to find out. But you must be willing to play guinea pig. The next time you go off on vacation, arrange to keep your dog out of the house for a day or two after your return. If you have fleas, you will know it immediately. Having fasted for the duration of your dog's absence, they will now desperately pounce on you and literally eat you alive. If there are no bugs to thus greet you, you can figure your house is flea-free.

Pruritus

Symptom: **Scratching.**

At any time of life, your dog can start what I call "that infernal, eternal scratching." Every time you turn your head, the dog is scratching.

Much of this problem, I have found, is nutritional. The dog has difficulty with impurities or chemicals or primary ingredients in the food. He may not be getting enough of the essential nutrients.

When a pet owner brings in a scratching animal and there are no fleas, ticks, lice, or other harassing insects at work, I will immediately resort to nutritional tactics. A chronic scratching problem can develop into serious trouble if the disturbance is not confronted. Endless scratching can open up the flesh, resulting in dangerous infections.

Immediately I will have the animal put on a good preventive program. The various nutrients, working together as a team, will attend to any nutritional imbalances which may be involved. Some of the vitamins and minerals, we have seen, have the ability to detoxify ingested chemical agents that may be causing irritation. The supplements will enhance the function of sluggish organs. For instance, if the kidneys are slowly failing, the added nutrients will stimulate the functioning tissue and help prevent further degeneration.

I will also put the animal on a higher dose of vitamin A than usual. I am in a hurry to stop the scratching and end the continual irritation and damage to the skin. Vitamin A seems to help accelerate this. Vitamin A is the skin vitamin. It has the ability to lubricate the skin, repair damaged areas, and stimulate hair growth. Many dogs will scratch an area so intensely they will create bald spots.

I usually suggest 10,000 to 20,000 IUs of vitamin A, depending on the size of the dog and the severity of the condition. As soon as the dog is doing well, we pull him off the high A and down to the regular preventive dose. I have not had any problems with these higher levels of vitamin A. Usually within ten days you can expect to see some welcome improvement.

I will inquire into the type of food the dog is eating and often suggest the client change to products that have fewer impurities and chemical additives.

If the scratching is extreme, I will administer cortisone injections to the dog. In these cases, the animal has often done so much damage to the skin that some of the areas may be highly inflamed or even broken through. Cortisone is an anti-inflammatory agent and will eliminate the tendency to scratch.

Scratching can often be caused by parasites, as I explained earlier in this chapter. Scratching can also be the result of an allergic reaction. Something in the dog's food or environment isn't tolerated. The substance or combination of substances cause the release of histamine, a body chemical that creates all kinds of mischief, including watery eyes and runny nose and itching skin. Vitamin C and pantothenic acid are marvelous antihistamine agents.

Sometimes a dog will have a thyroid problem, just like a human. I will run a thyroid function test and if I find a shortage of thyroxine, the active hormone of the gland, I put the animal on a thyroid preparation and in a few days the scratching diminishes.

Chronic or acute scratching can reflect a serious internal disorder. See a veterinarian for a diagnosis.

Sebaceous Cysts

Symptoms: **Grapelike lumps develop on the skin of the animal. They come to a head and discharge (by themselves, or if you squeeze them) a cheesy material.**

Now and then when brushing an animal, people will notice a lump on the skin about the size of a small grape. It can be anyplace. The back, sides, legs. The lump is likely a sebaceous cyst. You can tell it is nothing more serious when it comes to a head and breaks open, discharging a substance that looks a little like Roquefort cheese.

The cyst is actually a capsule formed under the skin. Inside the capsule the cheesy exudate is produced. I have opened some of these lumps and found hair inside, so the problem in some cases could be the result of ingrown hair. But I have seen other cases where there is no trace of hair. The reason for this growth isn't always clear. Again, we may be dealing with a nutritional defect. I say this because I have had good success using vitamins, particularly vitamin A, to prevent recurrence in dogs with a history of cysts.

The cysts seem more prevalent among thick-haired dogs like the Keeshond, Samoyed, and Husky. One severe case I treated involved a Keeshond that developed cysts quite readily. I would surgically remove one and a few weeks later another had developed. The owner was becoming desperate. Draining the cysts was futile. They would only fill up again with the cheese.

I decided to try a relatively large dose of vitamin A—20,000 IUs daily. The A was added to the dog's food. For a two-month period we observed that no new cysts had developed. In the meantime I had been removing the cysts that were already present.

I felt that the animal was healed and I discontinued the vitamin A. In a few weeks' time a new cyst started to form. We decided that the dog had a specific need for extra vitamin A and maintained him on this level. He developed no further cysts.

I am not sure exactly how the vitamin A works in this situation. Vitamin A is known as a skin feeder and a major factor in healthy skin. It has no effect on cysts that already exist but it does seem to prevent others from forming.

I have not found these cysts to be a serious problem but I would recommend that they be removed. Over the years I have seen about a dozen cases where the cysts developed into benign tumors. There is not much good in popping open the cyst yourself because it will only fill up again. Cysts should only be removed by a veterinarian.

As far as prevention of future cysts is concerned, a good diet with a full range of vitamin and mineral supplements is advisable. The vitamin A in the multi, along with everything else, should keep cysts from developing. If this doesn't help, then you might have to treat the condition with some extra A. You can buy tablets or capsules in 5,000 IU or 10,000 IU strength. Try the lower level for a few weeks first and see if that works. You might have to go up to 10,000 or 20,000 before you find a minimum level to prevent the problem. Then stick with that level.

Seborrhea

Symptoms: Scratching, with flaking skin that drops off like dandruff.

This is a very common condition associated with endless scratching and scaly, flaking skin all over the body. Thick flakes of dead skin drop off the dog like the ugly clutter of dandruff that accumulates on a person's shoulders. There is also a rough hair coat.

We don't know much about the cause. It may stem from allergy. It may be from impurities in the food that are not eliminated by the kidneys and that recirculate throughout the system.

Many years ago, before I had become interested in vitamins, I faced the challenge of curing a young Sheltie with a bad case of seborrhea. I put the dog on cortisone to stop the itching. To some degree this measure helped, but not to the satisfaction of the client who decided to consult with a specialist.

The specialist did nothing different. For three years, the animal was kept on cortisone. The scratching and flakiness did clear up but the dog was left with a dry, dull hair coat. The drug had also made the dog extremely lethargic. At the end of the three years, the cortisone became ineffective and the scratching and flaking returned as of old.

The client came back to see me. Since I had seen her last I had started to use vitamin C in my practice. I asked her if she would be willing to try some for the dog's problem. I didn't know for sure if it would help but I thought it was worth a try.

In ten days the condition began to improve. The dog made a gradual comeback and in three months the skin and hair coat were in fine condition. The dog was much friskier.

Whatever was causing the problem, allergy or impurities, the vitamin C was acting as a detoxifier and general immune system stimulant.

Many of the B complex vitamins are known to be essential for skin health. Seborrhea is often associated with deficiency in one or more of the B vitamins, particularly B_2, B_6, and biotin. Nowadays I prefer including the entire range of B vitamins in any skin treatment. Vitamin A is important also. It will help lubricate the dry skin that is sometimes found with the seborrhea condition.

I am often asked by dog owners about dealing with stiff, dry, and even scaly-looking skin and a lackluster hair coat. I have to attribute this condition to a lack of good nutrition. These dogs are usually eating nothing more than a commercial dry dog food and from this kind of diet I am convinced they are getting unbalanced and insufficient nutrition. Usually I have been able to turn around the dry skin and poor hair coat problem with vitamins and minerals.

For seborrhea, for the dry, stiff skin with the poor hair coat, the prevention plan is the best medicine.

24

Spinal Problems

Degeneration of the Spine (Spinal Myelopathy)

Symptoms: **Poor appetite, pain and sensitivity in the spinal region. Progressive loss of control of the hind leg muscles with accompanying dragging of the paws, swaying of the hind end, and reduced ability to walk and jump. Eventually develops into a hind quarter paralysis and can move forward, affecting the forelegs and the brain. Most frequently seen in aging dogs.**

For years a man named Vernon Castle has been a client of mine, but I could never get him interested in vitamins until the day he walked into my office with a very distressed dog. Kini was eight, a German shepherd suffering from an obvious spinal problem. She was having difficulty walking, was swaying in the hind end, and couldn't jump or rear up on her back legs.

I examined the dog but I wasn't able to determine if she had a ruptured disc or spinal myelopathy. I suspected the latter. Just to be sure I recommended to Mr. Castle that he take her to the veterinary school at the University of California at Davis, a two-hour drive away. The school has excellent facilities and can do the kind of intricate testing and examination for spinal problems that I am not set up to do. Spinal myelopathy is a type of disease that is extremely difficult to diagnose because you first have to rule out other possibilities such as hip dysplasia, traumatic injuries, ruptured disc, or tumors.

What happens in this condition is a deterioration of the tissues in and around the vertebrae. The cause may be related to the aging process. The breakdown causes inflammation and some degree of pressure on the spinal nerves that supply the hind quarters. Difficulty in control of muscle movement and walking develops into a paralysis. The animal goes down in the hind quarter and pathetically drags himself around on his front legs. I have seen forelegs become affected also. The legs get stiff and unsteady and eventually the animal is down altogether and can't get up. Such dogs are usually put to sleep.

At Davis, Kini was examined. The diagnosis of spinal myelopathy was made with the suggestion that the dog be euthanized. But the Castles refused to let the dog be put away and returned to San Jose to see me. I had suggested to them that vitamin C might be able to remedy the problem.

Kini was left with me and I started therapy. For three days I administered the routine of vitamin C intravenously twice daily. When the Castles returned, the dog was eating better and appeared more stable in the hind quarters. I then prescribed oral vitamin C along with multiple vitamins and minerals.

Two weeks later, Mr. Castle called to say the dog had improved to such an extent that he was going to buy some vitamins for himself and his wife. I heard from him again some time later. He told me that his chronic migraine problem had been helped considerably by the supplements.

I remember this case vividly because here was a situation where the master learned a trick from his dog.

Over the years I have handled about thirty cases of spinal degeneration and managed, with vitamin C, to heal about twenty-five of them. In the beginning the dogs were put to sleep because there was nothing that could be done. I remember years ago a male terrier cross who had such intense pain in the lumbar region that he walked about stiff-legged, his back arched like a cat, in a strained effort to relieve himself. The dog had a poor appetite, high fever, and a moderate loss of muscle control in the rear legs. I feebly applied antibiotics to control the fever. There was no favorable response. I referred the dog to Davis where the diagnosis of spinal myelopathy was made. The dog was euthanized.

Some years later, after I had begun using vitamin C in my practice, I was presented with an old Labrador retriever.

There was the similar lack of appetite, fever, and a general list-lessness. At Davis, spinal degeneration was diagnosed. I first tried different antibiotics but in forty-eight hours there was no change. With standard forms of treatment having failed, I obtained permission from the owner to attempt something new and untried: vitamin C.

After sixteen hours, the temperature returned to normal, the appetite improved, and the patient's activity increased. After three days the dog was put on oral vitamin C, six grams daily in his food. The improvement was progressive. Within three months the dog was normal again.

The client was impressed to the point that he purchased kilogram quantities of vitamin C and vowed to keep the dog supplied with it for the rest of its life.

Junkyard dogs are known for bites as big as their barks. They're mean. One such junkyard dog turned up in my office one day looking considerably less than mean. H was his name. The letter of the alphabet. This dog was part German shepherd and part pit bull and was used as a guard dog to prevent thieves from entering a San Jose junkyard. By the owner's account, this dog had been the meanest of the mean. But now, at nine years, H had developed a posterior paralysis that looked like a case of spinal degeneration. The owner didn't want any elaborate diagnosis or to make any trip to Davis, so I went right ahead with vitamin C therapy.

We hospitalized H for a few days and gave him injections of sodium ascorbate. The earlier you can catch a condition like this, the better and quicker the response. H had been down two days. C got him up in three. After four days I felt he could go back to the junkyard. The animal was in no apparent pain and was eating better. I instructed the owner to give the dog oral supplements on a daily basis if he wanted to keep H on his feet and on the job.

The employees at the junkyard didn't maintain the program regularly and in a short time, old H was down in the hind quarters and back in the office again. I repeated the treatment and the dog was on his feet again in a couple of days.

This time I made a strong plea to the owner about the necessity of keeping the animal on vitamins. The lesson was apparently learned because the last I heard, H was his bristling old people-eating self again and effectively keeping the junkyard free of intruders. H was maintained on three grams of vitamin C a day along with the other essentials.

This was a case in point of the necessity of maintenance. People bring in an ailing dog, but after it improves on a therapy program the owners will often neglect the vitamins. Invariably, the dog will revert to its weakened state and I'll see it in the office again with the same symptoms. I keep telling my clients that prevention is a lifetime discipline. It will save them veterinary bills and time and wear and tear on their animals. Some have to learn this lesson the hard way.

I feel spinal degeneration comes about through deterioration of collagen in the spinal tissues. Remember that a dog's ability to make ascorbic acid diminishes with age and the vitamin is needed both for the production and maintenance of good quality collagen.

By treating an animal with vitamin C, we are improving the collagen and rebuilding the degenerated ligaments and tissue of the spine. Sometimes I will have people bring in animals that have been paralyzed and down for six months. If the deterioration goes beyond a certain point I can't really offer much hope. If an animal goes down, I like to see it as early as possible. In these cases the deterioration is still minimal and treatment can usually bring the dog back on its feet in a short period of time.

A dog owner with such a downed pet can confidently apply the prevention program to his or her animal if no local veterinarian can be found to go along with the vitamin therapy. Be sure to administer the recommended doses.

In carrying out this program on your own, keep in mind that intravenous injections—the "shots" a doctor or a veterinarian will administer—work considerably faster than oral administration.

You may recall the case of Kurt, the Doberman in the opening chapter with spinal myelopathy, whose owner administered the vitamin C by mouth for two months and brought the animal back to its feet again. Recovery can take months. You will have to be patient.

Ruptured Discs

Symptoms: **Paralysis in the hind quarters and legs with urinary and fecal incontinence. A common problem with dachshunds and to a lesser degree with Pekingese, cocker spaniels, and poodles.**

Long, low, and tubular, the spirited little dachshund pays a heavy price for his world-famous shape: a tendency to back problems and ruptured discs. The ligaments holding the vertebrae firmly together become lax and a vigorous tug here or there and a disc is damaged. Should the fibrous tissue of the cartilagenous disc become torn, which is often the case, the jellylike substance inside oozes out and inflames the area of the spinal nerves. This causes interference with the transmission of nerve messages to the rear. What follows is paralysis in the hind legs—partial or complete, gradual or sudden—and a loss of ability to control bladder and rectal function.

This may be related to collagen weakness. I have found that the dachshund bad back problem responds very well to vitamin C treatment.

Some years ago I met a schoolteacher couple that owned a cabin near ours up in the Sierra Nevada mountains. The man and his wife had two older dachshunds. The dogs were very active and frisky for their age. The male dog suffered from a chronic back problem and periodically would drag in the hind quarter. I suggested vitamin C. The couple purchased some drug store vitamin C tablets in 500 milligram strength and afterward whenever the animal started dragging his behind they would pop a tablet down his throat twice a day. In a few days, the dog would be back to normal. If they neglected the C for any length of time, the animal started to drag again. Eventually the couple made it a point to maintain the dog routinely on vitamin C.

Irving Eldredge of Tirvelda Kennel in Virginia successfully used vitamin C to rid a cherished fifteen-year-old dachshund of excruciating back pain.

"The dog was having attacks of trembling every day," El-

dredge told me. "Whenever we picked her up she would scream
with pain. We started giving her 1,000 milligrams of vitamin C
and a Bufferin and overnight the attacks stopped and she has not
had the problem since. She gets around fine now with no apparent discomfort."

In my practice I have yet to see a dachshund that was maintained on a vitamin and mineral program have any back problem. I have advised dozens of dachshund owners how the simple
addition of vitamin C daily to the dog's food effectively reverses
an early case. In the more serious cases, my routine approach is
to inject the downed dog with sodium ascorbate for three to five
days. Normally this is all the time it takes to bring the animal
back to its feet.

The vitamin C is apparently contributing to improve the quality of the collagen in the animal's entire body. In the trouble
zone of the spine, stronger collagen means stronger ligaments
and restoration of disc integrity. It also means less pain.

My vitamin C experience with canine spines has a human parallel. Dr. James Greenwood, Jr., professor of neurosurgery at
Baylor University, has been using vitamin C for years in dealing
with human back ailments. Twenty-five years ago he was suffering personally from increasing back pain and rigidity. The standard treatment proved ineffective, and as he suffered so did his
golf game. Greenwood was aware of the relationship of vitamin
C to connective tissue and strong bones and cartilage. He started
taking some daily. His condition began to improve and he could
start swinging the golf clubs again. When he slacked off, forget-
ting the vitamin, the back misery returned. Greenwood resumed
the vitamin C regimen and has followed it methodically ever
since. His patients have also been getting vitamin C during all
this time.

He reported that a "significant percentage" of patients with
disc damage were able to avoid surgery by the use of approximately 750 to 1,000 milligrams of vitamin C daily. In many cases,
when the patients stopped the vitamin C, the symptoms returned. When the patients resumed taking the vitamin, the symptoms disappeared.

Using the vitamin C in surgery cases, Greenwood observed

that it greatly reduced the rate of reoperations, a frequent problem with disc patients.[1]

Vitamin E Works Too

Fred Heying, the retired Southern California breeder of champion dachshunds, has found vitamin E a wonderful preventive and therapeutic agent in fighting back problems. He told me of his experience with it:

> *This has been the main reason we have used vitamin E for years. We put our animals on a routine dose of 200 IUs per day and if we feel there is any trouble brewing from this disc disease we just bounce up the dose to 800 or 1,200. Then there's no problem. We have sold dogs to people and told them to use vitamin E the same way and it works for them also.*
>
> *For years the Dachshund Club of America has been soliciting contributions to finance a research project on disc disease. They have some laboratory working on it. I told them that we just didn't have any problems since we started using vitamin E. They couldn't believe it. I said rather than looking for something as a cure when the dogs already have it, why not get something to prevent it. We think that vitamin E is the best preventive of all. We feel it is almost a miracle in fact.*

Heying mentioned that he has a lemon orchard on his property and his dogs always eat the citrus fruit when they fall to the ground. Skin and all. That's an extra forty milligrams of vitamin C from each lemon.

The effectiveness of vitamin E against the dachshund spinal problem may be the result of two of the vitamin's special talents. First, as an antioxidant, it may be preventing the harmful peroxidation process in the cells of the spinal region. Peroxidation is associated with tissue degeneration and aging. Second, vitamin E enhances transportation of nutrients through the bloodstream. It may be bringing a better supply of nourishment to the spinal tissues and thus keeping them more robust and better able to withstand wear and tear.

As Heying says, better to prevent than to cure. My recommendation for all dachshund breeders and owners is a prevention program with solid amounts of vitamins C and E.

Vitamins *vs.* Laminectomy

I always suggest to clients they try vitamins before considering a laminectomy—surgical removal of the damaged disc. There are several good reasons:

1. Surgery is always a risk. An animal can die from anesthesia. Moreover, spinal surgery is a delicate procedure. I have heard of cases where animals came out of this operation and did not walk again.

There is no risk with vitamin therapy.

2. Usually you have to bring an animal to a veterinary school or a veterinary neurosurgeon to perform the operation.

You can administer vitamins at home.

3. A laminectomy will cost $500 and up.

The vitamins cost a few dollars.

4. A surgery patient has to convalesce. Activity is limited. There is a return trip to have stitches removed. There is a constant vigil for infection.

With supplements, the animal stays at home and is encouraged to be as active as possible.

Most of the clients in my practice are working-class people. Few of them can afford a $500 operation for their dogs. The vitamin program done at home offers them an effective and much cheaper alternative.

25

Trauma:
Injury, Shock, Surgery

Injury is a jolt of stress to the body. If serious enough, it can cause shock and death. Shock is a condition of general body collapse. The circulation system breaks down and brain and organ function comes to a halt.

Any time I am presented with a dazed, injured dog, I routinely administer vitamin C intravenously. The C reduces the level of shock and rapidly brings about a restoration of bodily functions. In short order, the animal is more relaxed and I am able to go ahead and treat the injury. Pain is also diminished.

Years ago whenever an animal was brought in to my hospital following an accident, I would use a common analgesic drug called Demerol. Occasionally after receiving the drug, a dog would become distressed and die. I was puzzled by this response and tried to find an explanation. There were no clues in the brochure that accompanied the medication and nothing pertinent in the medical literature. Finally one day while reading a veterinary journal, I came across a small article stating that Demerol, when given during a state of shock, could cause adverse reactions. The drug, it seemed, united with histamines and could cause an animal to sink deeper in shock. This is apparently what happened in my cases.

After I began using vitamin C, I found some references about how this vitamin prolonged survival time and reduced mortality rates in animals suffering from hemorrhage and shock. I then began administering vitamin C injections to my injury and shock cases and found this extremely safe and beneficial. I never encountered the negative response I had had using Demerol.

In my practice I have observed that dogs on a good overall vitamin and mineral program seem to be less traumatized after injury than other dogs. Supplement-fed animals seem to shake it off better. They don't display the heavy breathing, anxiety, and pale mucous membranes that you see in a typical shock-laden animal. Studies have shown that not only vitamin C but many of the B complex vitamins play important roles in connection with recovery from shock and injury.[1]

In my practice I do a good deal of surgery and have found that supplement-fed animals both cope with anesthesia better and heal faster.

Some dogs will go into what we call anesthesia shock. They will gasp and stop breathing. It is not a matter of too much anesthesia but seemingly a problem of the body handling the substance. The anesthesia in these cases can actually act as a toxin and affect the center in the brain that deals with respiration. I have never seen a supplement-fed dog stop breathing on the table. But in the course of a year I will have about a half-dozen or so animals that don't get supplements stop breathing on me.

The prevention program is effective in promoting fast healing. Vitamin C, vitamin A, vitamin E, and zinc are all known to speed the healing process. The supplements also protect the animal against infections by stimulating the immune system.

26

Tumors

Tumors, benign and malignant, are afflictions of both man and beast. Except for tobacco usage and occupational exposures, animals are subject to all the other tumor-causing factors that affect humans: viruses, solar radiation, X rays, certain chemicals, radioactive elements, foods, drugs, and changes in endocrine function.

In 1971, the National Cancer Institute published a survey documenting the incidence of domestic animal tumors at a dozen U.S. and Canadian veterinary schools. The survey included 6,000 canine tumors. Here are some of the findings:

Malignancies were found to occur in 40 percent of cases. Risk increased with age. Crossbred dogs were said to be at a substantially lower risk than most purebreds. Small breeds tended to be at low risk for all tumors, as were collies and German shepherds.

The skin was the most frequent site of canine tumor growth and 20 percent of skin tumors were malignant. After skin, the most frequent tumors were in the mammary glands of bitches (46 percent malignant), digestive system (33 percent malignant), and the blood and lymph system (95 percent malignant).

Tumors of the mammary gland were the most common in the female dog. The ratio of female to male with this condition was about 50 to 1, the same as in people. Four canine breeds—the miniature poodle, English setter, German short-haired pointer and the pointer—were said to have the highest risk for mammary tumors.

Ovarian tumors are infrequent in the dog but testicular tumors are more common. Boxers, Weimaraners, Shetland sheepdogs, and German shepherds were indicated to have the highest risk for this type of growth.[1]

According to another National Cancer Institute study, cryptorchism is a contributing factor to testicular tumors. Cryptorchism is a condition where one testicle doesn't descend into the scrotum but remains locked in the abdominal cavity. The NCI study says cryptorchid dogs have a risk for tumors of the testicle that is nearly fourteen times higher than that of normal dogs. In my own practice I recall two old German shepherds with this condition. The undescended testicle in each case had developed immense tumors—the size of softballs—and had to be removed surgically.

In the extremely malignant blood and lymph cancers, the most common manifestation in dogs involves tumors of the lymph nodes. The boxer and English pointer seem to have a high risk for this condition.[2] These malignancies, which usually first appear as lumps or bumps in the neck, occur typically in an animal five to ten years of age.

Symptoms, in the case of tumors, involve the usual swelling and other expressions of illness depending on the organ or part of the body involved.

My attitude toward tumors is essentially to try to prevent them. Leading scientists have repeatedly found nutritional deficiencies present in cancer patients. Drs. Ewan Cameron and Linus Pauling, who have conducted an intense nutritional investigation of cancer, believe that vitamins hold special promise in enhancing resistance and retarding malignancies, "with ascorbic acid probably possessing the greatest promise of all."[3] I feel if an animal is on a good vitamin and mineral program he is going to have a strong immune system that can neutralize the viruses, chemicals, pollutants, additives, and abnormal cell growth that are involved in this disease process. I believe an optimally healthy animal at the cellular level is a lesser risk for cancer.

In his excellent book *Cancer and Its Nutritional Therapies,* biochemist Richard A. Passwater quotes the late cancer expert Dr. Hardin Jones of the University of California: "You see, it is not the cancer that kills the victim; it's the breakdown of the defense mechanism that eventually brings death."[4]

Vitamins and Minerals Against Cancer

Ever since 1925, researchers have connected vitamin A deficiency with cancer. According to Dr. Michael Sporn of the National Cancer Institute, well over half of all human cancer starts in epithelial tissue, the top layer of cells that form the lining of the respiratory tract, urinary tract, gastrointestinal tract, of skin, glands, and internal organs.[5] This situation holds true not only for humans but for all mammals. Epithelial tissue is dependent upon vitamin A for normal development.

Researchers have determined that vitamin A helps prevent cancer by protecting the vital nucleic acid inside the cells, by influencing normal cellular proliferation and keeping mucous membranes healthy.

Over the years, animal studies have repeatedly shown that supplemental vitamin A greatly reduces a whole variety of experimentally induced cancers.[6] Dr. Raymond Shamberger of the Cleveland Clinic, after a series of animal tests, wrote: "Vitamin A retards the growth and inhibits the induction of benign and malignant tumors."[7] Vitamin A thus seems protective whether a recognized deficiency exists or not.

Going alphabetically, we see that tumors have been experimentally provoked in mice deficient in B_1, B_2, B_6, and choline, one of the lesser known B vitamins. Baboons deficient for two to six years in B_6 alone, even with all other known nutrients present in their diet, developed signs of liver cancer. Baboons totally deprived of B_6 all died of liver damage within six to eight months after the start of the experiment.[8]

Liver and brewers' yeast have been found to provide protection for rats that were fed a banned food coloring agent known to cause liver cancer.[9] Liver and brewers' yeast are good sources of B complex vitamins. In still another experiment, the addition of the B vitamins to a normal diet of rats was shown to increase resistance to connective tissue malignancies.[10]

Vitamin C has scored some high marks in fighting cancer. Dr. J. U. Schlegel of Tulane University found that by adding vitamin C to the drinking water of laboratory mice—already known as

good producers of vitamin C—the animals resisted bladder tumor formations when implanted with a proven bladder carcinogen. Schlegel has also found vitamin C effective in preventing recurrences of tumors in the bladders of his human patients.[11]

Laboratory animals such as rats have been shown to dramatically increase their internal production of vitamin C when challenged with cancer-causing chemicals. A dog is not known to have this similar ability. Furthermore, an old dog that is the most likely to develop a tumor has a diminished ability to produce ascorbic acid altogether.

Despite promising research over the years, the medical establishment has been slow to change a closed attitude toward a possible cancer-vitamin C connection. In 1969, a team of National Cancer Institute scientists exposed vitamin C (sodium ascorbate) to a culture of cancer cells and found it to be highly lethal to the cancer. They felt the advantage of vitamin C as a potential anticancer agent was that it was "remarkably nontoxic to normal body tissues, and may be administered to animals in extremely large doses (up to 5 or more grams per kilogram of body weight) without notable harmful pharmacological effects." The researchers were so impressed they suggested future chemotherapy should concentrate on cancer-killing and nontoxic compounds like vitamin C rather than the toxic compounds that are commonly used, which are harmful to both cancer and healthy body cells.[12] Their suggestion went unheeded.

During the seventies, Drs. Cameron and Pauling reported positive results using vitamin C on seriously ill cancer patients. They said that megadoses of vitamin C reduced pain and dependence on pain-killing drugs and improved poor appetites, stimulated mental alertness, and brought on a sense of well-being. There is little doubt, they wrote, that administering high levels of the vitamin "is of real value in extending the life of patients."[13]

The successful work of Cameron and Pauling, however, has barely stirred a reluctant medical profession to take vitamin C seriously. By 1981 there was still no large-scale work underway by major cancer research institutions.

Cameron and Pauling believe that the principal value of increased vitamin C is to make the natural protective mechanisms

of the body more effective. Vitamin C maintains the strength of collagen and the stronger this intercellular cement, the greater is the resistance of tissues to the infiltration and spread of tumors. Some malignancies are caused by viruses, and we have seen how high doses of vitamin C have a powerful effect against viruses. Yet another facet of vitamin C in the tumor picture is its ability to detoxify chemical agents, such as nitrites, that are known to cause cancer.

Vitamin C, vitamin E, and the trace mineral selenium are the body's natural antioxidants. These are the nutrients that protect the body's cells against the harmful effects of peroxidation. They all have the common denominator of improving the immune system in general and improving resistance to cancer specifically.

Using all three of these antioxidants together, biochemist Richard Passwater reported reducing chemically-caused cancer in mice to about 10 percent of the expected level. He noted that mice given supplements thrived and lived longer than mice not given supplements. "The antioxidants slowed the aging process as a secondary factor and prevented cancer as a primary factor," he wrote.[14]

Dr. Gerhard Schrauzer of the University of California at San Diego conducted a study with female mice susceptible to breast cancer. Schrauzer reduced the incidence of cancer from 82 percent to 10 percent merely by adding minute amounts of selenium to the animals' drinking water.[15]

Supplemental zinc has also been shown to be effective. Mice were injected with cancer cells and 60 percent of them remained clear of expected tumors when they received a daily zinc supplement within two days of the injection. The zinc was believed to stimulate cellular defense mechanisms.[16] The combination of a low zinc diet and a tumor-causing chemical produced malignancies in 79 percent of rats in another experiment. If the diet was adequate in zinc, only 29 percent developed tumors.[17]

Vitamin Therapy

The customary treatment for pet tumors is surgical removal. If the tumor is malignant, chemotherapy is also used. In my prac-

tice, I have either removed the tumor myself or recommended the client bring the animal to a specialist.

Where tumors are involved, I am reluctant to suggest vitamin and mineral therapy to clients. Often, a pet owner allows a tumor to develop to the point where any course of action other than immediate removal may be dangerous to the animal. People have brought in dogs with massive and pussy tumors. Sometimes the tumor has been hidden under a thick matting of fur and not noticed. Sometimes it is just plain negligence. An owner will shrug his shoulders and mumble something about the lump not growing in size. Meanwhile, I am staring at a grapefruit-sized tumor.

Whether large or small, benign or malignant, external or internal, a tumor is a frightening matter and people understandably want their pet free of it as soon as possible. Once a tumor is removed I will encourage a client to put the animal on a vitamin and mineral program for future protection or at least on extra vitamin C to help the healing process.

I have read letters-to-the-editor in popular nutrition magazines describing successful home treatment of pet tumors with vitamins and minerals. This doesn't surprise me. However any such attempt should be conducted under the guidance or at least with the knowledge of a trained veterinarian who can monitor progress.

I am aware of few veterinarians who have used vitamins and minerals to treat tumors. One is Dr. H. H. Robertson, of Higgenville, Missouri. As a rural veterinarian with a mixed practice, he has found vitamin C useful in treating both large and small animals. Robertson uses a combination of C along with E to cure many canine tumors. His method is injecting intravenously one gram of sodium ascorbate per pound of body weight daily along with an intramuscular injection of 400 IUs of vitamin E. This treatment continues for five days. Afterward, the animal is sent home with a supply of vitamin C and instructions for continued daily administration of the vitamin. An average tumor takes about three weeks to resolve, Robertson has told me.

In Ireland twenty years ago, Dr. N. H. Lambert reported using smaller amounts of vitamin E alone and found this rendered tumors more operable or even made surgery unnecessary.

In a summary of twelve cases of canine tumors, Lambert said he used up to 200 IUs of vitamin E daily. He made the following observations:

— Tumors considered inoperable due to their inaccessible position and diffuse nature often responded to such an extent that they were soon operable, and after removal healing took place with great rapidity.

— Internal tumors reacted favorably. Even though complete regression may not occur, it appears that in some cases no further growth takes place.

— The life-span of otherwise doomed animals has been prolonged for as long as five years.

— After surgery, animals showed a very marked improvement in general health and well-being, appetite, and in luster of coat.[18]

My own therapeutic experience with vitamins and tumors in small animals is essentially limited to cats. The experience is so promising however that I would like to briefly mention it here since there are many readers who own both dogs and cats.

Feline leukemia is the most common form of cancer affecting cats. The disease is viral in nature and isolation of the responsible virus in recent years has set off a major research effort to develop a workable vaccine. Meanwhile, many cats are succumbing to this dreaded disease and many others are being euthanized to prevent carriers from infecting others.

For the past few years, I have worked closely with two California catteries. The objective was to prevent or eliminate feline leukemia.

When the first cattery opened I was invited to apply my vitamin C concept to the leukemia problem. One female adult had been purchased for breeding purposes. Three blood smears submitted to the lab revealed the cat to be a carrier. The animal was then placed on the vitamin program. Ten weeks later three more blood smears were submitted and this time the results were negative. This brought a phone call from the laboratory pathologist.

"This animal was positive two months ago and now it's negative," he said. "What are you doing?"

There were five such cases in the past three years at this cattery. The entire cattery is on vitamin C and, at the time of this writing, we are in the third generation of offspring without a single appearance of leukemia.

At the second cattery there was a serious problem with leukemia when I was consulted. The situation was so bad that a local veterinary school had recommended a cessation of breeding to prevent a spread of the disease. Over a two-year period, six adult cats had consistently showed positive for leukemia in semiannual testing. The entire cattery was placed on vitamin C, and when retested six months later, all felines were negative. The owner of the cattery has told me that feline leukemia is no longer a problem.

Medical research into the use of interferon in viral-caused cancer has been intensifying in recent years. Interferon is the protein substance produced by cells when challenged by viruses. Vitamin C has been found to increase the interferon production in animals and it may be precisely this increased output that is the healing factor at work with the cats. The C is also protecting the animals against high levels of toxic metals present in the food.

Stronger immune systems. Increased interferon. Better quality collagen. More effective detoxification of cancer-causing chemicals. More tumor protection for your animals. These are the results of a solid vitamin and mineral maintenance program.

Viral Disease

The name of the game is prevention. Dogs on supplements don't come down with viral diseases like distemper, hepatitis, or kennel cough. Animals built up to optimal health do not suffer from chronic subclinical scurvy, the subtle vitamin C deficiency that is a standing invitation for germs and viruses. Animals built up to optimal health will produce good antibodies in reaction to immunization shots. They will not, as unhealthy animals often do, come down with the symptoms of the very disease they have been immunized against.

In my approach to canine medicine, I use two weapons to fight viral disease. One is standard: immunization. The other is not so standard: supplementation.

I feel the immunization strategy alone doesn't cover the flanks. These are the weaknesses:

1. Immunizations are available for only a limited number of viral conditions, namely distemper, hepatitis, rabies, and kennel cough. There are no vaccines for the odd viral diseases and flus that come and go every year.

2. Antibody levels diminish with time. That's why annual booster shots are recommended. But owners forget to revaccinate.

3. A vaccine may not produce adequate antibodies at the time of inoculation if the animal is weak, stressed, or unhealthy. Vaccination is no guarantee of good immunity. If the body is not up to par then the antibody production will be low and the animal won't be protected adequately. A typical example is the Australian shepherd I mentioned in Chapter 9. The dog was fighting a mange infestation and was immunized for distemper. No immu-

nity was built up because of the animal's stressed condition. Six months later, the dog was ill with distemper.

The vitamin and mineral program will boost your dog's immune system and protect him from the failings of immunization. Why be satisfied with partial protection? Why protect your dog from only a few viruses and not all of them?

Viral disease in a dog can be an extremely serious matter. I don't recommend forcing vitamins down an animal's throat once you start seeing symptoms. *See a veterinarian immediately.* Ask your veterinarian about supplementing along with the prescribed medication. He should not be opposed to this. Vitamins and minerals do not impair drugs but in fact increase their effectiveness and at the same time build up the animal's natural defenses. Another reason for supplementation is that drugs can cause biochemical imbalances and nutrient irregularities, and the supplements will protect the animal against this possibility.

Keep one thing in mind. If your animal does come down with a viral disease, there is no drug in your veterinarian's arsenal that will control the virus. The most commonly prescribed medications are antibiotics and steroids. The antibiotic will affect only the bacteria that usually accompany a viral infection. A steroid will treat inflammation. Neither one lays a finger on the viruses. If the disease involves a serious strain of virus like distemper or hepatitis, the dog can die. If the strain is minor, like a mild human flu, then the illness will just have to run its course.

There is one way to stop the virus cold. It is so simple that the medical establishment scoffs at it.

Since about 1965 and, by now, in hundreds of cases, I have found that the intravenous use of vitamin C (sodium ascorbate) is highly effective in treating viral diseases. Any viral disease. It is dependable and absolutely nontoxic. I don't know of any other substance that has the same ability. I have not seen a single viral disease in all these years that did not respond to vitamin C treatment.

The successful therapy depends on using it in sufficiently large doses. Much, much higher than the routine levels I recommend for prevention. Generally I will use a half gram of sodium ascorbate intravenously per pound of body weight twice a day. This is the key: big enough doses. Vitamin C is not a drug but if it is

administered in large enough doses it acts pharmacologically
and deactivates the viral disease process. If any doctor or veterinarian tells you it doesn't work, this is simply due to the fact that
he or she either has never used vitamin C or never used large
enough doses.

Dr. Fred Klenner, the senior medical practitioner of vitamin C
therapy in the world and author of numerous scientific articles
on vitamin C's virucidal potency, calls it "more effective than
any drug in the pharmacopeia." His work years ago with humans
inspired me to try the vitamin C approach on small animals.
Klenner emphasized that the key to success lay in using large
enough doses. Other medical men had reported inconclusive results with small doses.

For an adult, Klenner's vitamin C payload against viral infections ranged from 4.5 to 17.5 grams every two to four hours
around the clock. A total of 27 to 210 grams per day! Compare
this to the NRC's recommended daily allowance for humans of
45 milligrams. Acute viral infection can be a matter of life and
death. Klenner discovered it calls for saturation of the tissues
with vitamin C, and he used doses well beyond the limits of
therapies tried before. With this kind of "heavy firing," Klenner
has cured hepatitis (within a week), viral pneumonia, polio,
herpes simplex, measles, chicken pox, mononucleosis, influenza,
and other viral conditions. He reported success after success in
an age before the powerful vaccines had arrived on the medical
scene. And vaccines, keep in mind, can deal with only one type
of virus. Vitamin C deals with them all.

In summing up his rather remarkable results in a southern
medical journal in 1949, Klenner made some remarks that are ap-
plicable today—more than thirty years later—when the virtues of
vitamin C are still being debated:

> No one would expect to relieve kidney colic with a five-
> grain aspirin tablet. By the same logic we cannot hope to
> destroy the virus organism with doses of vitamin C of ten to
> four hundred milligrams. The results which we have re-
> ported using vitamin C may seem fantastic. These results,
> however, are no different from the results we see when ad-
> ministering the sulfa, or the mold-derived drugs against

many other kinds of infections. In these latter instances, we expect and usually get forty-eight to seventy-two hour cures. It is laying no claim to miracle-working then when we say that many virus infections can be cleared within a similar time limit.[1]

Klenner applied his therapeutic touch now and then to ailing animals, curing a number of dogs suffering from distemper.

The dosage factor alone, he said, has misled many veterinarians to disregard the value of ascorbic acid in dealing with viral disease, because as they would see dogs dying with distemper they knew that the dog could make his own vitamin C. "What they did not appreciate was that even the animal could not make enough vitamin C under certain conditions."[2]

Over the years a scattering of doctors have used Klenner's big doses with success, but the medical profession as a body has not followed his promising example. The reasons are rooted in the drug, surgery, and crisis orientation of modern medicine and a parallel disregard for nutritional and preventive medicine.

A sweeping Japanese study, published in 1975, was one of the more recent scientific projects providing firm support to the claims that large doses of vitamin C are effective in both the prevention and treatment of viral disease. Dr. Akira Murata, a microbiologist, studied the effect of vitamin C for seven years on a wide variety of bacterial viruses—viruses that attach themselves to bacteria inside the body. He found they were all inactivated by the vitamin. Working along similar lines at the Fukoka Torikai Hospital, Dr. Fukumi Morishige, head of the hospital's surgical service, found vitamin C therapy effective in treating patients with infectious and serum hepatitis, measles, mumps, viral pneumonia, herpes zoster (shingles), herpes facialis, encephalitis, and certain types of meningitis.[3]

As do Klenner, Linus Pauling, and other vitamin C advocates, I believe that any virus is incapacitated within a few minutes after the intravenous administration of a sufficiently large dose of the vitamin. Let me give you an example. Distemper is a highly contagious and deadly virus to dogs. I have placed unvaccinated dogs in prolonged close contact with other dogs ill with distemper, but first I gave the diseased animals an initial injection of sodium ascorbate. Never have any of the unvaccinated dogs acquired the disease. That's how quick-acting and powerful is vitamin C!

Vitamin C *vs.* the Virus—How It Works

First, let's look at a virus, the little organism that packs a big punch. It is smaller than a bacterium, smaller than a cell, and to see one you need an electron microscope. Scientists have measured different viruses and say they range in diameter from the 1/1,250,000 inch polio virus up to the 1/100,000 inch pox virus. More than two hundred different viruses capable of inflicting acute illness in man and beast have been identified.

A virus is basically a speck or filament of nucleic acid, the chemical essence of all living cells, surrounded by protein and fatty matter with an outer coat of protective protein. Viruses have outer spikes or tails used for attaching purposes. This is what they use to grab onto bacteria or animal cells. Once attached, the nucleic acid is injected into the host organism and carries out its apparently sole function: reproduction. Scientists have observed how one single virus can invade a cell and in twenty-five minutes reproduce a new generation of two hundred viruses. The host cell is destroyed. The new viruses either burst out explosively or file out in a more orderly fashion. Whatever their style, they leave with one thing only in mind and that is to plunder new cells and repeat the cycle. In this way, tissue and eventually normal bodily functions can be overwhelmed and destroyed.

Viruses are carried in the air, passed on from animal to animal, or person to animal, or vice versa, or picked up from contaminated objects.

Guarding against this harmful process is the body's police force, the immune system. The major elements in the system are interferon, leukocytes, and antibodies. Studies have shown that vitamin C is essential to all of them. These components, when functioning at maximum capacity, will prevent the multiplication of disease-causing viruses and bacteria. Conversely, when they are not functioning well, when the immune system is weakened by stress, by chronic subclinical scurvy, and by poor nutrition, the cellular community becomes more vulnerable to attack. The police force is depleted.

Interferon, discovered in 1957 and recently making big headlines, is a hormonelike protein substance produced by the cells any time they are threatened by viruses. In 1970, Linus Pauling hypothesized that vitamin C is "involved in the synthesis and activity of interferon in preventing the entry of virus particles into the cells."[4] A few years later, experiments conducted by Dr. Benjamin V. Siegal at the University of Oregon confirmed the expectations of Pauling. Siegal fed large doses of vitamin C to a group of mice for several months. Keep in mind that mice produce their own vitamin C, as do most animals, and are in fact considerably more efficient producers than dogs. Siegal then infected the mice with a virus that causes leukemia. He similarly infected another group of mice that did not receive the extra provisions of vitamin C. They had to rely on their own natural production. Blood tests revealed twice as much interferon and less cellular damage from leukemia in supplement-fed mice than in the control group.[5]

Interferon has been found to be effective not only against the virus that provokes its production, but against other unrelated viruses as well. Antibodies are effective only against a single organism and are called up into this biochemical warfare much later than interferon. Thus interferon seems to be the first line of defense.

Why don't we and our animals all take interferon then instead of vitamin C or drugs whenever we are ill from virus? Interferon is just too expensive. It is so complicated to prepare with present technology that a pound of it would cost between $10 and $20 billion to produce, *Time* magazine reported in a cover story in March 1980. In a 1972 experiment, British researchers gave sixteen volunteers a nasal spray of interferon one day before and three days after exposure to common cold viruses. Another sixteen were exposed to cold germs but received no interferon. "The result seems miraculous," *Time* reported. "None of the sixteen sprayed subjects developed cold symptoms, but thirteen of the unsprayed did." The only catch: Interferon for each individual spray cost $700.[6]

A scramble among the big drug companies to produce cheap

interferon promises affordability in the future. In the meantime, vitamin C is a comparative bargain.

Viruses have the unwelcome habit of stirring up dormant bacteria and thus causing secondary infections. Wherever you find a viral infection you usually find a bacterial infection as well. Here is where another line of immune system defenders rush into action. Leukocytes and macrophages are white blood cells that have the ability to engulf and destroy encroaching bacteria. A combined term for these cells is phagocytes, from the Greek word *phagein*, to eat. The phagocytes contain particularly high concentrations of vitamin C and whenever they swarm into a battle zone of infected tissue, they take on extra vitamin C molecules just as battle-bound soldiers load up with ammunition.

The antibodies are chemical substances secreted by specialized cells in the lymph glands in reaction to the presence of microorganisms in the body. For the first few months of life, the newborn baby or pup is protected by antibodies transferred from the mother across the placenta before birth. Afterwards, the infant has to produce its own antibodies. Immunizations put a mild form of the disease into the young animal and, if it is healthy, the specialized cells will secrete the antibodies to combat the particular invader. Then, if the animal is exposed to the same disease later on, the specific antibodies will be present in the system and mobilized into action. It is strictly a one-on-one situation. Antibody A doesn't take on Disease B, only Disease A.

Antibodies are somewhat like reserve soldiers. It takes time for them to reach the front lines. Antibodies in force take up to six days to join battle after a foreign substance asserts its presence in the body. During this time, the specialized cells are literally gearing up for battle. They multiply, then produce and release the antibodies.

The foregoing has been an attempt at simplifying what is an extremely complex and not thoroughly understood system. One thing is clear: an animal that is minimally nourished, that is fighting off the effects of dietary toxins and harmful metals like lead, is not likely to put up as stout a defense as a supplement-fed animal.

The immune system, like any system in the body, depends on an ample supply of all nutrients. The whole team. Zinc has been found to play an important role in some white blood cells' ability to combat viruses and fungi. Any shortages in the B complex vitamins, particularly pantothenic acid and B_6, inhibits the performance of the immune system and prevents the production of good antibodies after immunization.

In the aging process, there is a slowing down of the immune response. This is partly due to peroxidation and free radical activity that impair the function of cells involved in "defense work." Vitamin E, as well as vitamin C and the trace mineral selenium, are the main agents that combat this destructive process.

Protect your animal's immune system with regular immunizations and supplements. If you follow this simple advice you shouldn't ever have to worry about the following canine viral problems.

Distemper

Symptoms: **High temperature, coughing, pussy discharge from eyes and nose, lack of appetite, vomiting, diarrhea, slimy foul-smelling stool. There is often a hardening of the foot pads. If treatment is delayed or not given, infection spreads to the nervous system, causing involuntary twitching of muscles, often in the temporal muscles of the head and in the limbs. There can be a posterior paralysis or convulsive seizures. If the disease reaches the nervous system, the animal will probably die.**

A four-month-old, 25-pound Doberman pinscher was brought into my office. The animal had not been immunized against distemper and just the week before had been impounded in the local humane society facility. There, in all probability, the animal had picked up a distemper infection.

The temperature was 104 degrees with the typical pussy discharge from the eyes and nose. The dog had bronchitis, was coughing, had no interest in food, was listless, and had a hardening of the pads, another typical symptom of distemper.

I administered intravenously 12.5 grams of sodium ascorbate

at 10 A.M. In a half hour the temperature dropped to 102.5 and continued steady at this level. A second injection was given at 5 P.M. The following morning there was a great improvement, a normal ration of food was eaten, general activity was noticeably improved, the discharges diminished slightly, and temperature was now at 101.5. The two injections were repeated leading to marked improvement on the third day. Temperature was hovering at 101.5, the bronchitis and coughing appeared lessened by half, the digital pads were not quite as hard as on admittance, and only a very slight trace of discharge remained from the eyes and nose. The patient was lively and barking, the appetite was good.

The fourth day saw the temperature drop to 101.3 with no facial discharge. The pads were almost normal. The appetite was excellent and the dog extremely active. The sodium ascorbate treatment was given twice again that day.

On the fifth day, the dog was released and thereafter kept on one teaspoonful (four grams) of sodium ascorbate a day, added to its food. One month later, I had the dog returned for a distemper immunization and upon examination, it was found normal in all respects.

Several years ago, a lady brought in a ten-month-old Irish setter named for Marshal Matt Dillon of TV's "Gunsmoke." Dillon, the dog, had been diagnosed by another veterinarian as having a hopeless case of distemper. The vet recommended the dog be destroyed.

The case was presented to me just before a Labor Day holiday when I had planned to take my family up to the mountains. I told the woman I wouldn't be able to handle the case because the vitamin C therapy took five days and I had a commitment to be away over the holiday.

She pleaded with me to take on Dillon and finally wore me down. I said I would treat the dog and cancel my plans. Not only did I encounter some heavy flak at home, which was to be expected, but Dillon himself proved to be a resistant and ungrateful patient. As I proceeded with the routine vitamin C therapy of a half-gram of sodium ascorbate per pound of body weight twice a day, Dillon, sick as he was, fought me off whenever I approached with the needle. Because of the holiday week-end, I was working alone and had to practically sit on the dog before I could get the needle in a vein. Most dogs are very weak and docile in this condition. But not Dillon. He was as tough as his namesake.

Twice a day I fought that big dog, and Dillon came to hate my guts. But after five days, I was able to break the persistent high temperature and bring it down to the 101 range and normal.

The vitamin C therapy calls for uninterrupted treatment. Two injections a day for about five days. Treatment broken off in the middle permits the virus to take the offensive again.

If ever I saw a dog glad to see its owner, it was Dillon. And if ever I saw a dog not so glad to see a veterinarian, it was Dillon. There were occasions for him to come back for vaccinations and checkups. The first time he returned, he saw me and dashed to the corner of the waiting room and cringed, as if to say, "no, not again." Dillon is about six now and doing well. We have him on a good prevention program which has kept him healthy over the years, but I haven't ever really been able to make a pal out of that dog.

Over the past fifteen years I have successfully treated about two hundred cases of distemper with vitamin C. The frequency of cases has dwindled in recent years because more owners are aware of immunizations. While important gains have been made in immunization against canine distemper, the practitioner is still confronted often enough with the problem of what to do with the dog that is already sick with distemper. The fate of an unattended dog is a horrible death, and euthanasia just doesn't carry the professional dignity it did a generation ago. Thus, the vitamin C treatment offers the veterinarian a useful tool and the dog owner a source of hope.

In 1967 I published a paper reporting on the first twelve successful cases I treated with vitamin C. Two years later, Dr. Joseph Leveque, a Las Vegas veterinarian, confirmed the effectiveness of this therapy with a follow-up paper in the same veterinarian journal. Dr. Leveque, who is a regular user of vitamin C, summed up the results of sixty-seven cases of distemper with the remark that "the recovery rate can be markedly improved by including ascorbic acid in the treatment regimen."[7]

As a note of interest, a Las Vegas neurologist became interested in Dr. Leveque's work with vitamin C and began applying it to some of his own patients with favorable results. The neurologist has used it successfully several times in treating patients with viral encephalitis, a condition similar to distemper in dogs.

The distemper virus is a powerful and highly contagious microorganism commonly picked up by dogs from such things as feeding and drinking utensils, grooming brushes, excreta from infected animals, and contaminated particles in the air. So contagious is the virus that many veterinarians will not even allow a sick dog into the hospital. The vet will go out to the car and examine the animal there.

The virus will cause lung congestion in almost every case, as well as damage to the digestive and urinary tract. Sometimes the skin may be involved, usually on the underside of the body.

As a dog owner, the first signs you notice are when the dog stops eating and seems listless. The animal may or may not have diarrhea. You can allow this to continue for about three days because many an animal will become lethargic for different reasons. I strongly recommend that every dog owner acquire a rectal thermometer. In cases like this, the temperature should be checked. Normal for a dog is between 101 and 102. If there is any elevation, such as 102.5 or more, then you know something is wrong. Bring the animal to the vet immediately. If you have no thermometer and the dog goes three days and is still listless, not eating, and developing a cough or diarrhea, by all means take him to the vet.

Keep in mind that your dog can still contract distemper even though he was immunized. Don't delay beyond three days. Distemper is a very startling disease. It hits an animal hard. It can kill in two weeks if the infected animal is weak.

If allowed to progress unchecked, the virus will attack the nervous system and move up into the brain. Whenever I see the animal twitching, in the temporal muscles or the muscles of the legs, then I know the virus has reached the nervous system. Even if I can defeat the distemper infection, the nerves have been permanently damaged. The jerking motions will remain. I have treated some animals in this stage of the disease and afterward they were left with the twitching. They twitch in the waking state and in the sleeping state. Sometimes when they are asleep and twitching they will utter little whimpers, as if in some kind of pain. It is a very exhausting thing for an animal and rather pathetic to see. Most dog owners will despair and ask that the dog be put to sleep.

It is extremely important to bring the dog in as early as possible. Don't wait for the animal to become dehydrated and weakened from days of diarrhea. Don't wait for the virus to strike the nervous system. Bring the animal in early. This is when the animal has the best chance to survive.

It is important to allow an animal a good several months of recuperation after a serious viral illness like distemper. It will take that long for the dog to regain full health. The tissues have been severely devitalized. I have to caution people now and then about not subjecting their dog to the usual amount of work, play, or activity too soon after discharge. Like a human who has been seriously ill, the dog too needs to rest and regain strength. Taxing it unduly can invite problems.

One month after discharge I recommend that the animal be vaccinated.

Obviously, a good vitamin and mineral program will help speed up the recovery process.

Influenza

Symptoms: **The same as for humans, including vomiting, diarrhea, elevated temperatures, apathy, lack of appetite.**

There are no immunizations for influenza because there are just too many different types of viruses around. One year the Asian variety makes the rounds, the next year the London type, or the Russian type, etc.

For this reason it is vital for your dog to have a strong immune system to fight off the perennial viral challenge. A good prevention program, with plenty of vitamin C, will keep the interferon and white blood cells strong and able to deal with the passing parade of microorganisms.

Many times the influenza is picked up in the owner's household. Whenever there is an outbreak of human virus I invariably see dogs brought in suffering from the same symptoms. I will ask the client about any incidence of flu in the house and whether the dog has been around any sick persons. Usually, the answer is yes, my daughter or son or husband has had the flu and the animal had contact with that person or had contact with food that was partially eaten by that person.

Typical was a case in the winter of 1973 during the "London flu" epidemic. A client brought in a two-year-old poodle. The woman had taken the dog to an emergency clinic during our absence on holiday and was told that a heart murmur had been detected. The disease symptoms included violent vomiting, listlessness, lack of appetite, and a 103-degree temperature. The clinic had administered phenobarbital to stop the vomiting and referred the animal to me for further treatment the following Monday. When the dog was presented to me for examination, the vomiting had stopped. Temperature was 102.5. There was no appetite. The dog was apathetic and had a slight ventricular murmur.

I asked the woman if anyone in the house had the flu. She said that the entire family had had it for the last week. This bit of information helped me to make a diagnosis of "London flu." Among humans, this particular virus can adversely affect the cardiac muscle and cause a murmur. It had done just that in the poodle.

I had the dog for one work day and gave it two intravenous treatments of a half gram of sodium ascorbate per pound of body weight. The client refused further hospitalization, so I gave her some vitamin C powder and told her to give the dog one teaspoon (four grams) the following morning. The next afternoon, the dog was returned. The temperature was 101.5. The animal was eating subnormally but had become somewhat more active. I gave it another injection of vitamin C. On the third day, the client called in and said the dog was back to normal. The following week we monitored the heart and found it normal—no murmur.

Using this same kind of treatment, which is considerably less intense than the therapy for distemper, I have had good results in about three hundred influenza cases.

The thing to remember is that the dog can catch your flu. If you or anybody else in the family is ill, try to keep the dog at a distance. Smart prevention should include keeping the animal away from sick individuals and not letting the dog eat any leftovers from an ill person's plate.

Dogs can also pick up influenza viruses from other dogs. This is where the protection of a supplementation program is felt. Several years ago one of my clients was participating in field trials with his German short-haired pointers. A rash of influenza broke out during the contest, as sometimes happens when many dogs are brought together. All of his four dogs were on vitamins and minerals and not one of them came down sick.

I have seen supplement-fed trial and show dogs demonstrate this kind of resistance over and over. These dogs are being given the best protection and best chance for maximum performance through supplementation.

Kennel Cough (Contagious Canine Respiratory Disease)

Symptom: **A persistent hacking cough. Extremely contagious. Can lead to bronchial pneumonia if not treated.**

Kennel cough is like those TV detective shows. If you've seen one you have seen them all. The kennel cough script goes like this:

Mr. and Mrs. Smith are going off on vacation for two weeks and leave their pet dog at a local kennel. When they return the dog has a cough. Nothing else, just a cough with a slight gagging sound afterward. Perhaps a bit of white mucus will come out. The dog is eating and otherwise acting normal. The cough doesn't seem to bother the dog much. But it bothers the hell out of the owners. So the owner calls the veterinarian.

"I think my dog has something caught in his throat," the owner says. "He's got this hacking cough."

"Is the dog pawing at it?" the vet asks.

"No."

"Has the dog recently been boarded at a kennel?"

"Yes."

"Does the cough sound like this?" and the vet renders an impression of the kennel cough he's been hearing for years.

"Yes, that's it," the owner says.

"OK, bring the dog in right away."

Kennel cough is the creation of a highly contagious virus that seems to thrive wherever dogs accumulate. A high percentage of dogs in kennels, grooming parlors, pet shops, animal shelters, dog shows and trials, spay clinics, and veterinary hospitals become infected. Seldom is the isolated household pet affected. The virus is believed to be most commonly picked up from contaminated feeding or water bowls or contact with any other kind of contaminated object. A dog can brush against a virus-laden surface and later lick his hair coat and thus pick up the disease.

Kennel cough strikes fast. Leave a dog in a grooming parlor for an hour, or overnight in a kennel, and when you pick him up he is coughing. Many a store-bought puppy has kennel cough.

I have heard of cases of dogs becoming ill with kennel cough and dying from complications. The condition was not treated. In two weeks or so, the animal was becoming progressively poorer and the infection migrated deep down into the lung tissue, causing pneumonia and death.

The cough, the pneumonia, can be prevented in two simple ways.

The first is immunization. Good, ever-improving vaccines are readily available through a veterinarian.

The second way is through regular supplementation. When the time comes to board a dog, leave the supplements and instructions on how much to administer with the kennel operators.

You may ask, well, why do I need the supplements if the dog is immunized? I have already explained why but the reasons are well worth repeating.

Immunization is no guarantee of protection. One Florida veterinarian, writing about the prevalence of kennel cough in his area, says that this disease is the most common infectious condition of dogs in south Florida "despite widespread vaccination."[8]

An animal may be stressed or unwell at the time it is immunized and if this is the case it is not likely to develop good antibodies. Moreover, the potency of the immunization may have waned. If you are planning to board your dog any time in the future, it is a good idea to ensure that the vaccine is still potent. Reimmunize if you are in doubt.

Many people have a mistaken idea altogether about immunization in relation to kennel cough. There have been many occasions when people would rush into my office a day or two before kenneling their animal and want a vaccination. They believe the dog will have instant protection. This is not the case. It will take a minimum of ten days to build adequate immunity against kennel cough. Furthermore, a strange new surrounding like a kennel can be very stressful to a dog. If he has just been immunized and is immediately stressed, chances are he will not develop immunity. The vaccination should be given weeks in advance.

Dr. Hans Kugler, an expert on nutrition and aging who lives in Southern California, told me of an experience he had with kennel cough. He acquired two dogs, a dachshund and a shepherd, from the local pound. Both of them had bad kennel cough.

Tapping his household supply of vitamins and minerals, Kugler began administering vitamin C, selenium, and a thymus gland concentrate to the dogs. The thymus gland is one of the organs in the body that activates the immune system.

The vitamin C doses were given orally, starting at 200 milligrams per pound of body weight and increased gradually to a maximum of 500 milligrams per pound. Kugler reported that within ten days the kennel cough was gone.

I don't expect you to start playing doctor in this manner. What you can do is provide your animal with supplements as an adjunct to your veterinarian's treatment.

But remember: *Once you hear the cough, see the vet.*

My treatment includes a half-gram of sodium ascorbate per pound of body weight twice a day. Often, a single injection, along with a steroid drug to stop the coughing and an antibiotic for the bacteria, will clear up the condition. If the disease is advanced then it can draw out to several injections. A supportive vitamin and mineral program greatly helps the recovery process.

Backyard or household dogs will sometimes come down with a similar cough even though they haven't been around other animals. This is usually an acute bronchitis brought on by cold weather or the sudden drops in temperature that we frequently have in California. Come October or November, I will see a dozen dogs a week with this bronchitis condition. The history of the cough is different but the symptoms and treatment are the same as kennel cough.

Canine Viral Hepatitis

Symptoms: Fever, lack of appetite, vomiting, intense thirst, abdominal tenderness.

This is an acute viral infection with an affinity for puppies, affecting the liver and inner lining of blood vessels. It has often been confused with distemper because some of the symptoms are similar. However, hepatitis does not as a rule have the discharges from eyes and nose as does distemper. There is usually no coughing.

Very effective vaccinations have been developed and are readily available. Vitamins and minerals will bolster the immune system further and guarantee production of necessary antibodies.

I haven't seen a hepatitis case in years.

Parvovirus

Symptoms: Lack of appetite. Severe and protracted vomiting. Diarrhea, often becoming bloody. Rapid dehydration, especially in pups. A high temperature is common. Dogs of all ages are affected. Mortality is highest among young puppies.

The headline in the August 7 San Jose *Mercury* was typical of press reports that began appearing around the country during 1980.

"Contagious Virus That Can Kill Dogs Spreads to County," the headline read.

Parvovirus had arrived in town.

Some puppies at the Santa Clara Valley animal shelter were said to have died from the virus and there were epidemics reported among canine populations in Seattle, Salt Lake City, and Portland, Oregon.

In November, *Time* magazine was saying that parvovirus had killed two thousand dogs in Britain and an estimated fifteen hundred in the Minneapolis–St. Paul area in the previous three months.

Parvovirus seems to be a new, highly contagious disease in dogs caused by a tiny virus strain with a reputation for afflicting rodents, swine, cattle, and cats. Scientists think maybe a mutation of the cat virus is responsible for the disease among dogs. Whatever the origin, the parvovirus is known to spread through the feces of infected canines or through dog-to-dog contact. A larger danger obviously exists where there is a brisk traffic and mix of animals, such as at kennels, pounds, and veterinary hospitals.

According to the Cornell Research Laboratory for Diseases of Dogs, which first identified the parvovirus in 1978, the chronology of the disease is as follows:

First there is a cessation of appetite and a depressed behavior for twelve to twenty-four hours before other signs appear. Vomiting, usually severe and extended, is the next typical symptom, followed by diarrhea which often becomes bloody. High fever is common and may exceed 105 degrees in pups.

The virus also can attack the heart and often does with staggering swiftness and severity in pups twelve weeks and younger. When the virus attacks the myocardium (heart muscle), there is so much damage to the muscle that the heart just cannot pump enough blood and the pup dies of heart failure. Pups thus stricken are most often simply found dead. Survivors may have significant scarring. As these animals grow, the damaged hearts cannot meet the increased demands, and the puppies may die weeks or months later.

At the time of this writing, Cornell was developing a vaccine promising to offer long-lasting protection. The vaccine that has been available—but in very short supply because of the heavy demand—utilizes the cat virus, and the duration of immunity following vaccination is questionable.

When parvovirus reached the San Jose area, I began getting calls from worried dog owners who had heard the worst.

"Do you have the vaccine?" people wanted to know.

"No, none is available," we'd tell them.

"What can we do?" they desperately asked.

If the caller was one of our clients we would ask if their animal was getting vitamin C every day. Usually they said yes. If not, then we strongly urged them to start.

"Keep the dog on vitamin C and this will keep the immune system strong and hopefully prevent parvovirus," we would tell them.

I have not heard of a single case of parvovirus among dogs receiving either vitamin C alone or vitamin C along with a general vitamin-mineral program. These are dogs who for the most part did not receive any vaccine.

In treatment, I found vitamin C, in even heavier doses than I use for other viral conditions, to be effective in the dozen or so cases I saw during the latter half of 1980.

This is significant considering the swiftness of the disease. One day we received three calls in the morning from dog owners whose animals were showing the symptoms of severe vomiting and profuse bloody diarrhea. These were young dogs and it doesn't take long for small puppies to dehydrate and go downhill fast. Before they could bring their dogs to the hospital in the afternoon, these three individuals phoned to say the dogs had died.

Normally for virus conditions I would use a half-gram of sodium ascorbate intravenously per pound of body weight. And this is what I used on Kazan, a year-old spitz, who was the first parvovirus case brought in.

After a few days I didn't seem to be making satisfactory headway so I decided to step up the dosage to two grams per pound. And this worked very well. It worked so well that I continued this dosage with all the other cases, also administering medication and fluids to offset the symptoms of vomiting, diarrhea, and dehydration.

The vitamin C controls the virus in about forty-eight hours. The animal starts to show signs of recovery. The vomiting subsides. There is still some diarrhea but it is no longer bloody.

Reference Notes

Chapter 2

1. Dr. Philip R. Lee of the University of California Medical School at San Francisco, as quoted in "The Medical School Where Nutrition Isn't a Dirty Word," *Prevention*, June 1977, p. 146.
2. Quoted in "Scientist Tells Senate of Critical Need for More Nutrition Training Programs," *DVM*, November–December 1978, p. 1.
3. Lyle A. Baker, "Veterinary Corner," *International Academy of Preventive Medicine Bulletin*, Winter 1980, p. 3.
4. Personal communication with Anne Rogers Clark.
5. Personal communication with Irving Eldredge.

Chapter 3

1. Francis Sheridan Goulart, "Bone Appetit-Rating Pet Foods," *Consumers Digest*, November–December 1979, p. 6.
2. Paul M. Newberne, "Problems and Opportunities in Pet Animal Nutrition," *Cornell Veterinarian*, April 1974, pp. 159–60.
3. Goulart, p. 6.
4. Patricia P. Scott, "Nutritional Implications in the Feeding of Pets," *Veterinary Record*, June 24, 1978, p. 543.
5. *Vitamin Assurance for Pet Foods*, Roche Animal Nutrition and Health Manual 102, Hoffmann-La Roche, Inc., Nutley, N.J.
6. Newberne, pp. 164–65.
7. *Dishing Up the Dog Food*, Department of Health, Education, and Welfare Publication No. FDA 73-2035, as excerpted in *Consumers Research Magazine*, August 1975, p. 18.
8. Goulart, p. 8.
9. "Packaged Dog Foods," *Consumer Reports*, July 1960, p. 354.
10. Newberne, pp. 165–66.
11. Phyllis Lehmann, "More Than You Ever Thought You Would Know About Food Additives," Part III, *FDA Consumer*, June 1979, p. 12.
12. Jacqueline Verrett and Jean Carper, *Eating May Be Hazardous*

During the next forty-eight hours we give the animal a mul-timineral tablet and a protein concentrate along with the vitamin C. This helps to strengthen the dog who up to now has not touched any food. Around the fourth day we find the appetite returning and the animal becoming livelier. In five days we have been able to send our cases home.

Both in prevention and treatment, vitamin C can play a big role in this most current and worrisome of canine viruses. But surely you'll agree that prevention is the best way to go.

to Your Health (Garden City, N.Y.: Anchor Press/Doubleday, 1975), p. 121.

13. Ruth Winter, *A Consumer's Dictionary of Food Additives* (New York: Crown, 1978), p. 124.

14. A. E. Sloan *et al.*, "Effect of Order of Mixing on AW Lowering Ability of Food Humectants," *Journal of Food Science*, Vol. 41 (1976), p. 536.

15. Newberne, p. 166.

16. Verrett and Carper, p. 53.

17. Lester Hankin *et al.*, "Lead Content of Pet Foods," *Bulletin of Environmental Contamination and Toxicology*, May 1975, pp. 630–32.

18. James G. Fox *et al.*, "Lead in Animal Foods," *Journal of Toxicology and Environmental Health*, January 1976, pp. 461–67.

19. James G. Fox *et al.*, "Analysis of Lead in Animal Feed Ingredients," *American Journal of Veterinary Research*, Vol. 39, No. 1 (January 1978), p. 167.

20. E.G.C. Clarke, "Lead Poisoning in Small Animals," *Journal of Small Animal Practice*, Vol. 14 (1973), pp. 183–93.

21. Warren C. Ladiges *et al.*, "Bacterial Pathogens in Dry Dog Foods," *Journal of the American Veterinary Medical Association*, July 15, 1974, p. 181.

22. Paul J. Pace *et al.*, "Salmonella in Commercially Produced Dried Dog Food," *Journal of Food Protection*, May 1977, p. 317.

23. "Pet Food Firm Hit on GMPs," *DVM*, August–September 1979, p. 13.

24. Alfred J. Plechner, "Food Mediated Disorders," *California Veterinarian*, June 1978.

Chapter 4

For general reading on Vitamin C and its medical applications, see Dr. Irwin Stone's book, *The Healing Factor: Vitamin C Against Disease* (New York: Grosset & Dunlap, 1972).

1. I. B. Chatterjee, "Evolution and the Biosynthesis of Ascorbic Acid," *Science*, December 21, 1973, p. 1272.

2. J. V. Lacroix *et al.*, "Ascorbic Acid Blood Levels in the Dog," *North American Veterinarian*, May 1942, p. 329.

3. *Ibid.*, p. 329.

4. Work of I. B. Chatterjee, cited in Dr. Carl C. Pfeiffer's *Zinc and Other Micro-nutrients* (New Canaan, Conn.: Keats Publishing, 1978), p. 180.

5. Irwin Stone, *The Healing Factor: Vitamin C Against Disease* (New York: Grosset & Dunlap, 1972), p. 155.

6. Pfeiffer, p. 180.

7. J. J. Doyle, "Effects of Low Levels of Dietary Cadmium in Animals," *Journal of Environmental Quality*, April–June 1977, pp. 111–15.

8. M. R. Spivey Fox *et al.*, "Cadmium Toxicity Decreased by Dietary Ascorbic Acid Supplements," *Science*, September 4, 1970, pp. 989–91.

9. Sidney S. Mirvish, "Blocking the Formation of N-Nitroso Compounds with Ascorbic Acid in Vitro and Vivo," presented at the Second Conference on Vitamin C, New York Academy of Sciences, October 9–12, 1974. Melvin Greenblatt, "Ascorbic Acid Blocking of Aminopyrine Nitrosation," *Journal of the National Cancer Institute*, April 1973, p. 1055. I. A. Wolff and A. E. Wasserman, "Nitrates, Nitrites and Nitrosamines," *Science*, July 7, 1972, p. 15.

10. Steven R. Tannenbaum, "Nitrate and Nitrite: Origin in Humans," *Science*, September 28, 1979.

11. W. J. McCormick, "Ascorbic Acid as a Chemotherapeutic Agent," *Archives of Pediatrics*, April 1952, p. 152.

12. I. B. Chatterjee, *op. cit.*, p. 1271. Natarajan Subramanian *et al.*, "Role of l-Ascorbic Acid on Detoxification of Histamine," *Biochemical Pharmacology*, Vol. 22, No. 13 (1973), p. 1671. Sherry Lewin, *Vitamin C: Its Molecular Biology and Medical Potential* (London: Academic Press, 1976), p. 84.

13. E. Cameron and L. Pauling, "Vitamin C and Cancer," *International Journal of Environmental Studies*, Vol. 10 (1977), p. 303.

14. W. M. Ringsdorf, Jr., and E. Cheraskin, "Vitamin C and the Metabolism of Analgesic, Antipyretic, and Anti-inflammatory Drugs," *Alabama Journal of Medical Sciences*, Vol. 16, No. 3 (1979), p. 218.

15. Ringsdorf and Cheraskin, p. 219.

16. Linus Pauling before the U. S. Senate Subcommittee on Health, quoted in *A Physician's Handbook on Orthomolecular Medicine*, Roger J. Williams and Dwight K. Kalita, editors (New York: Pergamon Press, 1977), p. 48.

17. *Ibid.*, p. 48.

18. Stone, pp. 142–45.

Chapter 5

1. *The Complete Book of Vitamins*, by the staff of *Prevention* magazine (Emmaus, Pa.: Rodale Press, 1977), p. 311.

2. Roger J. Williams, *Physicians' Handbook of Nutritional Science* (Springfield, Ill.: C. C. Thomas, 1975).

3. Erwin DiCyan, *Vitamins in Your Life and the Micronutrients* (New York: Fireside Books, 1974), p. 40.

4. Benjamin E. Cohen *et al.*, "Vitamin A–Induced Nonspecific Resistance to Infection," *Journal of Infectious Diseases*, May 1974, p. 597.

5. Satoshi Innami *et al.*, "Polychlorobiphenyl Toxicity and Nutrition," *Journal of Nutrition Science and Vitaminology*, Vol. 20 (1974), p. 363.

6. *Nutrient Requirements of Dogs*, National Research Council's Subcommittee on Dog Nutrition, National Academy of Sciences, Washington, D.C., 1974, pp. 17–18.

7. Fred Hale, "Pigs Born Without Eyeballs," *Journal of Heredity*, March 1933, p. 105.

8. Philip O'Neill, "The Effect on Subsequent Maze Learning Ability of Graded Amounts of Vitamin B_1 in the Diet of Very Young Rats," *The Journal of Genetic Psychology*, Vol. 74 (1949), pp. 85–95.

9. Tom D. Spies, "The Natural Occurrence of Riboflavin Deficiency in the Eyes of Dogs," *Science*, October 22, 1943, p. 369.

10. Roger J. Williams, *Nutrition Against Disease* (Bantam Edition; New York: Pitman, 1971), pp. 146–47. Richard B. Pelton and Roger J. Williams, "Effect of Pantothenic Acid on the Longevity of Mice," *Proceedings of the Society for Experimental Biology and Medicine*, December 1958, p. 632.

11. Adelle Davis, *Let's Get Well* (New York: Harcourt, 1965), p. 160.

12. I. Szorady, "Pantothenic Acid and Allergy," *Acta Paediatrica*, Budapest, Vol. 4 (1963), p. 73.

13. Personal communication from John M. Ellis.

14. Williams, *Nutrition Against Disease*, p. 62.

15. Paul M. Newberne and Vernon R. Young, "Marginal Vitamin B_{12} Intake During Gestation in the Rat Has Long Term Effects on the Offspring," *Nature*, March 23, 1973, pp. 263–64.

16. *Vitamin Assurance for Pet Foods, op. cit.*

17. Herbert Bailey, *Vitamin E—Your Key to a Healthy Heart* (New York: ARC Books, 1971), p. 35.

18. *Ibid.*, pp. 40–49.

19. N. H. Lambert, "Clinical Experiences with Vitamin E in Dogs and Cats," *Proceedings of the Third International Congress on Vitamin E*, September 1955, p. 610.

20. Mohammad G. Mustafa, "Influence of Dietary Vitamin E on

Lung Cellular Sensitivity to Ozone in Rats," *Nutrition Reports International*, June 1975, pp. 473–76.

21. Ching K. Chow *et al.*, "Influence of Dietary Vitamin E on the Red Cells of Ozone-exposed Rats," *Environmental Research*, Vol. 19 (1979), pp. 49–55.

22. Cheryl F. Nockels, "Protective Effects of Supplemental Vitamin E against Infection," *Federation Proceedings*, June 1979, p. 2134.

23. Ben E. Sheffy *et al.*, "Influence of Vitamin E and Selenium on Immune Response Mechanisms," *Federation Proceedings*, June 1979, p. 2139.

Chapter 6

1. A. C. Ivy, "Biology of Cancer," *Science*, November 14, 1947, p. 456.

2. Tadashi Suzuki *et al.*, "Effect of Dietary Supplementation of Iron and Ascorbic Acid on Lead Toxicity in Rats," *Journal of Nutrition*, Vol. 109 (1979), p. 982.

3. N. P. Singh, "Intake of Magnesium and Toxicity of Lead," *Archives of Environmental Health*, May 1979.

Chapter 8

1. Williams, *Nutrition Against Disease, op. cit.*, p. 53.

2. *Ibid.*, pp. 60–61.

3. E. Cheraskin, W. M. Ringsdorf, Jr., and J. W. Clark, *Diet and Disease* (New Canaan, Conn.: Keats Publishing, 1968), pp. 111–13.

4. Williams, *Nutrition Against Disease, op. cit.*, p. 55.

5. *Nutrient Requirements of Dogs, op. cit.*, p. 3.

6. Martin Zucker, "Childbirth Made Easier With Vitamin C," *Let's Live*, October 1979, pp. 22–30.

7. Lambert, *op. cit.*, p. 618.

8. F. G. Darlington and J. B. Chassels, "A Study on the Breeding and Racing of Thoroughbred Horses Given Large Doses of Alpha Tocopherol," *The Summary*, February 1956, pp. 2–10.

9. Lambert, *op. cit.*, p. 618.

Chapter 9

1. Archie Kalokerinos, *Every Second Child* (Melbourne: Nelson, 1974).

2. "Should Your Pet Travel by Air," *Consumer Reports*, March 1973, pp. 200–1.

3. A. E. Axelrod *et al.*, "Effects of Pantothenic Acid, Pyridoxine and Thiamine Deficiencies upon Antibody Formation," *Journal of Nutrition*, Vol. 72 (1960), p. 325.

4. Adelle Davis, *op. cit.*, p. 120.

5. Paavo Airola, *The Miracle of Garlic* (Phoenix: Health Plus Publishers, 1978), pp. 25–28.

6. Wendell O. Belfield and Irwin Stone, "Megascorbic Prophylaxis and Megascorbic Therapy: A New Orthomolecular Modality in Veterinary Medicine," *Journal of the International Academy of Preventive Medicine*, Vol. II, No. 3 (1975), p. 24.

7. C. Gregoire, "Barlow's disease or vitamin C deficiency in the dog," *North American Veterinarian*, March 1940, p. 164.

8. Hans Meier *et al.*, "Hypertrophic Osteodystrophy Associated with Disturbance of vitamin C Synthesis in Dogs," *Journal of the American Veterinary Medical Association*, June 1, 1957, pp. 483–91.

9. J. R. Holmes, "Suspected Skeletal Scurvy in the Dog," *Veterinary Record*, July 21, 1962, pp. 801–13.

10. Maria Vaananen and L. Wikman, "Scurvy as a Cause of Osteodystrophy," *Journal of Small Animal Practice*, August 1979, pp. 491–99.

Chapter 10

1. Louis-Paul Dugal, "Vitamin C in Relation to Cold Temperature Tolerance," *Annals of the New York Academy of Sciences*, April 2, 1961, pp. 307–17. Louis-Paul Dugal, "The Influence of Ascorbic Acid on the Adrenal Weight During Exposure to Cold," *Endocrinology*, May 1949, pp. 420–26.

2. W. L. Weaver, "The Prevention of Heat Prostration by Use of Vitamin C," *Southern Medical Journal*, May 1948, pp. 479–81. "Keep Cool with Vitamin C," *Prevention*, July 1977, pp. 106–10.

3. Stone, *op. cit.*, pp. 164–65.

4. Milton L. Scott, "Environmental Influences on Ascorbic Acid Requirements in Animals," *Annals of the New York Academy of Sciences*, October 9–12, 1974, p. 151.

Chapter 11

1. Williams, *op. cit.*, pp. 127–38.

2. Adelle Davis, *op. cit.*, p. 33.

3. L. H. Chen, "The Effect of Age and Dietary Vitamin E on the Tissue Lipid Peroxidation of Mice," *Nutrition Reports International*, December 1974, pp. 339–44. See also A. L. Tappel, "Will Antioxidant Nutrients Slow Aging Processes?" *Geriatrics*, October 1968, pp. 97–105.

4. Denham Harman *et al.*, "Free Radical Theory of Aging," *Journal of American Geriatrics Society*, Vol. 25, No. 9 (1977), pp. 400–6.

5. Personal communication from I. B. Chatterjee.

6. I. B. Chatterjee, "Aspects of Ascorbic Acid Biosynthesis in Animals," *Annals of the New York Academy of Sciences*, April 21, 1961, pp. 50–51.

7. Lacroix, *op. cit.*, p. 331.

8. Ewan Cameron, Linus Pauling, and Brian Leibovitz, "Ascorbic Acid and Cancer: A Review," *Cancer Research*, March 1979, pp. 663–81.

Chapter 16

1. Francis M. Pottenger, Jr., "The Effect of Heat-Processed Foods and Metabolized Vitamin D Milk on the Dentofacial Structures of Experimental Animals," *American Journal of Orthodontics and Oral Surgery*, August 1946, pp. 467–85.

2. Mitsuo Kamimura, "Anti-inflammatory Activity of Vitamin E," *Journal of Vitaminology*, Vol. 18 (1972), pp. 204–9.

3. Alfred J. Plechner, "Food Mediated Disorders," *op. cit.*, and "Food-Induced Hypersensitivity," *Modern Veterinary Practice*, March 1977, p. 225.

4. K. W. Chamberlain, "Clinical Signs and Diagnosis of Atopic Disease in the Dog," *Journal of Small Animal Practice*, Vol. 19 (1978), pp. 493–505.

Chapter 18

1. Harvey L. Edmonds, Jr., *et al.*, "Spontaneous Convulsions in Beagle Dogs," *Federation Proceedings*, September 1979, pp. 2424–27.

2. Donald B. Tower, "Pyridoxine and Cerebral Activity," *Nutrition Reviews*, June 1958, p. 161.

Chapter 19

1. L. O. Brooksby, "A Practitioner's Experience with Selenium-Tocopherol in Treatment of Cataracts and Nuclear Sclerosis in the Dog," *Veterinary Medicine/Small Animal Clinician*, March 1979, pp. 301–2.

Chapter 20

1. N. H. Lambert, *op. cit.*, pp. 611–17. This article is the source of all the material on Lambert in this chapter.

Chapter 21

1. Adelle Davis, *op. cit.*, p. 111.
2. Susan D. Cole, "Canine Hip Dysplasia: The Controversy," *Dog Fancy Magazine*, October 1979, pp. 24–27.
3. Gerry Schnelle, *Radiology in Canine Practice* (Evanston, Ill.: North American Veterinarian, 1945), pp. 48–56.
4. J. W. Bardens and H. Hardwick, "New Observations on the Diagnosis and Cause of Hip Dysplasia," *Veterinary Medicine/Small Animal Clinician*, March 1968, pp. 238–45.
5. Wendell O. Belfield, "Chronic Sub-clinical Scurvy and Canine Hip Dysplasia," *Veterinary Medicine/Small Animal Clinician*, October 1976, pp. 1399–1401.

Chapter 23

1. Clive M. McCay, *Nutrition of the Dog* (Ithaca, N.Y.: Comstock Publishing, 1949).
2. Frank Král and B. Novak, *Veterinary Dermatology* (Philadelphia: Lippincott, 1953), quoted in Mark Morris, *Nutrition and Diet in Small Animal Medicine* (Denver: Mark Morris Associates, 1960), p. 31.
3. Personal communication to Dr. Wilfrid E. Shute.
4. N. H. Lambert, *op. cit.*, p. 617.
5. *Ibid.*, p. 618.
6. Belfield and Stone, *op. cit.*, p. 21.
7. Lacroix, *op. cit.*, pp. 329–31.

Chapter 24

1. James Greenwood, Jr., "Optimum Vitamin C Intake as a Factor in the Preservation of Disc Integrity," *Medical Annals of the District of Columbia*, June 1964, pp. 274–76.

Chapter 25

1. S. M. Levenson *et al.*, "Ascorbic Acid, Riboflavin, Thiamin, and Nicotinic Acid in Relation to Severe Injury, Hemorrhage, and Infection in the Human," *Annals of Surgery*, Vol. 124 (1946), p. 840.

Chapter 26

1. W. A. Priester and Nathan Mantel, "Occurrence of Tumors in Domestic Animals," *Journal of the National Cancer Institute*, December 1971, pp. 1333–44.
2. Howard M. Hayes, Jr., "The Comparative Epidemiology of Selected Neoplasms Between Dogs, Cats and Humans," *European Journal of Cancer*, Vol. 14 (1978), pp. 1299–1308.
3. Ewan Cameron and Linus Pauling, "The Orthomolecular Treatment of Cancer," *Chem.-Biol. Interactions*, Vol. 9 (1974), pp. 273–83.
4. Richard A. Passwater, *Cancer and Its Nutritional Therapies* (New Canaan, Conn.: Keats Publishing, 1978), p. 18.
5. *Ibid.*, p. 97.
6. U. Saffiotti *et al.*, "Experimental Cancer of the Lung," *Cancer*, May 1967, p. 857.
7. Raymond J. Shamberger, "Inhibitory Effect of Vitamin A on Carcinogenesis," *Journal of the National Cancer Institute*, September 1971, p. 667.
8. Henry Foy *et al.*, "Histologic Changes in Livers of Pyridoxine-Deprived Baboons—Relation to Alpha, Fetoprotein and Liver Cancer in Africa," *Journal of the National Cancer Institute*, November 1974, p. 1295.
9. Kanematsu Sugiura, "On the Relation of Diets to the Development, Prevention and Treatment of Cancer," *Journal of Nutrition*, Vol. 44 (1951), pp. 345–59.
10. Roger Williams, "Concept of Genetotrophic Disease," *Nutrition Reviews*, September 1950, p. 257.

11. J. U. Schlegel, "The Role of Ascorbic Acid in the Prevention of Bladder Tumor Formation," *Journal of Urology*, February 1970, p. 155.

12. L. Benade *et al.*, "Synergistic Killing of Ehrlich Ascites Carcinoma Cells by Ascorbate and 3-Amino-1,2,4,-triazole," *Oncology*, Vol. 23, No. 1 (1969), pp. 33–43.

13. Ewan Cameron and Linus Pauling, "Supplemental Ascorbate in the Supportive Treatment of Cancer," *Proceedings of the National Academy of Sciences*, September 1978, pp. 4538–42.

14. Passwater, *op. cit.*, p. 129.

15. Cited in Passwater, p. 140.

16. Allen D. Woster *et al.*, "Zinc Suppression of Initiation of Sarcoma 180 Growth," *Journal of the National Cancer Institute*, April 1975, p. 1001.

17. Paul M. Newberne and Y. Y. Fong, *Science News*, February 11, 1978, p. 88.

18. N. H. Lambert and Eileen Parkhill, "Preliminary Clinical Report on the Treatment of Tumors in Cats and Dogs with Vitamin E," *Veterinary Record*, May 2, 1959, pp. 359–62.

Chapter 27

1. Fred R. Klenner, "The Treatment of Poliomyelitis and Other Virus Diseases with Vitamin C," *Southern Medicine and Surgery*, Vol. 111 (1949), pp. 209–14, and "Massive Doses of Vitamin C and the Virus Diseases," *Southern Medicine and Surgery*, Vol. 113 (1951), pp. 101–7.

2. Fred R. Klenner, "Significance of High Daily Intake of Ascorbic Acid in Preventive Medicine," *Journal of the International Academy of Preventive Medicine*, Spring 1974.

3. Akira Murata, "Virucidal Activity of Vitamin C," *Proceedings of the First Intersectional Congress of the International Association of Microbiological Societies*, Tokyo, 1974, pp. 431–36.

4. Linus Pauling, *Vitamin C, the Common Cold and the Flu* (San Francisco: Freeman, 1970), p. 45.

5. Brian Leibovitz and Benjamin Siegal, "Ascorbic Acid, Neutrophil Function and the Immune Response," *International Journal of Vitamin Nutrition Research*, Vol. 48 (1978).

6. "The Big IF in Cancer," *Time*, March 31, 1980, pp. 60–66.

7. Wendell O. Belfield, "Vitamin C in Treatment of Canine and Feline Distemper Complex," *Veterinary Medicine/Small Animal Clinician*, April 1967, pp. 345–48. Joseph I. Leveque, "Ascorbic Acid in

the Treatment of the Canine Distemper Complex," *Veterinary Medicine/Small Animal Clinician,* November 1969, pp. 997–1000.

8. Keith W. Powell, "Use of Canine Adenovirus Type 2 Vaccine to Control Kennel Cough Syndrome," *Veterinary Medicine/Small Animal Clinician,* June 1979, p. 801.

Index

Acknowledgments

Thanks to Wayne Harris of the Hilcoa Corporation in San Jose for providing pertinent ideas and invaluable grounding on nutrient function and fortification practices; to Dr. Irwin Stone, who knows just about all that is known about vitamin C; to Dr. Wilfrid E. Shute, who has healed the ailing hearts of both man and dog with vitamin E; to Fred Heying, one of the most successful dachshund breeders, for sharing his experiences of how vitamin E made healthier and more potent dachshunds; to Anne Rogers Clark of Cecilton, Maryland, and Doris Wear, also of Cecilton, for sharing some of their kennel tips and experiences with me; to Irving Eldredge of Middleburg, Virginia; to Dr. Hans J. Kugler of Redondo Beach, California, an expert on aging, for explaining some of the complicated processes of aging; to Dr. John M. Ellis of Mount Pleasant, Texas, for sharing some of his vast knowledge of the workings of vitamin B_6; to Margaret Hickel, who keeps the worms off her dogs with garlic and parsley tablets; and a number of well-informed government officials for providing important background information about pet food manufacturing practices.